With All My Heart
A Life In Gospel Music

Lily Fern Weatherford
and
Gail Shadwell, Ph.D.

Alliance Press

LIMITED AUTOGRAPHED EDITION

#189/400

To my dear friends, Bernard & Carole, Thank God for His peace thru old trials. I love you both "With all My Heart"

Lily F. Weatherford

Copyright © 1999 by Lily Fern Weatherford and Gail Shadwell, Ph.D.

All rights reserved. No part of this book may be reproduced in any form whatsoever, by photograph or xerography or by any other means, by broadcast or transmission, by translation into any kind of language, nor by recording electronically or otherwise, without permission in writing from the publisher, except by a reviewer, who may quote brief passages in critical articles and reviews.

Printed in the United States of America.

ISBN: 1-890704-59-8
98-598

Alliance Press

1527 Brighton Drive • Carrollton, TX 75007 • (800) 970-1883

Address all correspondence and order information to the above address.

Dedication

My dedication of this book has four parts, coinciding with the purposes of writing it.

First, I dedicate the book in loving memory to my husband, Earl Weatherford, who was an integral part of my life for forty-seven years and will be in my heart forever.

Second, I dedicate it to my children, Susan Marie Weatherford Cunningham and Steven Earl Weatherford, without whom the story would have no "spice." They are a vital part of my life and I appreciate their loving support.

Third, I dedicate the book to friends and family who loved me and encouraged me to write it.

Finally, I dedicate this book to the never-failing God, who brings us through whatever we have to face in life, if we just believe.

Romans 8:38,39—"For I am persuaded, that neither death, nor life, nor angels, nor principalities, nor powers, nor things present, nor things to come,

Nor height, nor depth, nor any other creature, shall be able to separate us from the love of God, which is in Christ Jesus our Lord."

Lily Fern Weatherford

I dedicate the book to my family and friends for their support during my intense involvement in this project over the last year and a half, and to my co-author and subject, Lily Fern Weatherford, whose kindness, honesty, sense of humor and gracious spiritual guidance resulted in a friendship I will treasure forever.

Gail Shadwell, Ph.D.

Acknowledgements

There is one acknowledgement that cannot be left out of this book. In an effort such as this, there is always one who sees the vision, who perseveres no matter what the obstacles and discouragements. There is one who goes beyond the call of duty and works countless hours, days, weeks, months and even years, without complaining--the one who "labors with love."

The one who spent those hours attempting to make this book the best it could be is Gail Shadwell. She reminded me of deadlines with love and patience, urging me on to finish the task. Her consistency and perseverance completed the work. Ever faithful and true to her word, she is my unsung hero. Thank you, Gail, my co-author and my dear friend.

Lily Fern Weatherford

I wish to acknowledge Lily Fern's willing cooperation in researching the story of her life. I appreciate her graciousness through hours of interviews and phone calls, no matter how tight her schedule might have been. I appreciate the research, production, photography and editing assistance of Nelle and Myrna Shadwell, Kay and Lee Campbell, John and Jan Ferchow and Angela Jakes.

Lily Fern and I both wish to express our gratitude to her friends, family and Southern Gospel colleagues for materials submitted for inclusion in the book, and to Jon Hughes of Alliance Publishing for her patient assistance.

Gail Shadwell

From The Authors

January 2, 1998
Lily Fern Weatherford
Paoli, Oklahoma

When Gail and I decided to write a brief note to explain how we came to write this book and what we hoped to accomplish, I had to think back over the years and examine my motives.

The first thing that came to mind was the large number of people over the years who have asked questions about how long I have been doing this work, why I do it, how we got started, how they could get started and so forth. Many times I heard the statement, "You ought to write a book!" Some have asked for the "inside story" of life on the road. Well, this is definitely the inside story! You will read about the pitfalls, the sorrows, the joys and the fun. The main point, though, is that we must all trust the Lord and the word of God. You can still be happy, no matter what happens, if you have faith. You can take situations that seem impossible and turn them over to God. He can't do anything for you until you turn it over to Him. I want to express what happens when God has His way in a life.

As we spent hours and days in interviews and taping, I realized the importance of humor in our lives. You will find some pretty wild experiences in this book, and I know I could not have handled them without the ability to laugh--at the situations and at myself.

Another point I want to get across is that God makes a way, even when you think there is no way out. Sometimes we humans think we know best, but after a situation is over and you thought it went wrong, down the road you can see why it was for the best. Remember, God always answers prayer, but He may not always say "Yes." The Weatherfords have had their share of miracles--but we have also had times when things didn't go the way we thought they should. Later, we would see what could have happened if we had gotten our way--we see why it was best the way it happened. We have included examples to explain that, as well as examples of some of the miracles that happened.

If one person can benefit from my experiences, this book will have been worth the effort. Gail can testify that I have laughed as I remembered and told some of the old family stories, and that I have been brought to tears by painful or tender moments from my past.

I was thinking of a book before Earl went to live with the Lord, and I remember him saying, "You need to get busy on that book." Well, Earl, I would rather have done it with you here to share it, but I'm getting it done at last.

When you read this book, remember that I write it with love and "with all my heart."

January 3, 1998
Gail Shadwell
Elgin, Illinois

Although my most vivid childhood memories include services in a small Methodist Church, my journey into the academic world took me far from my roots. My mother filled my life with music. She is a talented pianist and our home rang with her spirited playing. My sisters and I still love crowding around the piano and singing--enthusiasm compensating for short-comings in talent. Mother knew the work of many gospel groups, so she was excited by the advent of the Bill and Gloria Gaither video tapes.

To humor her, I watched some videos with her. Not only did I respond to the joy and good fellowship evident in those videos, but I was struck by the voice and manner of Lily Fern Weatherford. I went to a live performance of The Weatherfords. They were smooth and professional, and I felt the personal dignity of the woman whose apparently effortless singing witnessed her faith. Later, I found myself humming "Weatherford" songs.

Some family members and I attended the Grand Ole Gospel Reunion in South Carolina, where I got to talk to Lily Fern. If I have had a spiritual experience in my life, that was it. I had gone through a stressful, challenging period, but had not shared it with anyone. No one could have been more surprised than I, when, as I chatted with Lily Fern, I asked her to pray for me sometime. Almost embarrassed, I stood in the crowd of people around her. I can't explain it, but there seemed to be a special energy field around us as she turned her full attention to me, those remarkable eyes conveying warmth and strength. She stepped closer, put her arm around me and said, "I'll be glad to pray for you, Gail, but I'm going to do it right now. When people ask me to pray for them, I don't wait. I do it right then, if I can. Now, we'll stand here as though we're just talking quietly, and I'm going to pray for you." And she did--a strong, beautiful prayer in that melodious voice, and there was a feeling that I can only describe as "electric." For that time, not one person came to talk to her, although they had lined up, waiting. I have never seen people back off as they did that night. Even my family seemed to stay at a distance. I felt as though time stood still until she finished that prayer. I still don't understand it, but I can tell you that when Lily Fern Weatherford prays for you, you have been *prayed* for!

Now, having researched her life over the past year and a half, I am even more impressed by the intensity of her personality and her faith. If you know Lily Fern, you already know why we chose the title of the book. Not only does she often use the expression, "with all my heart," that is the way she lives her life. Because of my association with her over this period, it is also the way I am approaching the book. Lily Fern is a very real person, with an outlandish sense of humor, a keen enjoyment of life, awesome talent, unwavering love of family and friends and a legacy of life-long devotion to her God to share with all of us.

Personally, I found our long conversations and interviews fascinating and the innate honesty and goodness of the woman inspiring. She did not hold back. If I asked it, she answered it. You will find that this is not a "picture book" or public relations piece. It is a real life told in down-to-earth terms. I know you will enjoy her story.

Note:

We have chosen to use a predominantly "interview" style for this book. Since we had access to friends, peers and family members, as well as all of Lily Fern's own memories, we combine a narrative style with the actual words of some of the people involved, whether from interview or correspondence. We believe it will make the book more lively and enjoyable for you.

LFW/GS

FOREWORD

When I think of Lily Fern Weatherford, the first words that come to mind is "a gentle spirit." I know it takes all types to get the Lord's work done, but thank God for the gentle spirits in our world.

My earliest memories of Earl and Lily were when they would stop by our house with the entire group. Gloria would always have a good meal prepared for them and then, after that, we would go into the family room, gather around the piano and sing through something new that we had just written: "In the Upper Room," "Lovest Thou Me," or "Have You Had a Gethsemane?"

When she would take those last verses and drive their meaning home, again, I would say Thank God for that "gentle, sweet spirit."

Still today, through all the heartaches, tough times, and struggles, when you are around her, that sweet spirit permeates everything that happens. And what a classy voice! There is none like hers. She was one of the first female stylists in our field. She was so smooth and she made the other three male singers sound regal! It was an incredible combination!

> Bill Gaither
> Alexandria, Indiana

Lily Fern performing at Gaither taping

Table of Contents

1. Living Legend..1
2. Genesis and Exodus...7
3. The Promised Land...23
4. Leaving the Nest...41
5. Building the Dream...65
6. Filling the Void...89
7. The Young and the Restless..105
8. Trials and Tribulations..121
9. Music and Miracles...131
10. One of God's Singers Goes Home...................................147
11. A Life Examined...165
12. A Living Legacy..189

Afterword...221

Appendix..223

Chapter One
Living Legend

RP: The experts...insist that she is the greatest female singer who has ever stepped on a gospel stage and sung a song. She is a lady of great class, great dignity, and still is every bit the singer she was thirty-five, forty years ago. You proved last year, as she stood on this stage and sang to you, that she's one of your very favorites, too. So I'm honored to present tonight our Living Legend Award to Lily Fern Weatherford.

With these words, Roy Pauley, versatile singer, outspoken *Singing News* columnist and music critic, inducted Lily Fern Weatherford and her late husband, Earl, into the distinguished company of gospel greats designated as "Living Legends" at the Grand Ole Gospel Reunion, on August 8, 1992.

Lily Fern stepped to the microphone to accept the plaque, but had to wait while the audience roared its approval and cameras flashed. When the applause subsided she said, "I am completely overwhelmed." Her voice broke as she added:

LFW: And I'm very proud. I'm proud that my name's engraved on this with Earl Weatherford's. We were married for forty-seven years. We worked together side by side twenty-four hours a day, forty-seven years. The night before Earl died, I talked to him. He couldn't talk back. He was on a respirator. And I said, 'You don't have to talk. We've lived together so long we know what each other's thinking.' And I said, 'I know you love me, Earl. And I love you—with all my heart. We've made some beautiful music together.'

Any fan of The Weatherfords knows that this was probably one of the most harmonious and productive working relationships gospel music has ever known and they did, indeed, make "beautiful music together."

Since Earl's death in 1992, Lily Fern and her son, Steve, have carried on

With All My Heart

the Weatherford music ministry.

At an age when most people are retired or considering retirement, she is on the road at least eleven months a year, singing in churches and auditoriums coast to coast. The Weatherfords perform before audiences as small as a tiny country church congregation and as large as the 24,000 member Saturday evening audience of the National Quartet Convention in Louisville, Kentucky.

With the advent of the Southern Gospel videos produced by Bill and Gloria Gaither, Lily Fern's following has grown dramatically. Although The Weatherfords as a group and Lily Fern as an individual had their own loyal "fans" all over the country prior to the Gaither tapes, new audiences are becoming aware of their tremendous talent. Lily Fern is featured on several of these popular videos, many of which have gone "gold" or "platinum." Lily Fern attributes much of the current popularity of The Weatherfords to the Gaither tapes.

> LFW: A lot of people thought we weren't singing any more, even before Earl died. Now they see the Gaither videos and the Weatherford name is becoming known again.

Not only do Lily Fern's fans admire and enjoy her, so do her peers. For example, Dr. James Blackwood, loved and respected as a singer and a gentleman, expressed his respect and regard for her as both a singer and a lady. In his opinion, Lily Fern's unique voice and ability to blend with others made her the woman who sounds like "a wonderful male tenor." He adds, "She is not only my favorite lady who sings gospel music, she is a dear friend as well."

One of the matriarchs of the pioneer gospel family, The Speers, echoes Dr. Blackwood's evaluation. Rosa Nell (Speer) Powell commented, "I know that she is a fabulous singer and a good person."

Dr. Blackwood and many others of her peers have indicated that The Weatherford's "In the Garden" album is the benchmark for Southern Gospel albums. Many attribute "The Weatherford sound" to the voice and talent of Lily Fern.

Born in Bethany, Oklahoma, on November 25, 1928, Lily Fern Goble has come from the depression "dust bowl" to the bright lights of the stage, proving that one woman can, indeed, do it all. She has been a wife, a mother, a grandmother, a performer, and a business woman. Perhaps more important, she has been a friend, a Christian and a role model for thousands during her long career.

She has known great sadness and great joy. She loves her God and tries to serve him faithfully. Her story, extending over seven decades, from the Great Depression to the very gates of the twenty-first century, has the pathos and joy that epitomize the Christian life.

When discussing Lily Fern's performance at the National Quartet Convention in 1996, her sister-in-law, Martha Goble, voiced what her friends know: "She is anointed. There is no question that God has His hand on her life."

At a performance of The Weatherfords, when Steve introduced his mother as a winner of the Grand Ole Gospel Reunion "Living Legend Award," Lily Fern stepped forward and quipped, "I was very grateful to receive the Living Legend Award, but I noticed something about it—all you have to do is live long enough!" The congregation of the small Oklahoma church responded with laughter, but, as people familiar with Lily Fern's work, they knew better.

Lily Fern Weatherford is one of the pioneer ladies of Southern Gospel. She and Earl have been the backbone of The Weatherfords, a group responsible for the early experience of many of today's gospel favorites, such as Glen Payne, George Younce, Henry Slaughter, Armond Morales, Jim Hamill, and the list goes on. As a matter of fact, at the first national quartet convention held on the west coast, The Weatherfords received a standing ovation as they performed and then brought out of the audience a large group of former Weatherfords to join them. That event was so well received that they repeated it at both the Grand Ole Gospel Reunion and the National Quartet Convention in 1997. Any time there is a mass gathering of Southern Gospel performers, there will be a reunion of former "Weatherfords."

Neil Enloe, long-time member of the popular "Couriers" quartet, had a humorous comment on the importance of The Weatherfords to beginning performers:

NE: Earl probably gave more aspiring gospel singers a chance than any other group manager. He was always introducing a new member. We Couriers often joked about the Weatherfords. They probably never knew it until now, but we did. The joke went like this: 'A best-selling book would be, *The Weatherford Quartet Personnel Directory*, even if it just sold to those whose names were listed.'

When told of this comment, Lily Fern laughed and said, "Oh, yes. We knew!"

A former Weatherford singer, Doyle McAlister, once said, "My time with The Weatherford Quartet was the greatest experience in my gospel career. They are the 'University of Gospel Music!'"

With Earl's death in 1992, Lily Fern faced the prospect of going on without her life partner. As she puts it, "My son, Steve, has carried me since I lost Earl." Steve had been with the group for years, so he and Lily Fern now form the nucleus of the group.

They still travel extensively, performing at the National Quartet Convention in Kentucky, The Great Western Convention in California and the Grand Ole Gospel Reunion in South Carolina, as well as on their own extensive tour circuit.

They have gotten a newer bus and are planning at least one new recording project. When Kenny Payne left the group in 1997, they acquired the smooth and talented Jamie Caldwell, who blends beautifully with the "Weatherford sound."

Lily Fern has been heavily involved with writing this book and with plans to record an album that will be a companion to it. The titles will be the same. She says the title is appropriate for both, because she is living and singing with all her heart. She feels that another solo album is way past due. Her sense of humor becomes evident when she discusses her only solo album to date:

> LFW: Solo albums don't sell as well as a group album, but really, in fifty-four years I should have more. Somebody asked me one time about 'A Place of Peace,' my one and only solo tape, and asked if it sold well. I said, 'Oh, yes! I've sold that thing since 1963 and the other day I had to re-order on it. Yes, I ordered the second thousand. It's really sold!' Well, that's not quite true. I have re-ordered on it more than that.

With all the excitement generated by the resurgence in the popularity of Southern Gospel, Lily Fern has emerged as one of the most respected singers in the field. She says she and Brock Speer are the oldest Southern Gospel singers still singing in their original groups.

Recently, Lily Fern received notification of another award for her life's work, being the only gospel singer ever to be honored to date with the "Living

Legacy Award" of the Women's International Center, located in San Diego, California. The Center's founder, Gloria Lane, announced the award:

> GJL: Lily Fern Weatherford's glorious singing is indeed inspirational. She is a beloved gospel singer whose resonant voice makes her a favorite among the thousands who have attended her concerts and heard her on television, radio and recordings. She will receive a 'Living Legacy Award' at our 15th Anniversary Award Ceremony in San Diego on March 7, 1998, along with former First Lady, Betty Ford, actress/humanitarian Anne Jeffreys and others.

In May of 1998, Lily Fern is scheduled to receive an honorary doctorate in humanities from Oakland City University in Indiana.

A list of awards won by The Weatherfords and Lily Fern will be found in the Appendix, as well as a list of former members of The Weatherfords and a listing of tapes and CDs still available.

While this book is primarily an attempt to recount the life of Lily Fern Weatherford, her life is interwoven with the ministry of The Weatherfords, the history of Southern Gospel and the remarkable relationship of Lily Fern and Earl.

The material has been gathered by over a year of interviews, letter writing, phone calls and general research. In order to give the reader the widest possible view of Lily Fern's life, both a third person narrative and exact quotations and recollections by Lily Fern are used, as well as quotations from peers, family and friends, as appropriate. In some cases, conversations between Lily Fern and others have been recorded. The use of initials to indicate the speaker seemed the simplest way to help the reader understand who is speaking in any quotation.

While some refer to her as "Lily," we have chosen to use "Lily Fern." When asked if she prefers to be called "Lily" or "Lily Fern," she responded, "I suppose in the profession it's 'Lily Fern.' I don't really care, but my dad cared. He always said, 'Her name is Lily Fern!'"

Any material spoken or written by Lily Fern is so indicated by initials and inset paragraphs, or quotation marks.

She has stated to her co-author the desire to be honest and to tell things just as they are, with the exception of omitting names in any situation where to include them would cause difficulty for anyone else.

This is a life and a philosophy. From Lily Fern's parents, through her growing up years, her marriage, her children and her career, it is also a picture of America's history through the eyes of one family, with all its highs and lows. It is also a history of one woman's spiritual journey, presented with the hope that it may inspire or comfort anyone needing to believe in miracles and the faithfulness of God.

Perhaps the simplest summary of Lily Fern's belief came from her years on the staff of beloved evangelist, Rex Humbard at The Cathedral of Tomorrow. She says it was there that she learned that God's power is limited only by our own lack of faith. The story that follows, from her childhood to her present success, is punctuated by instances of her solid faith in God.

Lily Fern and Charlie Waller, Producer of the Grand Ole Gospel Reunion.

Chapter Two
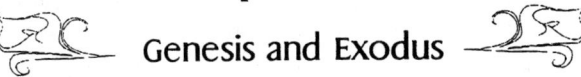 Genesis and Exodus

Lily Fern's paternal grandparents, George Thomas Goble and Myrtle Mary Goble, moved from Indiana to Kingfisher, Oklahoma, by covered wagon in 1900. Two years later, they received land near Apache, Oklahoma by lottery. Her grandfather participated in the great Oklahoma Land Run. Their first eleven children had been born at Honey Creek, Indiana, including Lily Fern's father, Alonzo Elmer Goble, known to everyone as "Lon." Their last six children were born in Oklahoma.

Her maternal grandparents, Everette Arthur and Elizabeth Vandora Summers, were married in Arkansas sometime around 1902, and later moved to Oklahoma. Lily Fern's mother, Lillie Alice Summers, born in 1905, was the second of their eight children.

Lily Fern's parents were married July 23, 1922, in El Reno, Oklahoma.

During their growing up years, both Lon and Lillie had to learn responsibility, mostly due to the size of their families. Lily Fern remarks on their background:

LFW: Mother came from a family of six brothers. Since she was one of the oldest, she had to help care for the younger boys. My dad came from a family of seventeen children, so everybody had to sort of raise themselves.

Their backgrounds were very different, however, in terms of education, religion and up-bringing. As Lily Fern explains:

LFW: Dad got to go to school very little. He said if he counted it all up, he probably had a fourth grade education, as far as time spent in school. They never went to church. In fact, he would sneak off once in a while and go to Sunday School or church, or if there was a church revival going on, or a tent revival around, but if his father caught him, he would punish him. And the punishment in those days in that family was not really easy to take.

When we were growing up, Dad told us many times about the things that his brothers used to do to each other, which they called 'playing tricks.' To me, they weren't very funny tricks. Dad told us things that the kids did. They never really had any toys or anything to play with, but one of their pastimes was to get two cats and tie their tails together and throw them over the fence and watch them fight until one died. That was their 'fun' in life. And when he would tell me that, I'd think, 'Oh, how horrible! That must have been awful!'

I remember Dad telling a story about one of his brothers doing something to another brother--I can't remember what it was--but I was just horrified that brothers and sisters would do those things to each other. Dad had one thumb nail that never did grow out all the way, because it was cut off when he was just a little kid, and he had an eyebrow that had a permanent scar clear across it. He said, 'You want to know how I got that bad thumb nail there? Well, we were pitching hay one day and a couple of my brothers were down below pitching hay and they weren't doing it like I thought they should, so I just threw the pitchfork down. One of my brothers was barefoot, and I pinned his foot to the ground with that pitchfork.' I thought that was awful, and he said, 'Don't worry. He got me back! He threw a hoe one time when I was chopping cotton and nearly cut the end of my thumb off, and that's why that thumb nail won't grow out. If that wasn't enough, that day after he got the pitchfork out of his foot, he pulled me down out of the hayloft and threw me on the ground and held me down....' And he explained how another brother filed Dad's eyebrow off with a file!

That was the way my dad lived. The kids were just kind of mean in those days, but the brothers and sisters all loved each other and were very devoted when they were older.

Comparing the lives of her parents, Lily Fern commented on the areas of music and education:

LFW: Dad, because he was an avid reader and self taught, seemed like a very educated man. Mother graduated from high school with high honors. I have her certificates to this day. She was the valedictorian of her class and a very brilliant woman.

Dad couldn't sing; he couldn't carry a tune if he tried to. But he loved singing and he loved music--all kinds of music. Mother could sing. She was a high soprano and all her family were great singers. They didn't put it to practice, but they were good singers. But Mother did. She sang in church and played the piano for the church.

While Lon and Lillie had differences in up-bringing, they seemed uniquely matched when they finally found each other. Lon's life changed significantly in the area of religion, once he began life with Lillie. According to Lily Fern:

LFW: My mother and daddy had a short courtship before they married. My father was not a Christian. He drank a lot and lived wild and rough. He met my mother, and she started him going to church, but he didn't get saved until after they were married. She took him to a really great old-fashioned tent revival in Kingfisher, Oklahoma. The crowds were so overwhelming that they decided at the close of that meeting, which lasted, I think, about six weeks, to establish a church in Kingfisher. It became the First Church of the Nazarene.

During that revival, my father was saved and felt immediately that he was called to preach. The evangelist in that revival and his family became life-long friends of Mama and Dad. The evangelist was M.P. Smith, and the other evangelist was J.W. Curtis. Those three families, the Gobles, the Curtises and the Smiths, were friends for many years. Although our lives and paths took us to different areas, we still managed to get together, and Mother always corresponded with the families.

At the close of that revival, they needed a pastor, and those days preachers didn't really feel the need to go to seminary. If they felt like God called them to preach, they just started preaching the *Bible* and that was it. Of course, they had seminaries in those days for preachers, but Dad didn't go to seminary. In fact, Dad was not an educated man at all, but he was a very smart man and he had a great deal of wisdom and he loved to read. He would read everything he could get his hands on, and after he was converted, he would read the *Bible* and study it. Then he would get the dictionary and study the dictionary. Thus, he became very knowledgeable and used good grammar. He had a beautiful style of delivery.

That First Nazarene Church in Kingfisher was his first pastoring experience, followed by the Nazarene Church in Yukon, Oklahoma, and the

Calument Church near El Reno. Recently, The Weatherfords sang at the new building of the Kingfisher First Nazarene.

Another change in their lives was the birth of their children. When they were living in El Reno, their first two children were born. Lily Fern's sister, Florence Marie, was born on September 11, 1923. Her brother, Meekly Everette, was born on January 25, 1925.

Approximately three years later, in Bethany, the baby of the family, Lily Fern, was born on November 25, 1928. Lon and Lillie were now responsible for three new lives. As Lily Fern put it, "I was born in Oklahoma during the depression, and it was very hard times." Her sister, now Florence Goble Squier, recalls the night their baby sister came into the world:

FGS: I remember the night that Lily Fern was born. It took everyone there to keep me out of the room. I knew something was going on in there, but they wouldn't let me in and I was really livid with them!

In an interview, Lily Fern asked her brother, Meekly Everette Goble, what he remembered:

MEG: All I remember about it is that Mother was home; she wasn't in a hospital. They had Flo and me go into another room. Dad said, 'You'll have to stay in here.' He was going to be out there where Mother was, with the doctor. And when you were born, Dad came and got us and said, 'You've got a new baby sister,' and he took us out to see you. We were so thrilled and excited, and what a wonderful occasion that was! Little did I know that I wouldn't have been so joyful, if I had known then what I was going to experience for about the next eleven years!

They shared a laugh as they recalled their childhood bickering. In a recent conversation, they discussed those growing up years and their relationship with each other and Florence:

LFW: There was a time when Meekly and Florence were much closer to each other, because they were closer in age. But I never resented that, because I just understood it. There was, oh, probably the first eleven years of my life that they just kind of tolerated me.

MEG: It was hard!

LFW: It was hard, he says! And I know why. I mean, I know I was a brat. I was spoiled and I could get away with a lot of things because I was Daddy and Mama's baby.

MEG: We've talked about our younger years, when we weren't quite so loving as we are now, and how we used to fight a lot. She was just enough younger to always be in my way. Sometimes I couldn't get her out of my way without pushing or hitting her. We did fuss and fight a lot when we were young. We got into a scuffle one day, and, of course, I was older and bigger and tougher then--I don't know if I am now or not! And I hit her or something, and she began to whimper. My dad, this time, was a little bit too close, so he just grabbed me and wrestled me to the floor and was sitting on my legs and holding my hands, and he said, 'Alright, Lily Fern. You just come and do whatever you want to him. You just kick him or bite him or hit him--just do whatever you want now to get even with him. He just picks on you all the time. This is your time to get even!' And she looked down at me and she said, 'Oh, no, Daddy! Let him up. I don't want to hit him!' All the times that she wished she could hit me, and when it came down to hitting me, she backed off!

LFW: The chance of a lifetime!

MEG: Yes, the chance of a lifetime, and she didn't take advantage of it! That was a funny story my dad used to tell on us.

LFW: I remember that time. Meekly had flipped me with a dish towel--he did that a lot--and, of course, I would cry and Dad would feel sorry for me, 'cause I was always his baby. He always called me his baby. He'd say, 'Where's my baby?' Anyway, Meekly flipped me with that dish towel and made Dad mad. They wrestled all the time, but just play wrestle. This time he got him on the ground and sat on him and held his hands down, and told me to do anything I wanted to him. And I took a run and I was going to kick him as hard as I could, but I got right up to him, and I could not do anything to him. I couldn't stand it to think that somebody would hurt my brother. I cried and I said, 'Daddy, please let him up. I don't want to hit him and I don't want to kick him. Let him up!' I know we would have protected each other against anything.

Florence remembers Lily Fern's earliest years, especially how she loved to sing even as a baby:

FGS: Before she could talk, she was singing and carrying a tune. And she'd keep on perfect pitch and right on key. She could even harmonize when she was just a little tiny girl, so her talent started that early.

Lily Fern recalls what her mother told her about her singing as a child:

LFW: Mother said that when I was very, very small, I was humming and singing tunes, when I was around eighteen months old. I couldn't say the words, but I could hum the tune, and they said I was singing harmony before I could talk plain. So, I've always wanted to sing. It was just second nature to me. Dad and Mother always encouraged me to sing.

Her own memories concur with those of her mother:

LFW: I sang everything! If I was playing, Mama could always find me, 'cause I was singing, wherever I was. And I had a song for everything, seemed like, and I can remember that. I remember being caught up in something, playing paper dolls or something, and I'd be singing-- whatever I wanted them to hear, I was singing it. I would sing, 'Now, you're going to the dance tonight. You're going to wear this dress.' Paper dolls were really the thing back in those days, and I always sang to them. I guess that's why I'm singing today. I literally have sung all my life.

Meekly recalls, sheepishly, that most of his growing years were spent asking Dad or Mama to "make her quit singing!"

Few pictures of Lily Fern as a child exist, but she describes herself as "always kind of chubby" with straight hair "unless I had a permanent." It was blonde, but grew darker as she got older.

Lily Fern didn't know many of her relatives as she grew up. She never really knew her father's parents. His father died before Lily Fern was born and his mother died in 1936:

LFW: I didn't know my dad's people that much until this generation. It's been about the last four years that we've been having a Goble family reunion and I've met a lot of cousins. Wonderful Christian people.

Her maternal grandmother died when Lily was very small, but she did get to know her maternal grandfather:

> LFW: He had remarried and Grandmother Dora, we called her, was really the only grandmother I knew. She was a sweet lady and a very kind person. I thought my grandfather was just wonderful. I was very close to most of my mother's brothers, also.

Despite the limited contact with relatives, the Goble children grew up in an atmosphere of encouragement and love. They were free to explore their talents, and they were given loving support and guidance. Lily Fern explains:

> LFW: Dad took pride in everything his children did. And if we failed, he made us believe that it was not a failure, because we at least tried. And he told us we should keep on trying and, if whatever we were striving to do was not being successful, to go to something else and maybe go back to that later.

> Mother was an immaculate person and she kept us and her home that way. Although she never had very much as far as earthly goods were concerned, whatever it was, you knew it was clean. But she and Dad would stop anything they had to do at any time, if they thought we had a problem. Consequently, we never thought we had very big problems, because we knew we could always go to Mom and Dad and they would take us to the Lord. What a way to base your life! The love of your parents and their faith in God is wonderful.

Not only were the Goble children sure of the support and guidance from their parents, they were confident of the love in the family. Even the economic problems seemed minor, given the security of the family unit. A conversation between Lily Fern and Meekly illustrates the point:

> LFW: I always knew that in our family there were five people who really truly loved each other. And I don't remember that we went around saying, 'I love you.' We just knew. I think that one of the ways that Dad really showed his love was how hard he worked to keep his family going. I don't remember thinking that we were in bad shape, being poor or anything. Do you remember that?

> MEG: Yes, I realized we were poor, because when you eat cabbage soup for about four months, every Sunday for your main meal, you realized that there wasn't too much money floating around to have any luxuries. But we did it. We survived, because of the love in our family.

Dad was always known as a real hard worker. He provided. Whatever he had to do, he did.

Lily Fern attributes much of her success and that of her siblings to the intelligence, intuition and strong religious foundation of her parents:

LFW: Dad had a lot of wisdom and common horse sense, which is what I call it. Now, I've studied a little bit of psychology, and I know Dad never did, but to me, he could have taught it, because he could just read a man's personality, just by being with him for a short while. I'm not so sure that isn't what the *Bible* means as the gift of discernment. Anybody could go to Dad and talk to him and immediately feel that things were going to get better. He just knew how to talk to them. When we children were growing up, we could go to Dad or Mother. It just seems like both of them were so suited to talk to people and help them with their needs. But I know the reason why, now. It's because the first thing they would both do was say, 'Well, let's just pray about it and ask God to direct and lead.' I never one time in my whole life had my mother or father, either one, say to me, or to anybody else who had a problem, 'Well, I think you should do this or that, and if you don't do this or that, it's just not going to be right.' They did not do that. They said, 'Let's go to God's word and let's go to the Lord and talk to Him and He will direct your path and shed the light on the subject that you need to know. If you're honest and sincere, he will lead you and guide you and direct you.'

I really believe that's the reason why, today, that my brother and his wife, my sister and her family, and Earl and our family have had happy marriages and happy families. We just always followed that. We just always realized that the first thing to do was to go to the Lord with our problems and it's never failed. God has never let us down.

The Goble children had their parents' time and attention for the serious issues they faced, and they also had time for fun, such as the imagination game Lon played with Lily Fern, when she was little. Meekly refers to the on-going game as "Farmer."

MEG: Lily Fern was my Dad's favorite; there's no doubt about it! Flo will attest to that. He loved all of us, but he sure was close to that girl. We didn't have television, and I doubt if, at that time, we even had a radio in our house. So, once in a while, they would get down on the floor and play. They liked to play 'Farmer.' They would either get down on the floor or she would sit in Dad's lap in his chair, and Dad would say in a deep voice, 'Who are you?' And in her squeaky female-trying-to-be-masculine voice, she would say, 'Well, I'm a farmer. Who are you?' He would answer, 'Well, I'm a farmer, too. What do you raise?' And she would say she raised corn and peaches and plums and whatever. Then she would say, 'What do you raise?' And he would say the same things, usually, but they were always 'raising' something that we would eat. One day, after they'd done this, oh, many, many times, they got into this, 'Who are you?' and, 'What do you raise?' and Lily Fern had an answer that Dad told us about and laughed about many times.

LFW: I remember him telling this story so many times and thinking it was just something else! This one day he pretended he didn't know who I was. He said, 'My name is Lon Goble. What's your name?' I made up some name, and he said, 'Well, that's interesting. What do you do for a living?' I said, 'I'm a farmer.' And he said, 'Well, what do you raise on your farm?' And I said, 'I raise windows.' Well, Dad thought that was really funny. Of course, I didn't know what he was talking about 'raising.' I didn't know much about crops, but I knew you could raise windows!

It took all the strength, hard work and wisdom that Lon and Lillie could muster to care for their little brood during those depression years. Anyone who has read the Steinbeck classic, *The Grapes of Wrath*, will understand the state so many people were in with the "Great Depression" and the economic disaster of the Oklahoma "Dust Bowl." The natural solution for a large number of people was to leave the heartbreak of Oklahoma's rural areas for the "Promised Land" of California. Lily Fern explains the reasons behind her family's decision to move to California, and it probably mirrors that of many other families:

LFW: After the Depression, Oklahoma was a rough, rough, hard place to live, unless you were really highly skilled in something or very wealthy. Dad leased a farm and it had a small dairy. I think he had about six or eight cows and he sold the milk. But later on, he finally did get a job in Oklahoma City at the Ford plant, where he learned the trade of painting automobiles. But he always had two or three and sometimes four jobs, and he was preaching, too. My dad did anything he could to keep his family comfortable and to keep food on the table and, in those days, it wasn't easy. The last year we lived there was so bad. Mother and Dad planted three crops the year before we left Oklahoma. I know what I heard Mom say was that one of them froze out, the second one was eaten by bugs or grasshoppers or something, and the last one was beaten down with hail.

During all this time, this Reverend M.P. Smith was pastoring a church in California's San Gabriel valley, in a little town called Wilmar. They kept writing back and forth and convinced Mom and Dad that they could do better if they moved to California.

For the Goble children, the trip from Oklahoma to California was a major adventure. Although their memories of events on the trip vary, because, as Meekly pointed out, they were just small children, the essence of it all was definitely "excitement." Since Lily Fern was the youngest, she turned to Meekly to help remember their adventures on that trek west.

LFW: Meekly, do you remember when we left Oklahoma to move to California?

MEG: Oh, yes. Very well. I wasn't really all that old, but I was seven and old enough to remember the main things that happened to us. We were very poor people. I think my father left Oklahoma with a '27 Chevrolet and somewhere around twelve dollars in his pocket. But we did have a hundred loaves of day-old bread that we took along with us. That sounds funny, but it's really true. We just left there knowing that we would have to work on the way to California on whatever jobs we could get--picking cotton or odd jobs or whatever to subsidize our travel. And the day before we left, my father and the man whose family came out with us, they went down to Oklahoma City to a bakery and got a hundred loaves of bread. I think they paid a penny a loaf for it. And we ate that until, I guess I could say 'til it got too moldy, but I wonder if we didn't eat some of it even moldy! We had lots of bread and fried potatoes on that trip.

We did find some odd jobs. We stopped a couple of times and picked cotton.

We made it to California, although we did break down in Buckeye, Arizona. Now, that was a very memorable night. We had to stay a couple of days there to get the car repaired. Then, of course, we had to borrow money from somebody to get it repaired. But we made it.

LFW: I really wasn't aware that we had to stop and work on the way, because I was only about four. I just remember vaguely a little bit about the trip out there. Can you tell about how long we had to wait and where we stayed while we were waiting for the car to be fixed?

MEG: Well, we were in Buckeye, Arizona, as I said, and we had no place to stay, except in the car. There were five of us. On the way to California, before we broke down, we had to sleep in the car. Mother and Dad had a mattress put down beside the car and Flo and I slept in the car. At Buckeye, we were in this car, trying to sleep, and we were right next door to a bar. They were really having a time that night, and Flo got scared and Dad had to convince her that everything was going to be alright, that he was there to protect her. She got so frightened from all the noise. They were just really cutting up over there, drinking and yelling. We always teased Flo about that, because she got so scared.

LFW: Weren't there two other families that went with us?

MEG: No, just the Curtises. They had five girls and one boy. There were eight of them.

LFW: Eight of them. But they were rich. They had *two* mattresses! Now, did they stay with us when we were in Buckeye, or did they go on?

MEG: No, they stayed with us. In fact, they had to stay, because he was the one we borrowed the money from to pay the bill! They were very close friends. These were people my father knew before he had me. This other man was a preacher, and they would preach in revival meetings together, or brush arbor meetings, really. Dad never was really a hired pastor. He served as a pastor, but he didn't get paid for it. But they did brush arbor meetings together and were very dear friends, and they got us to California.

Lily Fern has her own memories of the trip, most of which are fairly close to those Meekly relates, but which are probably a compilation of real memories and the stories she heard about the trip over the years:

LFW: Brother Curtis had been one of the evangelists in the meeting where my father was converted. The cars left together to move to California. We were all very, very poor 'Okies.' I never have seen the movie, 'The Grapes of Wrath,' but one of these days I'm going to watch it, because I've heard enough about it to know that that must have been what we looked like as we drove those broken-down cars with mattresses thrown on top. I thought the Curtises were rich, because they had two mattresses and we were poor, because we only had one! When we would stop at night, Dad would throw the mattress on the ground and Mama would make our pallet there, and my brother and sister slept in the car. I slept on the ground with Mother and Daddy.

We would start out early in the morning and they would cook breakfast before we left our campsite. Now, we didn't have campgrounds or anything back then. We just pulled over to the side, off the road, and would make a fire and cook supper at night and then breakfast in the morning. Lunch was just what we would happen to have left over from breakfast, or whatever.

I remember gathering around the campfire, and we sang songs and had contests, and the kids played games, and I always went to sleep in my daddy's arms, and he'd carry me and put me in bed.

She tells one story that she and Meekly recall as one of the funniest and most frightening parts of the trip:

LFW: One night we discovered we were closer to the road than we thought we were. We had all got settled and were asleep, and suddenly we heard this car coming. Mom and Dad said they thought it was awful close, and Dad raised up and saw these headlights coming right toward our mattress! Well, Dad jumped up, wearing just his shirt and no underwear--we were so poor that I'm not sure at that point that he even owned any--and started yelling, 'cause they were coming straight at us. It must have been quite a sight in the headlights! They finally swerved and slammed on their brakes. They threw gravel all over the mattress, and Mom grabbed me by the hair and drug me to the car, screaming like an Indian. Mother was part Indian. She was one-sixteenth Choctaw and one-sixteenth Cherokee, which, by the way, is the same amount and type of Indian blood that Earl had. Anyway, Dad finally got that truck stopped and it turned out to be some Indians, who had been partying a little bit too much and got off the road! I think this was someplace in Arizona.

Meekly recalls the same incident:

MEG: Sometime after we went to sleep, I remember my dad jumping off of his mattress, and all he had on was his shirt, but he was jumping up and down and hollering, 'Hey, hey, hey!' A car was coming right toward us. The man was drunk and was driving well off the road, and just about to run over all of us. My father ended up right a-straddle of the hood of the car, waving his hands, trying to get this fellow to see that we were there, that he was going to hurt us if he ran into us--and he certainly would have. This is another incident in the Goble history that is funny now, but it wasn't funny then.

With all their adventures, funny and serious, the Gobles managed to travel from Oklahoma to California, but they didn't quite make it to their final destination, the Los Angeles area, without a lengthy stop. Lily Fern has fond memories of that stop-over:

LFW: We got as far as a little town called Jacumba, California, where the families knew another family. We had to stay there, because we ran out of money and couldn't go on into Los Angeles. The Curtis family went on, and this family that we knew got us a one room cabin in a little courtyard. There were six little cabins there. I don't know how much they had to pay for the rent, but it couldn't have been very much. It didn't have a bathroom. Everybody had to use the same outside toilet, but we did have a shower and a little kitchen. And Dad got a job working in a dairy in Jacumba. I don't remember the name, but it is still going.

Jacumba is about one hundred and thirty miles east of San Diego, so we were considerably short of our final destination of Los Angeles. But we stayed there long enough for Dad to earn enough money for us to make the rest of the trip. He worked twelve and sixteen hours a day for three dollars a day and all the milk we could drink and all the lard we could use. So, many times the only thing we had to eat was biscuits and gravy, which still sounds pretty good to me. I love biscuits and gravy! But in those days we thought that was just awful. Mom, when she'd get this lard, if she could get enough flour, would make doughnuts, because it didn't call for a lot of sugar and they were filling. So we could drink milk and have doughnuts, and sometimes that's really all we had. But, you know, we didn't really feel like we were suffering. We got hungry for other things, but you could look at all of us today and realize we weren't hurt any!

I don't care what we had to do without or what we didn't have, we always had one thing--and that was love. We had security and unity in the family. There was never a day that went by--I don't care how tired Daddy was, or how hard he had worked that day--every night, before we went to bed, Dad would get the *Bible* down and we'd have prayer, even up until my brother and sister left home or got married. When I was little, I always got to sit on Daddy's lap, because I was the baby. When he got the *Bible* down, I'd run for his lap and crawl up in his arms, and my brother and sister would fight to see whose turn it was to share his lap. One or the other would get in his lap, and the other one would sit down around his knees, and Mom would pull a chair up as close as she could get to Daddy. I can just see the picture to this day of Mom sitting there with my dad, with her arm around his neck, and me in his arms and either Florence or Meekly sitting on his lap. We absolutely worshipped and adored Father, our daddy. And he would read the *Bible* and pray for whatever needs his family had that day. His main prayer was that his children would grow up and serve the Lord and meet him in Heaven some day.

Lily Fern admits that her memory of Jacumba and their life there was sketchy, so she turned to Meekly for a more accurate view:

LFW: Meekly, do you remember how long we had to stay in Jacumba? Was it like weeks or months or....

MEG: It was months. I finished a school year there. I know Dad worked awful hard at that dairy. That is one of the most memorable things about Jacumba, to me. Dad was what, in those days, was called a 'professional dairyman.' He didn't work too long in the dairy business, but he went to school to learn how to do the different operations in the dairy. It was before the days of automatic milkers, I guess you'd call them, and they milked those cows by hand. I think he had to milk twenty-six cows a day, and his hands got so sore, he would have to get up early before he would go to work in the morning, just to work his hands to get them to shut enough to squeeze enough to milk those cows. Such agony he was in! I remember how we all felt so sorry for him. Though we were young, we could tell that our father was really sacrificing at that job for our livelihood. It was such a trial for him.

LFW: I remember that while we were living in Jacumba, we didn't have money to buy candy or anything, but once a week, there was a vegetable and fruit truck that came through the courtyard, and they had oranges for a nickel apiece. Now that may not seem like a lot, but in those days, ten cents would buy a loaf of bread and fifteen cents would buy a lot of different essential foods. But Mama would sneak fifteen cents out of the budget every week and buy each of us kids one orange. I have never had an orange that tasted as good as those tasted, and I probably never will! It makes my mouth water to think about them. I've got an orange right here in front of me now, and I can guarantee you, it's not as good as those oranges were back then. And we would peel that orange down just part of the way and eat on it, so that the orange itself would not get dirty from touching it. Mama said if we peeled it all, we had to eat it all, but if you want to eat on it a little at a time, just peel part of it down and eat it so the orange doesn't get dirty. I remember us making that orange last for three days, before we would finally finish it. Good oranges!

None of the Goble children could agree on the exact circumstances surrounding one incident that occurred at Jacumba. Each had a slightly different version, but all recalled it. Lily Fern's version was slightly more colorful, if not entirely accurate:

LFW: It was getting close to Christmas time, and Jacumba is right on the border of Mexico. We knew Mexico was there, but we didn't know--I'm not sure my mother and dad even knew--that there was a line that you didn't cross. It was like fifteen feet from our back yard, where we played, and we didn't realize that we weren't supposed to go over there. Just over the line were these beautiful Christmas trees. So Mom and Dad and all us kids went over there and chopped down a tree. The next day, my sister and my brother and I went over there and started to bring that Christmas tree back home, and the Mexican Border Patrol started screaming and shooting, to scare us kids, just so we wouldn't be coming back over there.

MEG: As I remember, it was coming Christmas and we didn't have funds for a Christmas tree. Maybe Mother was with us, but as I remember, just the three of us kids went out to get a Christmas tree, and we walked and walked, and I think I remember crossing a barb wire fence, but anybody could have crossed it. It wasn't restricted in a military sense. It was just a low fence. We finally found our Christmas tree and brought it back home. I don't think our mother even knew what we had done, but in relating the story to other people in the neighborhood, they found out that we had gone into Mexico. Mexico was a friendly nation to us, but the police did patrol the border. Not too often, but they would come by occasionally, and they told us that if the Mexican police had come by, that we could have gotten into some trouble for being over in their country. It was amusing to us. Again, isn't it funny how we can laugh at things later, but how serious they were at the moment?

LFW: I related my story to Florence, and I told that they were there and shot guns in the air, but Florence said they just took the guns out and were yelling at us and were trying to frighten us off. I probably just remember the story as different people told it, because I was pretty young.

Obviously, there is no consensus among the Goble children as to what really happened that day, but somewhere in those three versions, there is a funny remembrance from the time in Jacumba.

Perhaps the best part of the story involves what happened after the tree arrived in the Jacumba cabin, with or without Border Patrol confrontations:

LFW: That night, Mom popped popcorn and we had some cranberries, and we all strung the popcorn and cranberries, even Dad, and put them on the tree. Mama had a little white towel she wrapped around the base of the tree, and that was our Christmas tree. I have never seen a Christmas tree more beautiful than that one was to us. I've spent many hours trying to decorate a tree and decorate my home. In fact, this last Christmas, I had a little tree, and my living room and dining room were so beautiful--we had the garlands and the lights and the tree ornaments that all matched a certain way, and it was very beautiful, but not as beautiful as that tree that our family decorated with popcorn and cranberries in that little cabin on the border of Mexico.

Soon, though, Lon Goble was to begin the final stage of a journey that brought him half way across the North American continent, from his birth in Indiana, to his final home on the Pacific Ocean. He finally got together enough money to take the family the rest of the way to their destination, Los Angeles or, more specifically, Wilmar, California.

He could not know then that the war he had fought in before his marriage to Lillie, World War I, had not really established a lasting peace and that a new conflict was brewing in Europe. So, they set off to find a peaceful and prosperous life in Southern California.

Chapter Three

 The Promised Land

Life did not improve automatically for "Dust Bowl" refugees when they reached the promised land of California. The country was still recovering from a stricken economy after the stock market crash of 1929. President Franklin Roosevelt's "Relief" programs were swamped with people struggling to get back on their feet. It was a time of homeless people, hoboes wandering the land, and, for those politically acute, awareness of a gathering cloud over Europe and Asia.

Lon Goble was able to use his wit, charm and intelligence to find work and get established eventually.

He hadn't been in California long before he became aware of the coming conflict in Europe and Asia. Perhaps his experience as a World War I soldier made him more alert to the situation. Lily Fern recalls that most of their acquaintances traveled out to the farms of Japanese farmers for produce, but Lon would not. He was suspicious of them. He said, "Someday they're going to own America."

He had fought in Germany and he used some of his experiences in his preaching, such as the sorrow and joy involved in missing soldiers being found:

LFW: I remember Dad used to preach a sermon, something about Johnny coming home. His scripture was Timothy II, 'Thou therefore endure hardness as a good soldier.' I loved to hear my daddy preach that sermon! He told about a lost son marching home in a parade and the joy of the mother. I get torn up when I think about it. When Dad told this story, it would just tear you up. Dad would tell that story and then give an altar call and the altars were filled! It was a beautiful story.

Fortunately, little Lily Fern was young enough to only know the excitement of a new home and a new life. She was too young to be worrying about war.

She was around five years old when the family arrived in the Los Angeles area, where she would live for the next decade.

Her memories include the difficult times and the many changes they faced upon arriving at their final destination:

LFW: We finally did get on over to Wilmar, and we lived with the Smith family for a while. They had six children, and the youngest boy was my age, and that was the meanest little boy I've ever seen in my life! But, we grew up to be very close friends. We even dated a little bit. Anyway, we lived there and Dad began to try to find a job, but he couldn't find work at first. This was in the early 1930's, and it was still during the depression. Somehow or another, though, we met this lady, who was the head official, or something, of the relief work in the Southern California area. She got Dad a job working for the WPA, which was called the 'Relief' in those days. Some members of the family think she was more than a little interested in Dad, who was considered quite a charmer then!

Reflecting on her father's charm, Lily Fern explains:

LFW: I don't think Dad was a flirt or even appeared that way, but he had a lot of sex appeal. A lot of women really thought he was cute as a button. He wasn't really a handsome man. I thought he was a good-looking man. He was very graceful and he loved to dance. Of course, Nazarenes didn't believe in dancing, but he could dance a jig like you never saw! He really was very graceful on his feet. I certainly didn't inherit that! Dad couldn't sing, couldn't carry a note in a bushel basket, but he sure did love to try. He was a charmer.

Whether it was by charm, intelligence or luck, Lon now had the means to support his family in their new home. The lady got Lon a job managing the commissary that distributed food and clothes from the government.

In an interview with Lily Fern and Meekly, they discussed the way their parents worked together to make a life for their family.

LFW: You know, Meekly, we were talking about how hard Dad worked, but Mama worked really hard, too.

MEG: Yes, our mother was a real hard worker, too. In fact, after we left Jacumba and came to Wilmar, Mother took in ironings to help make ends meet. I remember how she used to stand out in that hot garage, working over that mangle. The heat from the mangle itself was enough to destroy anybody, but when the weather was hot outside, it was a real trial for her to have to do that.

In my mind, I think I remember her charging five cents to iron a shirt. I don't remember all the price rates for sheets and whatever else she pressed, but that's how tough things were for the Gobles. But we had a strong relationship with each other and our parents had a strong relationship with the Lord, that guided us through. We all came out and survived.

Conditions had gotten a little better for the Gobles after Lon got his job. That is how they were able to rent a house and move out of the Smith home. Lily Fern remembers how, even in the midst of a battle for survival, their mother continued to work for the Lord.

LFW: We began to live a little bit better, because we finally got to rent a little three room house. The main reason we rented it was because behind the house there was a building that had been a garage. They converted that into a laundry, and behind the laundry was a room they had made into a bedroom and a little bathroom. Mama took in ironings to help support the family. Mama and Dad slept in the garage bedroom, and my brother and sister and I slept in the house.

Mama also found a job cleaning three homes a week, and they were these huge, what we would call 'mansions' those days, with six and eight bedrooms. They paid her very well. In fact, she had only worked a couple of weeks when two of the families raised her pay because she was such a wonderful housekeeper and cleaning woman.

Mama won two of those families to the Lord. One was a Catholic family with four children. Mama just lived the life! One day the wife stopped Mama to talk to her, and she broke out crying. Mama just led her to the Lord. The woman was frightened, though. She didn't know whether she was going to be able to tell her husband or not. But eventually he noticed a change in her life, so she told him what had happened, and he told her that if something could change anything as much as it had changed her, he wanted to know what it was. So, Mama led both of them to the Lord, and, of course, they started coming to church with all the children. Mama kept in contact with them for years and years, and the last contact she had, they were all still serving the

Lord, raising their families and going to church. So, her testimony went with her wherever she went.

She cleaned houses and took in ironing and still cooked and kept up her family. Dad got to bring home all the old vegetables that were rejected or not passed out to the other families on Relief. The vegetables that he brought home were what we would throw away today. We would say that they were rotten. But Mama said, 'Don't throw anything away. Bring it home.' She would put it in ice and crisp it up, and sometimes they were nice enough to even have the raw vegetables, and she'd fix celery sticks and carrot sticks and things like that. But, on the days that she had her heavy cleaning and heavy ironings, she always made a great big pot of vegetable soup and some cornbread, and that's what we ate all day long. Dad got other things, too. He got cheese and butter, and so forth, that were luxuries to us--and the day-old bread. It saved on our grocery bill an awful lot.

The Goble children had their jobs, too. Even little Lily Fern helped out. She recalls an incident during the performance of one of their weekly chores:

LFW: Our family was given three dollars a week for groceries from the Relief. That was probably 1934. We didn't have a car, so Mama would have to send my brother and sister and me to the store to get our groceries. We would carry all we could carry, a bag in each arm. And most of the time, my brother and sister had to go back for a second load. That's how many groceries we could get for three dollars a week in those days. But we always looked forward to going to the grocery store every week, because the grocery man always gave us a big jawbreaker.

Now, the jawbreakers in those days were like golf balls, and we *loved* jawbreakers! It was the only candy we ever had. During the summer, all us kids went bare-footed. We had one pair of shoes and we didn't have any money to buy an extra pair. They had to last a long time. All summer long, I had the end of both big toes knocked off.

Well, we started back from the store this one morning, and I had a bag of groceries in each arm. I put that jawbreaker in my mouth, and Florence and Meekly got ahead of me. Florence was five years older and Meekly was four years older than I, and they were really close. They had gotten ahead of me and I was running to try to catch up with them, when I stubbed my toe, knocked the end off of it again, and swallowed my jawbreaker! The toe hurt, but what broke my heart was the fact that

I had swallowed my jawbreaker. It had gotten half way down--wouldn't come up and wouldn't go down! I thought I was going to choke to death. Florence and Meekly realized there was something wrong, so they came running back. Florence put her groceries down and hit my back really hard and that jawbreaker came back up. You'll never know what relief is until you think you've swallowed your jawbreaker and you're not going to get another one until next week! I wasn't even so much concerned about choking; I was just worried that I had lost my jawbreaker. And then, instead of going down, it came up and I still had my jawbreaker! And we finally got home with the groceries, too.

After the Goble family's adventures with being on Relief in Wilmar, they moved again, this time to a more prosperous existence. Lily Fern was aware that they were still poor, but things were improving:

LFW: We lived in Wilmar until about 1936, and Dad got a job at General Motors painting cars. That was in Southgate, California, so we had to move to be closer to that location. We moved to Compton. That was the first house that my dad owned. He bought a one bedroom house, but it had a huge living room, a dining room, a great big kitchen--and it was modern! We didn't have to go outside to go to the bathroom. It had a huge back porch and a laundry room, where Mama could still take in laundries and ironings.

That was when we started to the First Church of the Nazarene in Compton. Now, after we left Oklahoma, Dad didn't pastor a church any longer. He did preach, however, whenever a pastor would be gone. They would call Dad to hold the pulpit while they were gone. So, he preached quite a lot, and started painting cars at General Motors and at home on the weekends. This just shows again how my dad worked to try to make a living for his family.

"Family" was the key word during this period, and they all worked together and played together. Lily Fern laughs as she tells a story involving family outings and her spunky sister, Florence:

LFW: On Saturday mornings, Daddy would usually paint one or two cars. He would get up at the break of dawn and my brother would help him, because if he could get through early enough, we could all go into town. Mom would get her groceries and it was just a fun day for everybody. If we had any money, we kids would go to the dime store. By then, Florence was probably about sixteen or seventeen.

Every Saturday, this Jehovah's Witness man with his two boys would come down our street and my Dad would argue with him. He loved to argue and he would have argued 'til doomsday! It would delay him from his work, but he was determined to get that work done before we could go.

Well, Florence had been working in the yard one Saturday, trying to get the yard fixed up a little bit. She had a hoe and was getting the weeds out of Mama's flower beds. She saw the man and his boys coming down the street and she decided to fix the situation! She knew they were headed right for our driveway, so she hid behind a bush with this hoe in her hand. When they got about even with the bush, she jumped out and scared them to death. She said, 'Do you see this hoe handle? If you ever come back in this yard, I'm going to make a collar out of it for you. I want you to hit that street and the next time you come by, you cross the road when you pass our house!' And they did! They never came back to our yard. They really thought she was going to knock them in the head with that hoe handle. But Daddy always got his work finished sooner after that and we got our trips into town!

Lily Fern was not quite as forceful as her sister. She had to deal with her shyness, such as in her early experiences in school:

LFW: I had been to kindergarten and first grade in Wilmar and when we moved to Compton, I started the second grade. In the second grade, I was just as smart as the next person, but I was always very timid and bashful in surroundings where I knew we didn't have the things that other people had, like with the kids at school. I was not timid with family and at church, or with friends, though.

But in second grade, the teacher intimidated me so badly, and when she would ask me a question, although I knew what the answer was, I was afraid to answer it. And I just didn't. It looked like I was not learning anything in that class, so she convinced everybody that I needed to be put back. So, I had to go through the first grade twice, but after I got out of her room, I had no problem, so I'm sure it was just my personality with hers. I always thought she picked on me.

She was such a contrast to my kindergarten teacher. When we were still in Wilmar and I was in kindergarten, my teacher realized immediately, I'm sure, that we were very much in need of various things. She wrote a note home to my mother one day, shortly after I started to kindergarten, asking if she could have Mama's permission to drive me home from school the following day, because she had a big box of clothes that she wanted to give us. Mama wrote back and said it was O.K. You know, in this day and age, we would be afraid to let our children ride even with a school teacher. But this teacher--I thought she was the most beautiful woman in the world. She was like an angel to me. She catered to me. It just seems like even then I recognized it. And now, I realize that she knew that there was a need in my life and she really, to me, was a true teacher. She just took me under her wing and, if she thought anything was wrong, she would come and talk to me, and she was so kind and so gentle with me.

When I got out of school that day, she put me in the front seat, and in the back seat were three huge boxes of clothes for all members of my family--shirts for my brother and father, dresses for my sister and me, and underwear, some of it new, some of it not. It had things in there for my mother. Up to that time, my sister and I had had to wear long cotton socks to school, and all the kids made fun of us for doing that in California. But in that box were bobby sox, and back then, I thought they were the cutest things--I just thought that was the cat's meow. And I thought I was the cat's meow when I put them on. I didn't have to wear cotton socks and cotton stockings any more to school!

After Lily Fern's bad experience with entering the second grade, her schooling seemed to go well, except for the problems created by moving frequently. She adapted easily, though, because it became a way of life, moving from school to school:

LFW: I did fine in school after the problem with that teacher. We lived in the Southern California area, around Compton and Lynwood, with five school districts. Grammar schools went from kindergarten through the sixth grade, the next from seventh through the tenth. Then you graduated and went over to the Compton Junior College, and that's where they had their eleventh and twelfth, and then on to college. I went to four grammar schools and three junior high schools. Mama and Dad moved that much when I was in grade school. It was always hard to have to be moved around from school to school, but Dad was always trying to better himself, and he always did.

Lily Fern's dreams were not timid or bashful. She continued to want to sing:

LFW: All my life, I had always had a desire to sing, and when anybody would come to our church with special music for revival or anything, I would sit there and just say, in my heart, 'That's what I want to do someday!' I would even fantasize that I would be singing up there someday, but never really thought that I would be able to do that. There used to be a black family that would come to our church and sing, and, oh, we loved to hear them sing! When I would go home, for two or three days I would just dream about being able to do what they were doing. There was one evangelistic party that came to our church several times. They were called the Mackey Walker Trio. It was a man and his wife and another evangelist. The woman played the accordion and they sang in a trio. The men would preach on alternate nights. I loved to hear them sing. I really believe, with all my heart, that that was where I really felt my first call to sing for the Lord, but I still didn't know how it could ever come to pass.

It was in Compton, also, where Lily Fern began to realize the depth of the love of her siblings for her. One incident sticks out in her mind from when she was still a child:

LFW: When we moved to Compton and were doing a little better financially, Mama and Dad would give us kids ten cents a week allowance. I don't know what all Florence and Meekly did with their allowances, but I always spent mine a penny a day at school for candy, and then on Fridays, I had six cents. I could buy candy and an ice cream. We thought we were living high on the hog!

But the Christmas of 1936, Mama and Dad gave each of us twenty cents to spend for Christmas. I don't have any idea what I did with mine. I probably bought candy! On Christmas morning, when I got up, underneath the Christmas tree was this life-size paper doll. It was hard cardboard, with all these paper clothes. My brother and sister had pooled their twenty cents each and bought me that paper doll. They didn't get a Christmas present. They used all their money on me! That's the kind of love that we had in our family. So, I always knew that my brother and sister really loved me, even though we were never really, really close when I was small. I was too much younger than they were. But that was quite a sacrifice, really, and I knew that they loved me.

As the Goble children approached and entered their teens, the family stabilized and achieved more financial security, but not without some funny and worrisome times. Lily Fern tells a family story involving her mother:

> LFW: We lived in this one house that didn't have a bathroom in it and the outside toilet was way out behind the house, of course. It was another of those things where Dad had sold our house and bought a better house, except that it was not modern. It did have a shower in back of the garage, so we could take showers, at least, but the outside toilet was in bad shape. It was almost full to over-flowing, the floor was weak, and it should have been moved to a new location. Mama kept saying, 'You're going to have to move that, because I'm afraid one of the kids is going to fall in.' Well, Dad just kept procrastinating and never did get it fixed, and one day, Mama fell in! Florence was home with her girl friend, and they heard her screaming, but it was so far from the house that they thought it was just the chickens making noise. She screamed until she was about to pass out, and she knew she couldn't afford to do that. The outhouse was a 'two-seater," and she had caught one elbow in one hole and one in the other. Finally, she made one last desperate lunge for the door with one hand, and reached the outside of the door. She pulled herself out and she was a mess, so she ran for the shower behind the garage. Before she could get to the wash house to take a shower, she had broken out completely in a rash--the inside of her nose, her ears, her mouth--and, of course, we had to take her to the doctor and he said she was probably the same internally. We didn't have penicillin in those days, but he gave her a couple of rounds of sulfa. She was in bed for about three days over that, but it's a wonder she didn't die!

Lillie Goble seemed prone to unusual incidents, but this was certainly the most dangerous.

Lily Fern was still something of a pest in the older children's lives, as younger children can be to their older siblings, especially when they reach the teens and begin to take themselves more seriously. Florence was dating the young man she would later marry, Earl Squier, when Lily Fern got into some mischief. In Florence's words:

> FGS: Earl lived in Escondido, California, when we were dating, and that's about a hundred miles away. Consequently, there were lots of letters going back and forth. We didn't have a phone, and it would have been too expensive anyway. So, he wrote me a lot of letters. I came home from school one day--I was going to college in Compton--and the

closet door in my room was closed. I could hear this giggling in there. I opened the door and Lily Fern and one of her girl friends were sitting in the closet floor. They had a whole box of my love letters out, reading them! I think it's funny now, but I sure wasn't amused at the time!

Florence and Earl Squier looked after Lily Fern, though, as seen in another incident, described by Florence:

FGS: When I was dating Earl, we took Lily Fern down to the Long Beach Pike [amusement park], and a bunch of sailors passed by us. Of course, Lily Fern was always such a pretty girl, but she was only about eleven or twelve, and they started hitting on her. Earl got mad and yelled at them to leave her alone, and they didn't, so he left the two of us and just walked up to them like he was really big enough to do anything about it. Again, it was a really big laugh after it was all over, but it was kind of scary at the time!

To this day, Lily Fern remembers the way she clung to Earl Squier for the rest of that outing:

LFW: The Pike was a fun place to go. It was a big recreation park on the beach near the main part of Long Beach. When the sailors started hitting on me, I was scared to death, because I was only about eleven or twelve. Earl Squier was not a really big guy, but he finally just had to tell them--I forget just what he told them. I remember I was scared and I never let go of his arm after that. Earl Squier has *always* stood twenty feet tall to me, regardless of his physical stature.

When World War II began, the Gobles were living in one of the most affected areas in the country, being on the coast and near military installations. As the nation reacted to the ever-present threat of invasion and the need for materials, Californians adjusted to a war mentality.

This is Lily Fern's memory of that period:

LFW: In 1942, the war broke out and they rationed everything. I don't remember all of the shortages now, except that I remember we could hardly buy sugar. We had to have food stamps--ration stamps--for everything. You couldn't get gasoline to travel anywhere--it was very limited. And butter and oleo were rationed. We had to buy oleo in the packages which seemed like nothing but a pack of lard with some yellow food coloring in it, and you mixed it up and that was your oleo, or your butter. Sugar, probably even flour--I don't remember, but they were all rationed. Because we had no gas, we had to take the streetcar in to church and everywhere we went. It was called Pacific Electric, which was the streetcar that ran from Los Angeles to Long Beach. So, we would walk two miles to the streetcar depot, and then take it to Compton, get off and walk about another mile or mile and a half to church. Then, when church was over, everybody had to do the same thing back. It was a whole state or town effort and we never did have to walk alone when we were going back to the streetcar, because the whole church was going back to catch a train or bus to somewhere. We'd go back and catch the streetcar and get to our stop, two miles from home, and it was always dark, of course.

Every Wednesday night, after church, we'd have a black-out--an air raid warning, where they would make you put all the lights out for practice. I remember one night Dad thought he would just strike a match, to see what would happen. We were outside and there were always airplanes flying over, because they were depicting air raids. Immediately, a big, loud voice came out from the sky, 'Put that light out!' So, they could see it right away. They had many air raid warnings, where they'd blow the whistle and you had to do what you were already trained to do-- either go to certain areas or take some shelter someplace. One night, though, we heard this and it was in the middle of the night. Nobody thought, and I don't think to this day that it was just a warning. We really thought it was all-out warfare, because there were planes shooting back and forth in the sky. You could see the gunfire. And we never did find out what that was. They put a hush on it immediately. We were pretty close to the ocean-- just about fifteen miles, or maybe a little less-- and down around Long Beach, San Pedro and that area, there were a lot of naval bases and marine bases, and the defense plants and the shipyards. I think, and a lot of others think that there was truly a plane that got over and we never did find out how or why--or what happened.

As all the children matured during this exciting time, they began to get closer, enjoying each other and understanding each other better. During an interview, Lily Fern and Meekly reminisced about some good times.

LFW: Meekly, before you went to the service--I think I was probably about twelve when the war came and you enlisted in the Navy and had to go. Before you left, I remember we got pretty close. We'd go out. We'd go roller skating or ice skating on Friday nights.

MEG: Roller skating.

LFW: Yes, it was always roller skating, but one night we went ice skating, and I just could not get the hang of that ice skating bit! My ankles weren't quite strong enough to hold me up, or something. But there was the cutest guy there, who kept wanting to skate with me, and I was bashful and didn't want to do it, because I couldn't skate. I had watched him and he was a good skater. You had seen him come up to me two or three times and ask me to skate and I would turn him down, so you came over and said, 'Next time that guy comes back, if you don't skate with him, I'm not going to ever bring you ice skating again.' So, I said, 'O.K.' Well, next time he came, I said, 'O.K.' I tried to tell him I could not skate well, and that he'd have to help me and so on. He was willing to do that. Well, at this particular ice skating rink, they never would let you know, but at any point of time while you were out there skating, they would play a certain song or hit a certain chord or something, and that meant that everyone went into the thing called, 'The Whip.' Do you remember that?

MEG: Oh, yes!

LFW: And what the whip was--it would start out with two people and they would skate around the rink and they'd grab two more, one person on one side and one on the other side, or one couple or something. Anyway, by the time it got to everybody, the one that was on the end of that whip--I mean, even the professionals could hardly stand up. Guess who got on the end of the whip? This poor kid who was skating with me, trying to help and hold me up. They came around and we had to get on it. He had to hold himself up and me! I never could figure out why, but he never asked me to skate with him again. But you took me roller skating and ice skating again. We got close before you went to the Navy.

MEG: Yes. Just before I went into the service, I was chasing with a kid--we ran around and were real close. The two of us were real good friends, and they lived just down the street from us. He had two sisters. One was maybe just a little older than you. The girls were growing up to where they could go skating with us when we'd go out. So we did get real close just before I went into the service. We were able to tolerate each other enough to where we could go get a hot dog together and enjoy each other. Then, I went into the service in the latter part of 1942, or the early part of 1943.

As Lily Fern's relationship with Meekly improved, so did her relationship with Florence. Apparently their mother had not recognized the improvement, as Lily Fern recalls in her reminiscence of another war-time experience:

LFW: My sister had gotten married and lived in San Diego. She worked in the defense factories with her husband. Then he was called to the service during the war--he went to the Navy--and Florence had to move back home. By the time she moved back, she was expecting her first child. Now, up to this time, although my brother and sister and I knew we all loved each other, they just kind of tolerated me. They never mistreated me or anything, but we would fuss and argue and get into scraps, like all brothers and sisters do. But I never did really get into a real big scrap or argument with my sister. She was just old enough, I guess, that she'd just say, 'Oh, well. Go on and mind your own business,' or whatever.

Well, when Florence had to move back home, I was about, oh, probably about twelve or thirteen. Mama set me down one day and said, 'Now, I've got to talk to you, because Florence is moving back home because Earl is going to the Navy.' Dad had sold the house we had and bought another one, but it just had two bedrooms. I had one bedroom and Mama and Dad had the other. She said, 'You're going to have to share the bedroom with Florence. She's going to have a baby, and she's going to be blue and upset because Earl's gone to the service, and at times she may be very depressed and very moody. I want you to treat her kindly. I don't want you to be unkind to her at all.' She didn't know it, but she didn't really have to tell me that, because I always looked up to my brother and sister so much, and admired them.

My sister has always been a very strong person, personality-wise. She has never let things really affect her on the outside that much, and I knew she'd be O.K., even if Earl was gone. Mama didn't have to tell me I had to be kind to Florence. I was thrilled to death that she was moving back home. I did everything I could and would have done anything she would have asked me to do. We never had one cross word all the time she was living there with us. In fact, we bonded even closer. We took long walks, because she wanted to get a lot of exercise. We lived about four miles from town, and we walked to town and back every day. We'd either go see a movie or just have lunch or something, and then come back home. We really had a great, close relationship from that time on.

To this day, my brother and sister and I are so very close, even though we're miles and miles apart. All of our families--the children are all really close.

So, she came back home and her husband got a weekend furlough. He came home and he knew then that he was going to be sent overseas. We took him up to Los Angeles, to the train station, and Florence was just within about a month of having her first baby. I just felt so badly for both of them, because I felt how hard it must be for them to have to say goodbye to each other. When they finally called Earl's train and he had to leave, I felt like I had to do something. I walked up to Florence and took her by the arm and was standing there with her. He turned and walked away. Florence started to cry, and, oh, it just broke my heart! It still bothers me to think about it. I turned and looked at Earl Squier, and I wish I hadn't, because when I did, he had the most helpless look on his face, as if to say, 'Oh, why do I have to leave?' He knew he had to go, and I said, 'Earl, she'll be O.K.' But I was crying, too. I said, 'We'll take care of her. She'll be O.K.' I was only about thirteen. And he went on. We've talked about that later. He said that was the most helpless feeling he ever had. And I think that day Earl Squier and I bonded closer, too. But we were really good friends anyway. I love him with all of my heart. He's just like an older brother to me.

Florence also recalls her gratitude to Lily Fern:

FGS: During the war, when Earl was in the Navy and I was pregnant, I moved home with my folks. My folks didn't want me to stay by myself while I was pregnant. So, I stayed there until Earl got out of the Navy, and Dennis, my oldest son, was born during this time. Lily Fern very generously gave up her room so Dennis and I could have a room to ourselves.

It seems that the entire Goble family grew closer during the trying times of a war atmosphere, as the children matured. As usual, the church formed a foundation for the family:

LFW: Florence came back home and had the baby, and then Earl was brought back home, and then stationed in Washington state for a while, and she went up to be with him after the baby was born. But before that, we had to go on with our lives just like we always had. Mother had gone to work in the defense plants, and Florence and I were there at home alone, except when I was in school.

Most of the time we lived in Compton, Dad was the Sunday School Superintendent and taught a Sunday School class. Mama and Daddy were always on the board. Mother was the secretary and treasurer of the church, so she had to be at every board meeting. I don't know why, but it seemed like the board meetings in those days lasted for hours and hours and hours. Well, actually, they did. And they'd always have them Wednesday night after church. Even as a little, tiny kid, I remember going to sleep on a church bench and waking up, thinking they must have left me. I thought, 'It's been too long. They couldn't be in a board meeting this long!' But they'd still be in the board meeting.

This dedication to church work, and Lillie Goble's tendency to get into strange situations led to one of the funniest and most humiliating experiences of Lily Fern's young life:

LFW: My sister had moved back home, Earl Squier was in the Navy and Meekly had been stationed in New Caledonia. Somehow, that bonded the family closer together. Isn't it funny how separation will sometimes bond a family closer together? But, anyway, Dad was teaching the 'unmarried' Sunday School class, which was supposed to be young people, men and women, boys and girls, from ages sixteen up to the point that they got married. Well, when all of the men went to the service, all of those married girls came back to Daddy's class, because it was just all girls now. I was in that class. I wasn't old enough to be, but I was. I just went in there because all my friends were in there. And, like I said, during the war, we couldn't get gas to go anywhere, so we had to take the bus or the streetcar for everything we did. But once a week, because we all had enough money to go out and eat and do things, that Sunday School class would have an outing. Most of the time, we would go to downtown Los Angeles on the streetcar and eat at Clifton's Cafeteria, which is still there, as far as I know. In those days, it was just really the thing to do! We'd eat at Clifton's Cafeteria and then, generally, go to the ball game, to see the Angels play ball at Angels' Stadium. Then, we'd go catch a streetcar and head home.

Well, we did this one time, and I'm sure we must have looked like Daddy's harem, because it was always Mama and Daddy and all these girls--between fifteen and twenty girls--and at that time, three of them were expecting! We went to eat and went to the ball game, and then came back to catch our streetcar back to Compton. Dad had told us all,

'Now, when we get to the station--we want to get there as soon as we can--we want to try to be first in line. We'll just all stay together to be there when those doors open. Then, Lily Fern and I will hurry ahead and get seats saved.' I knew it was true that when the doors opened, you had to run to get your streetcar, and a lot of times, if you didn't, you wouldn't get on. You'd have to wait for another streetcar, which was an hour. Besides that, the service men preempted anything or anybody. They always went first, and then we got what was left. The people would just run for their cars.

We were standing at the door, waiting for the streetcar to be announced and for the doors to open. There were four big sliding doors, and when they opened, you ran for your car. Pretty soon, they called for our train and opened the doors, and Dad and I took off like we said we'd do, to get seats.

Now, my mother weighed about two hundred and sixty pounds, and she got warm standing there, because there were about three hundred people crowding around, waiting to get through those doors. She took off her coat and threw it over her arm. Our group was first in line. Mama said she kept feeling something down around her ankles, and she thought it was her coat. She kept pulling it up and she couldn't figure out why she couldn't keep it up--it was just hanging over her arm.

Well, in a little bit, one of the girls came up to where Dad and I were holding seats, and said, 'You're going to have to go back and help your Mama. She's lost her pants.' And I thought, 'What in the world is this girl trying to tell me?' I just couldn't feature this, but I hurried back, and, sure enough, there was Mother! Now, you have to understand that, during the war, we couldn't get nylon panties, or even cotton panties. We had to use the old rayon panties and elastic was completely out of the question. We couldn't buy elastic. We couldn't buy underwear with elastic in it. So the pants were rayon and they either tied around the waist or buttoned, and both of them were an absolute nuisance, because half the time they would hardly stay up. Also, Mother was very heavy, and she wore a corset that had stays in it from the top to the very bottom. I mean, I don't know how she stood it. But she wore it all the time, except when she went to bed. She had rayon panties that tied around the waist. If you pulled a string on it, or caught a snag, it would just unravel and unravel and unravel. And it was hard to break. The only way you could get it loose was with a pair of scissors.

When Mother had started to run for the streetcar, she discovered that what was down around her ankles was her underpants! Let me remind you that there were about three hundred people standing around her, and I'm sure someone must have seen those pants around her ankles, but she wasn't even aware of it until she tried to start running. She stumbled on them. What had happened was that one of the stays on her corset had broken loose and had torn a hole in the rayon pants, and they had started to unravel and worked down. It was just hanging by strings up beneath her clothes. When she discovered what had happened, she began to try to get the pants loose, and she was going to just drop them and leave them--just keep running and leave them. Well, they were hung up and she couldn't get them loose. She couldn't get them up or down. When she pulled on them, they just strung out more and more.

By the time I got there, I could get the picture. My mother was crying and embarrassed and still trying to pull them loose. My sister was trying to help her, but she was almost ready to have her baby. She had her hand up Mama's dress, trying to pull them loose, and it was doing nothing but stringing. It was just rayon string all around, down around Mama's feet. Just before I got to where Mother was, a sailor went by and said, 'My God, somebody help that poor woman!' I was so embarrassed, but I ran to her. I knew something had to be done. I reached up and tried to break them loose, but they just strung more and more. We couldn't break them, and the streetcar was already blowing the whistle. It started to move a little bit, and I said, 'We're going to have to go, Mom! Just put your coat around your ankles--We're going to have to run.' My sister was on one side and I was on the other, and she stumbled into the streetcar and sat down with the first group of girls that were with us. She finally got those pants loose, but you can imagine what she had to do to get them loose!

Dad had developed a hearing problem and he had to be looking right at your mouth, or you had to speak very loudly to get him to understand what you were saying. Well, he came over to where Mother was sitting, and he was aggravated at her because she was late getting on the train. He said, 'My goodness alive, Mama! What in the world were you doing? I told you we had to hurry. What in the world were you doing?' She was embarrassed, so she whispered, 'I'll tell you later.' He said, 'What? What did you say? I can't hear you!' She said, 'I'll tell you later!' He said, 'Mother, you know I can't understand a word you're saying! What in the world were you doing?' By now she was aggravated, too, and she just screamed, 'Well, if you just *have* to know, I lost my pants!' Dad was very modest. He gasped, 'Mother! My goodness alive! You don't have to tell everybody on the train!'

It's a funny story to me now, but it certainly wasn't funny at the time. Later my dad did get a hearing aid, but, because he had been partially deaf for so long, all the noises and sounds nearly drove him crazy, so he quit wearing it.

My mother also lost her pants another time. I was probably thirteen. Mother and I went to a neighboring town to shop and, again, we were hurrying to catch a streetcar when she felt her pants come down around her ankles, so she just walked out of them, like they didn't belong to her. She kept right on going, and I kept right on going, too. I ran way ahead of her and acted like I didn't even know who she was! She didn't even look back.

Incidents such as these became humorous Goble family stories, in contrast to the emotional disruption caused by separation and changes in their lives during those times.

LFW: Meekly, after his training in San Francisco, was shipped overseas. He became a Pharmacist's Mate in New Caledonia. He called us one day and said, 'I'm going to be coming through San Diego, and I'll be able to get off the ship for about two hours.' So somehow--I don't know how Dad got the gas--but Mother and Daddy and Florence and I drove to San Diego to see Meekly before he shipped out. That was another really, really sad time. It was just really hard. You know, we just felt like that was the last time we'd ever see him, and I'll never forget when he hugged me and told me he loved me. He went to the Navy when he was seventeen and I was thirteen. I was just really, really heart-broken when he left. Of course, we were all devastated, but we tried not to show it. He shipped out at one o'clock in the morning. We cried all the way back to Los Angeles, which was about a two and a half hour drive.

So, the war years saw the maturing of the Gobles, bringing them together in an even more loving relationship and ending the petty squabbles of their childhood. They also saw the breaking up of the family unit, as each child assumed adult status. Florence had married early in the war years and had a child; Meekly had gone to war. And now, Lily Fern, though still a child by today's standards, was to embark on a relationship with positive and long lasting results.

Chapter Four

 Leaving the Nest

Lily Fern's early teens were filled with activity. While she did not particularly like school, she enjoyed participating in glee club. Her major activities had to do with the family and the church.

Lily Fern indicates that a lot of significant things happened after Meekly left for the service. In addition to meeting Earl Weatherford, she became acquainted with other people who became very significant in her life:

LFW: During the time he was gone, I met Earl. I met another girl who was a singer, Martha Brown. She and I and another girl, Dorothy Bright, formed a female trio. We had a really good little trio, and we sang on the radio every day for a preacher in Long Beach, California. We would go down once a week and help him make his transcriptions and he would play our tapes all week. Later, Bette Jo, one of Earl's sisters from Oklahoma, came out to California to live with us, and she sang bass. We had a female quartet that was very good.

Before that, I had sung duets with a girl named Marjorie Hanby and with my best friend, Wynema Shahan [King].

Martha Brown eventually became Lily Fern's sister-in-law. Dorothy Bright was to be one of The Weatherfords' first pianists and her son, Kenny Payne, grew up to be a "Weatherford."

Lily Fern was familiar with church music, of course, and attended singing conventions and church services, which led her to what would be her future life. She describes how she came to be involved in "gospel" music:

LFW: All the time that we were in Oklahoma, Mama and Daddy used to go to the Sunday afternoon singing conventions. If you'll think of the

Gaither videos, when we all sing together those old songs in the choir, that's a lot like those singing conventions. They would have them every Sunday afternoon someplace. Sometimes they'd have six and eight hundred people come out to those things.

At that time, a lot of the people from Oklahoma, Texas, Arkansas, Missouri and Kansas had moved to California to get work in the defense plants. They were hungry and homesick for that Southern Gospel music, although we didn't even call it 'Southern Gospel' music then. We just called it 'gospel music,' because there were only two kinds of Christian music then, that I knew anything about, and it wasn't 'Contemporary,' and it wasn't 'Christian Rock,' or anything like that. It was just gospel music, which was the shape notes, out of different kinds of songbooks, not just your ordinary hymnals. The other kind of singing was your conventional singing, using your church hymnals with the round notes.

Anyway, Mama and Dad were so glad to find out that they were having these in California, and they went every Sunday somewhere to one of those singing conventions. The singing convention people would have four or five song books that they would work out of that were in shape notes, and they represented the different companies. One was the Stamps-Baxter company, one was the Frank Stamps Quartet Company, and there was the Hartford Music Company and the Vaughan Music Company. There may have been more, but I can't remember them. We would go and different people would get up and lead songs that they had learned out of the song books. The first one or two that Florence and I went to, we had never seen shape notes before and it was just really strange to us. Florence was a good singer, too, but she never did really go into it like I did. She just wasn't interested. Meekly could have sung, too, but he didn't.

So Florence and I tried to learn to sing like everybody else did there, and we thought we were doing really well. We'd be singing along and we'd be down about the second line of the verse and first thing we knew, they'd be clear down on the chorus! It was different music--just entirely different. People can understand that when they watch the Gaither videos. That's what Dad and Mama were really hungry for, when they began to go to the singing conventions in California. And at one of those singing conventions is where I met Martha Brown, Dorothy Bright, and Earl Weatherford.

Leaving the Nest

Lily Fern remembers the circumstances that brought this other Oklahoma native to California and into her life:

LFW: There was a quartet around Southern California at that time, called Bob Jones and His Harmony Boys. Of course, everybody worked in the shipyards or in the defense plants or something, and Bob Jones worked in the shipyards. Earl had left Oklahoma after graduating from high school, and he started to college and ruined his knees trying to play football. He tried to join the service, but they rejected him because of his bad knees and his bad heart. So, he moved to California and got a job at the shipyards. It was there that he met Bob Jones and they began talking about singing and so forth, and Earl was just really elated that he found someone who was interested in singing!

Earl's first love was sports and he excelled in basketball all during high school. As a matter of fact, he won a scholarship to play basketball at the university in Norman, Oklahoma. He also excelled in baseball, but he loved football. He loved and watched any kind of sport. He was playing semi-pro ball for the shipyards, but when the basketball season came around, he played semi-pro basketball and softball for the shipyards. He worked nights so he could do that, because their games were usually early in the evening.

Well, he met Bob Jones and they started talking about singing, and Bob told him he had this quartet. He asked Earl if he was familiar with that type of thing. Earl told him how he would walk home every day from school at lunch, just to get to hear Frank Stamps' radio broadcast, which was on at noon every day. He would walk as high as four miles every Sunday afternoon to get to a singing convention. He loved singing, but his first love was sports. Then, when he met Bob, he started singing with him, plus still working in the shipyards and playing ball.

So, this one Sunday afternoon I went to the singing convention and Bob Jones came with his quartet. Earl was singing with him. I remember I was very impressed, mostly by his looks, because he was a little more than six foot two, weighed about one hundred and eighty pounds, broad shoulders, muscular, black hair, black eyes, tall, handsome--what else can I say? Sexy? Now, I never dreamed that I would even get to know Earl, other than hearing him sing at a singing convention once in a while. So, I saw him this first Sunday, and in a couple of weeks, we went to another singing convention and I saw him again. The following Sunday, Bob Jones came and brought his whole group to church that

43

morning.

While they were there, we were talking about this Sunday School class party that we were going to have. The Young People Society in the church, which we called NYPS, the Nazarene Young People Society, and Daddy's class had a contest to see which group could bring the most people to Sunday School for so many Sundays. We lost. The loser had to fix dinner for the winner. Dad had gone deer hunting and had gotten an elk, so he said, 'O.K. Our class will serve you elk steaks at the park.' We chose a date and decided to make it a 'tacky' party. I can't believe that people these days don't know what a tacky party is, but, it's simply what it says. You go as tacky as you possibly can!

And I did. I was just as tacky as I could be! I don't even know now what I wore, but I know I was tacky. And Bob Jones brought his whole group to that Sunday School class party, and they were all tacky! And Earl was *really* tacky! He even had his pants on backwards. I'm glad there weren't any dire emergencies while he was there. But, anyway, I got better acquainted with Earl. By this time, I was within four days of my sixteenth birthday.

Back then, we didn't have television. All we had was radio. All of our socials were Sunday School or church socials, and we played games and had *Bible* quizzes, and we always had a really good time. Well, that night, we were playing games and everything, but Earl and I managed to sort of slip away and we talked for a few minutes. He asked me if I would go with him to the singing the following Sunday afternoon. I told him I would, but he would have to come to Sunday School and church, and I'd meet him there and we'd go from there. I said, 'And then, I have to be back to my church on Sunday night.' I would not miss my church on Sunday night. He said, 'O.K.'

The first "date" for Earl and Lily Fern did not end too well, but fate, in the form of Lillie Goble, entered in. Lily Fern tells the story of the disastrous first date and how they finally resumed dating:

LFW: He came to church that Sunday, and, believe me, he wasn't tacky that morning, and neither was I! I knew he was coming and I really tried my best to look good. The piano player for his group needed a date, so I brought one of my girl friends to go with him. After church, we went back to Mama's house and she fixed dinner. Then, we got in Earl's car and went to the singing convention. Mother and Daddy came to the singing in their car, because that was the way I was going to get back home. Earl couldn't bring me back, because the quartet sang that night at another church.

So, we went and I sat down in the audience. Earl got up in the choir, because he was going to be singing in the class singing with the group. I noticed this pretty little gal sitting right in front of him, and he kept talking to her. She kept turning around and talking to him. I really didn't think too much about that until after it was all over and the singing convention had dismissed. Daddy and Mama and I were getting ready to go home, and I went to find Earl to tell him how much I enjoyed being with him that day. When I walked up to him, he was talking to this girl and her parents. It didn't take me very long to realize what he had done. He knew I couldn't go with him that night, so he had made a date with her to go with him to the other church. So, he dropped me off at the convention and picked her up and took her to the concert. When I found out what was going on, I was boiling! I told Mama and Dad. I was so mad all the way home, I just griped and groaned. Finally, Mama said, 'Oh, don't worry about it. You just as well get used to it, because I've invited him and the whole group over for supper Wednesday night.'

Lily Fern did "get used to it," apparently, by the time of the Wednesday night supper. Earl and the other men who worked at the shipyards shared rides, and, although Earl had the night off, he had to take one of the others to meet his ride after dinner. Lily Fern recalls how this ride saved the relationship:

LFW: He asked me to go with him. On the way, I wasn't really scared, because there were three of us in the car, but on the way back, I was really scared, because Earl was twenty-two and I was only sixteen. He was quite mature. The girl he took that Sunday afternoon I didn't know, but I had seen him at singing conventions two or three weeks before with a girl that I had known all my life, and I knew she was a pretty rough character, who would do anything with anybody. I thought, 'If he was running around with that girl, then he's liable to...no telling what he'll do!' So I was a little bit afraid of him coming back. I was afraid he'd make a false move toward me, but he didn't. He was a perfect gentleman. He asked me to go out to dinner with him on Saturday evening, and we did, and after that we really started dating.

That "real" first date was the beginning of their relationship and the origin of Earl's nickname for Lily Fern. When he came to pick her up, he asked where Lon was. She said he was going hunting, so he went to look for some "bullets." Earl thought it was funny that she used that term instead of "shells," so for years he called her "Bullets."

When Lily Fern describes what really attracted her to Earl, there is no question that she was totally captivated by the handsome singer:

LFW: Oh, he was a handsome guy! Tall, all muscle, black hair and eyes, a little tiny mustache like he always wore. He just swept me off my feet. I was sixteen and he was twenty-two, and when he even paid any attention to me, I thought, 'I have to be the luckiest girl in the world for him to even look at me!'

Earl Henderson Weatherford was born October 10, 1922. He always went by "Earl H. Weatherford." His mother, Mary Elvada Branum, was only thirteen years old when she married Elton Henderson Weatherford. She was only fourteen when Earl was born. As young as she was when she started dating Earl, Lily Fern is still puzzled about how Earl's mother managed with a child at fourteen:

LFW: That sounds bizarre to me, as I'm sure it does to a lot of people, but we have to remember that back in those days the girls grew up a lot faster than they do today--or what they should today. They're still having children even younger than that, but they're not married and they're not really responsible, but his mother was a very responsible young girl. She had to work hard on the farm in her own childhood. His mother's name was Mary Elvada, but we all called her 'Mamaw,' or 'Vade.'

Lily Fern describes what Earl told her about his background:

LFW: He was raised in Oklahoma; he was born in Pauls Valley, Oklahoma. Paoli, where I live now, is seven miles north of Pauls Valley. He grew up within a fifty mile radius of Pauls Valley, and lived there until he left Oklahoma and went to California. He was born where the Pauls Valley city park, Wacker Park, is now. At that time, of course, it wasn't a park and there were some houses, but they've all been torn down and there's been a park there ever since I can remember--ever since before we were married. I think he went to school in Paoli. Then, I think he finished out most of his school years in Washington. The other schools were all little country schools, I think, but he graduated from Washington, Oklahoma, which is about thirty-five miles west of where we live right now--maybe a little bit northwest.

He was a good student all through school. He made good grades, but I think the main reason he made good grades was really because in high school he was an all-sportsman. In those days, you had to make good grades or you couldn't be on the team. He managed to get good enough grades to stay on the basketball team, and he played other sports in other seasons, but mainly basketball. He excelled in all sports, and was a great fan, also. In his later years, and especially when he was so sick, before he passed away, his pastime at home was sitting before the big screen television watching ESPN. It didn't make any difference what it was in sports; he loved to watch it.

Earl was born in 1922 and was big brother to Bonnie Louise, Vernon Carol, Bette Jo, Bobbie Sue and Mary Lou. Bette Jo Williams remembers her big brother fondly:

BJW: My parents had two families. I was the youngest of the four older children. Earl was the oldest. Needless to say, I always looked up to my big brother. He teased me a lot, but always made me know he loved me very much. I can remember he always loved to sing, and expected us all to sing with him. I believe my love for singing and the desire to perform was passed down from him. He had a great influence on my life as far as singing gospel music. He always made me think I really was 'good.'

When Earl left his family and moved to California to begin working in the shipyards, his singing career really began, as did his life with Lily Fern.

Responding to a question about when she actually knew that Earl was "the one" for her, Lily Fern said it was "certainly not the first two or three times I dated him; it was probably on about our fourth date." When further pressed to tell what made the difference, she laughed and hesitantly admitted, "He really kissed me. And I thought, 'Wow, I never felt anything like this before!'"

When asked when she believes Earl really knew she was the one for him, she didn't hesitate: "He told me that the first time he saw me he told Bob Jones, 'I'm going to marry that girl!'" She analyzed some strong points in favor of their marriage:

LFW: We really had about the same religious beliefs. His mother was

Pentecostal; I was raised Nazarene. It's very similar as far as standards of living and the way you dress and so forth. Earl wasn't necessarily Pentecostal, although that's what he knew. Actually, when I met him, he wasn't really going to church. He was pretty wild! He was doing some pretty wild things. In fact, when I met him, he was dating Miss Los Angeles. She was Miss L.A. of 1942, and I met him in 1945. He carried her pictures with him, and after we started dating, he tore them up and burned them. I said, 'I don't know whether I like that or not. If you had to tear them up and burn them, was that to try to get her out of your mind?' But she was a beautiful thing! She was a tall, slender blonde. She was what I always wanted to be. I wanted to be tall, with long legs and a beautiful figure. And here I was, short, fat and with short legs. Well, I really wasn't fat when Earl met me, but she was such a beautiful girl I felt that way! I think the Lord meant for me to be six foot tall, and my legs just didn't get quite long enough.

Basically, I was just an innocent little girl, and he had been around, but I think it was a good combination, because I think he wanted to go back to his up-bringing. He wanted someone moral and innocent. In fact, I know he did. And he respected me for that.

They dated for a short time and he gave her an engagement ring on New Year's Eve, 1944. They were married in June of 1945.

Lily Fern did not sing with him full-time until after they had been married for a while. Before she started singing with him, she worked as a waitress, which is about the only job she ever held other than her singing career.

Lily Fern tells the story of her engagement, which reveals Lon Goble to be rather mischievous:

LFW: Dad and Mama knew that we were very serious about each other, and the very first thing that Earl wanted to do was to talk to Dad and Mother, to ask their permission to get married. Well, it wasn't hard for him to do that with my mother. He asked her and she said that it was all right with her, but she wanted me to finish school. At that time, I was only in the tenth grade.

We began to think of a way that he could get Dad off to himself to ask him if Earl could marry me, so we invited Earl over for dinner one night. My sister was still living at home at that time. She had had the baby, but she was living at home because her husband was still in the service. We all sat down to eat. Mother, Florence and I knew that Earl was there to ask to marry me, and Dad knew, too, but he just wasn't going to allow it to happen. Every time there was a lull in the conversation, Daddy would bring up something else, something completely off the wall, just to keep Earl from getting a chance to talk to him about marrying me. The whole evening went by, but we had even planned it to where Earl said that his roommate was going to be using his car, so that Dad had to go get him and take him back home. Bringing him to the house, Daddy evaded the issue and just kept rattling and talking, so Earl didn't get a chance. So, when it came time to take him home, we thought sure enough he would get a chance then. Now, Dad could not sing. He couldn't carry a tune in a bushel basket. We got in the car and Earl cleared his throat and was going to ask Dad, and Daddy started singing, 'Them bones, them bones, them dry bones, them bones, them bones, them dry bones,' all off key, you know, like there wasn't a tune to it? And he'd sing and finally he'd stop, and Earl would start to say something, and then Dad would start again, or he'd start off on some stupid conversation.

Finally we got to where Earl lived and Dad stopped the car and said, 'Were you trying to ask me something, young man?' And Earl said, 'Yes! I was going to ask you if I could marry Lily Fern.' After putting him through that whole evening of misery, Dad said, 'Why, Earl, I don't know of anybody I would rather have her marry than I would you. But,' he said, 'You're not going to get married right away. You're going to wait until she finishes school.' Well, we thought that was great--right at first, for a couple of days--and then we didn't want to wait any longer. We kept trying to push the date up, and they kept telling me I had to finish school, and of course I was not interested in school at all!

This is where Lon and Lillie discovered just how stubborn their little Lily Fern could be. Lily Fern regrets what she did, but she tells how she got her parents to change their minds:

LFW: We had moved to another town. Dad had sold our little house and bought another one. I'd had to change school in the tenth grade and I was not with the kids I had gone to school with for several years and I didn't like it. Really, the main reason I didn't like it was because I had met Earl and I just wasn't interested; my interests were somewhere else. I really thought, 'Well, I'm going to get married. I don't ever have to work again.' Funny joke! Anyway, I would slip out of school and go to a girlfriend's house, and did it so many times that the truant officer came and told Mama and Daddy what I was doing. I convinced them that I wasn't even going to try. I didn't want to go to school. What they should have done was just, you know, ground me or something--I was just spoiled and thought I had to have my way about everything-- and usually got my way about everything. I think they finally decided it was just a hopeless cause, so they let me quit school.

Today, Lily Fern says that the only real regret of her life is that she didn't finish her education. She will also say, however, that she had no doubts or fears about taking this major step in her life. She feels that the age difference was not a problem. She had always associated better with older people, so she was a mature sixteen-year-old.

Having attained the agreement of her parents, Earl and Lily Fern set their wedding date and made their plans. Lily Fern tells of a tender moment with her father that she treasures:

LFW: Three days before I married Earl, Earl had come over to see me one night and I was not feeling well. I was just really sick, so he didn't stay long. When he left, I just laid down on the divan and was feeling really bad. Dad was sitting in the rocker, and he said, 'Come over here, Baby, and let me rock you.' I went over and crawled up in my Daddy's lap, and he rocked me to sleep just like he used to do. I remember, I woke up a little when he was carrying me to my bed. I was really awake, but I didn't want him to know it. I just wanted to take all that in for myself one last time. He put me in bed and covered me up and leaned over me and prayed a prayer that the Lord would keep me safe. Then he kissed me on the cheek and said, quietly, 'I love you, Baby.'

That was the end of her life as a child with Lon and Lillie, and to this day, Lily Fern cannot talk about it without breaking down a bit. She says it still gets to her to remember the love they all had together in what she terms a "wonderful, wonderful life."

While her marriage was the most romantic and thrilling moment of Lily Fern's life, Lon Goble did not take the new situation very well as he lost his second daughter, his baby, to marriage. But he carried out his fatherly duties perfectly.

LFW: In June of 1945, Earl and I got married. Daddy and Mama gave me a beautiful wedding. I had a long white gown and it was just a wonderful wedding for a girl my age--I was sixteen. I remember, after the ceremony, as we started walking back down the aisle, Earl put his arm around me and whispered, 'I guess you know who you are now.' And I knew what he meant--that I was 'Mrs. Earl Weatherford,' which thrilled me to death. And I even get a thrill when I think about it to this day.

The day that we were married, after the wedding reception, Earl and I left and Mom and Dad stayed at the church to clean up and to get all the gifts home. They went home and began taking the gifts inside. They displayed them in the dining room. It was almost two o'clock in the morning when Dad brought the last gift in and put it on the dining room table. They started to go to bed, and Dad broke down and started crying. Mama said he cried like a baby. He said, 'Mama, our baby is gone; she's gone!' Mama said, 'She's not gone.' And he said, 'Yes, she's married, she's gone. That's my baby. That was my baby!' And I still was his baby 'til the day he died, but it just got to him that I had gotten married. Although he loved Earl, he could hardly take the fact that I was married. They went to bed, and Mama said in the middle of the night she heard him sobbing--he sobbed all night long. That's how close Dad was to all three of us kids. He just took everything real close to heart.

Perhaps Lon wept too soon. His daughter did not go far.

LFW: We had a little three day honeymoon. That was about all the money we had to rent a motel for three days. We rented it close enough to Mama and Daddy that we could go back home to eat breakfast, lunch and dinner! But it was a wonderful three day honeymoon, anyway. This was right after the war, so you still could hardly find anyplace to live. There was a shortage on apartments and homes, so we lived with Mother and Daddy quite a while.

Lily Fern started life with her new husband in Lynwood, California, but shortly after they were married, Bob Jones moved to Fresno, taking his group with him. Earl chose to stay in Lynwood and start his own group. Lily Fern was his "substitute" singer whenever he needed her. When she wasn't singing, she worked as a waitress in a little restaurant. They continued to live with her parents. His group was active, and he started a radio program in Long Beach, which, at one time, aired three times a day. Part of it was transcribed, of course.

Florence and Earl Squier lived in San Francisco at the time of Lily Fern's marriage to Earl. Florence recalls the effect marriage had on their closeness:

FGS: I didn't get to go to Lily Fern's wedding, because my husband, Earl, was in the Navy, and he was stationed up in San Francisco. We just didn't have the money to go home for the weekend, so we had to miss all of that. I didn't see very much of Lily Fern, because we were quite a few miles apart. We never really lived very close together, since she was married and I was married.

Florence was busy with her own family, but Meekly had a problem accepting the changes in Lily Fern's life. Getting to know Earl and witness the strength of the marriage helped him to finally accept it:

MEG: I left home and she was just a baby. She was twelve years old, and I looked at her when I left. She was just a real small girl. Most girls that are twelve are just babies. I was gone for three years, and when I came home, she had gotten married and was a young lady, a grown woman. But I always looked at her as still a small girl, because she got married so young. Though I loved Earl, I thought, 'This girl has gotten married too soon.' But they had a good marriage and things worked out for them. So, that turned out to be very good. It led her into the singing business, and everybody will have to attest that that's where she belongs, because she's the greatest female singer that ever sang. She's where she needs to be. Earl and I became very good friends.

I don't know how many people who knew Earl knew that there was another side of his life. Probably the people in Akron, Ohio would know, because he pitched for their softball and baseball teams, I guess. But he was a fantastic softball pitcher. He could really fire them in. He pitched fast ball, not slow pitch that they do today. We'd practice together. I used to catch him, and in our practice, he could really burn 'em in and just about burn me out! He was a real athlete. He had been playing on a team in Long Beach. Cosby-Sexton Electrical sponsored the team. When I got out of the service and came home, he talked me into playing on the team, too. They let me play with them a little bit. We had a lot of fun. The problem was that we were on a city league and we were in the YMCA league. That's two nights a week we were playing basketball, and if we practiced a night a week, that was three nights we were spending--having a lot of fun--but both of us had other commitments. So, we couldn't just keep doing that. He was committed to singing, and I was working in a small church at the time, where Martha, my wife, and I were depended upon to do most of the work in the church. I wasn't the pastor, but we were elected to offices in the church that demanded so much time, so we had to get our priorities in order and realize that we just couldn't keep doing that too long.

But we sure had fun! John was a real good--I call him 'John.' He called me 'John.' He was a good player and we depended on him on the team to do our scoring. He probably had more experience playing than any of the people on the team. We had a pretty good team. We won some games.

In a conversation, Meekly and Lily Fern reminisced about the relationship of Meekly and Earl, as well as the part Lily Fern played in Meekly's marriage to Martha:

LFW: Going back to that 'John' bit--I don't know how all that started, except that I think he just started calling you 'John' and then it was pretty handy later. Well, of course, Florence had already married, and she had married an 'Earl,' and then the grandkids started coming along. Florence's oldest boy is named 'Dennis,' but Earl Weatherford always called him 'Kokomo' when he was a little tiny baby. Because of that, my husband is known as 'Kokomo' to all the nieces and nephews. I think even Martha refers to him as 'Kokomo' a lot. But Earl was always 'John' to Meekly, and vice versa. And a lot of the singers in the earlier days, when we had Les and Raye Roberson and Armond Morales-- Armond still refers to him sometimes as 'John.' I've talked to Glen Payne, and he'd say, 'ol' John,' this and 'ol' John' that.

MEG: I want to also say that one of the greatest things that Lily Fern did for me was to introduce me to a brown-eyed girl with black, wavy hair, who later became my wife. She was a very beautiful girl and she's still a beautiful girl and a beautiful person. They used to sing a lot. Lily Fern wasn't in the quartet then. Earl had a male quartet, and the girls-- my wife, Martha, Lily Fern and Dorothy Payne would sing in trios at Youth for Christ and at other times. So I got the job of carrying those three pretty girls to different churches.

Of course, Lily Fern later attached to the male quartet, and then she was indispensable, once they got her in there. They saw that she was the quartet. She was the singer, and they had to have her. I always say that they had to have her to keep going. So I'm a little bit biased, maybe, but I sure love to hear this girl sing! She's a precious singer, because I know that every word she sings, she lives in her heart and in her life. I've always been grateful to her and Earl for introducing me to Martha.

I'd only been out of the service a short time. I got out in February and we were married in August. I got the best woman in the world to be my wife.

Now all the Goble children had found their mates for life, even though Meekly had his concerns at first for his baby sister. Lily Fern describes the relationships in this new, extended family.

LFW: When Meekly came home from the service, he was really, really broken-hearted that I had gotten married. He thought I was too young, but he really liked Earl and they became very good friends. They were good friends 'til the day Earl died. As a matter of fact, all of my family, my brother and his wife, my sister and her husband and all their children--we've all been very, very close. We just have a really good relationship. I don't remember one time that any of us ever had an argument after we grew up.

We all really cared a lot for each other. We did have a little confusion once in a while. Like I said, my sister married a young man by the name of 'Earl,' also. His name was Earl Dennis Squier, and their first son they named Dennis Earl, then when our son, Steve, came along, we named him Steven Earl, and then one of Earl's sisters married another Earl, and she named her first child Jimmy Earl--so we had a lot of 'Earls' in the family!

But the relationship between us and Meekly, Martha, Florence and Earl was very, very good. When Florence's husband got out of the service, they moved back to San Diego, and we lived close enough to do some of things together. Meekly and Martha and Earl and I did a lot of things together. We went to ball games and to the singing conventions and church together.

Earl maintained a strong relationship with his family in Oklahoma, as well. His sisters, Bette Jo Williams and Bobbie Sue Lanz recall their memories:

BJW: He was my best friend. After he and Lily were married, she and I became best friends, also. I spent several months with them in Compton, and have lots of good memories of those days.

BSL: I was number six of seven children. My younger sister and I were referred to as the 'second family.' There was a twelve year gap between the sister just older than me and me. All of our older siblings accused us of being spoiled rotten.

My earliest recollection of my oldest brother, Earl, was when I was either four or five years old, and we lived in Pauls Valley. He was already married, living in California, and had his first quartet. I remember him coming home for Christmas with his wife, Lily Fern, and what a fun time it was. I don't know why, but even at that early age, he seemed like an idol to me, someone I looked up to.

I loved to go to Earl and Lily's house to visit. They lived in Lynwood, California. They would take us to Knotts Berry Farm and all the fun places, and, of course, we would go to their concerts. Earl had nicknames for all of us and mine was "Shorty Bob," because I was tall for my age and hated it.

So, for the most part, Earl and Lily Fern began their marriage with harmonious family relationships. At the same time they began their lives together, Lon Goble was prospering and was still the focal point of the family. Lily describes some of these times:

LFW: Not long after Earl and I were married and Meekly and Martha were married, Dad had bought a corner lot in downtown Lynwood and started his own business. On that lot there were shops that he leased out, and the back part he had for himself. He had learned to repair old automobiles and wrecked automobiles. He would buy these old cars and fix them up and resell them, or people would just bring their cars in to have them painted. This was right after the war, and you couldn't buy automobiles, so people were spending their money on getting their cars fixed up, which was a very good business for my Dad.

Earl had his group, but Meekly and Earl worked for my Dad. Meekly moved away from home when he married, and about that time, Dad sold the house we were in and bought another house, and we lived there until Earl and I left California.

Lily Fern and her father shared more than the deep love for the family. They both had passionate tempers that would flare occasionally. Lily Fern recalls several incidents where Lon lost his temper:

LFW: While Earl and Meekly were working for my daddy, he had to have a new water line dug, so he had them digging the ditch. They tried to look halfway decent when they went to work, no matter what they had to do. This man came in one day, and he did not like Earl. He thought Earl was trying to be a hot dog, I think. He said to my dad, 'What are you doing with that big shot out there digging that ditch? That guy doesn't know his ass from a hole in the ground.' It made my dad so mad--and this was a big job that Dad was giving an estimate on, which meant about nine hundred dollars for Dad. The man had a fender off his car and Dad was going to put it on and fix the car up and paint it. This made Dad mad. He took that fender and threw it, and he said, 'You get yourself out of here and when you come past my property, turn and look the other way. I don't want you near this place!' Dad lost the job because of that, but he was standing up for his children, and Earl had become one of his children.

Another time that my dad lost money over his temper, it was because he was a staunch Democrat. I mean to tell you, he would argue all day long between Democrat and Republican. It was when Franklin Roosevelt died, and some guy came in with a big job for Dad--I mean like a fifteen hundred dollar job for Dad--and he said, 'Well, I'm glad the old S.O.B. died. He should have died a long time ago!' That made Dad so mad he ran him off his property and lost that job. He said, 'Don't you ever come back here again! Don't come for anything!'

Lily Fern got the brunt of Lon's temper once, when she was trying to be helpful. She laughs when she tells the story:

LFW: Daddy was not a very neat person around the house. Once while Earl and I were living with Mama and Daddy, Daddy came home from work in the middle of the day, and I had cleaned house. Daddy went to his bedroom. He came out and said, 'What did you do with that envelope that was on top of the chest-of-drawers in there?' I said, 'Well, I suppose I threw it in the trash.' Oh, he went to pieces! That's the only time I ever remember my dad talking cross to me. He said, 'What in the world would you do a thing like that for?' Well, what it was, somebody had paid him for a job, and it was four hundred dollar bills. He said, 'Where is the trash?' I led him outside to where I had already started to burn the trash. He raked through that trash and burned his hands and pulled that envelope out. It was half burned, but he took the remaining part of the bills to the bank and got the four hundred dollars, but he was so mad at me. He said, 'Leave my stuff alone from now on!'

Again, the fruit doesn't fall far from the tree. Lily Fern has been known to lose her temper, too. She tells of an experience during her brief career as a waitress:

> LFW: I worked in a little coffee shop downtown in Lynwood. Their specialty was barbecue sandwiches. My boss made it himself and it was very good. When he made the barbecue, you could smell it all over town, and everybody would come in for barbecue sandwiches. One day, he had made the fresh barbecue and this guy I had never seen before came in. He sat up at the counter and ordered a barbecue sandwich. You got a barbecue sandwich and french fries for twenty-five cents, and coffee for a nickel, so his bill was thirty-one cents. I served his sandwich and people were eating barbecue sandwiches all up and down the counter. He ate about half of it, and as I walked by him, he pushed back his plate and stopped me. He said something was wrong with the barbecue. I was really busy and had more people than I could handle. I had the whole front and back by myself, and it made me mad. Of course, I was just a kid and I really had a bad temper back then. I said, 'Well, did you have to eat half the sandwich and all the french fries before you realized there was something wrong with it?' He said, 'Well, there's something wrong; I won't pay for it.' I just asked the person next to him, 'Sir, was there anything wrong with your sandwich?' He said, 'No. It's delicious.' I asked two or three people and they all said it was O.K. I turned back to him and I said, 'You're going to pay for that sandwich, whether you like it or not.' He really put up a fuss and came to the cash register. I said, 'You owe me thirty-one cents.' I made him pay it. Later the boss told me, 'You should have just let him go. He didn't deserve it, but you should have just let him go.' I said, 'He was going to pay for that sandwich if I had to climb over that counter and get it out of his hide!' He was going to pay for that sandwich, because he made me so mad.

Lily Fern eventually learned to control that temper, she says now, but she stood up for herself more than the average wife of that time, as evidenced by how she came to be a full-time quartet member in a day of all male quartets.

> LFW: When I met Earl, I didn't even dream that I'd be able to do such a thing as sing for the Lord. Earl started his own group, and, of course, he started out with a male group. One of the members of the group would quit, for some reason or another, so he would bring me in the group and I started singing with them. He would keep me in there until he'd find another singer, and then he'd put me out and have a male group again, for a while. And this went on for, oh, a long time after we

got married, so I finally said, 'Hey, if you want me to sing, then you're going to have to let me sing and quit pushing me out of the group and then bringing me back in. But, if you want a male group, then get one that will stay with you.' Well, I guess he realized that he couldn't find one that would really stick like I would, 'cause I was married to him! But that isn't the only reason; I think he finally realized that he needed me in the group, and then I sang with him all the time.

Lily Fern was not even sure that she could be a gospel singer at first, even though she had been approached at a singing convention by the uncle of singer-actress Joan Leslie to try popular singing for the movies. During that time, Lily Fern was just happy being with Earl and enjoying church and music.

She remembers, also, some funny incidents during the early years of her marriage and her career, which, taken together, may indicate that she and her mother had some similar experiences. The first involves her mother:

LFW: One of the funniest things that ever happened to Mama was after Earl and I had been married about a year. We decided to go back to see his mother and dad, who lived out in the country on a farm near Paoli, where Earl's dad farmed and hauled hay. Mother's daddy, my grandfather and my step-grandmother lived in El Reno, which was about eighty or ninety miles north and west of Paoli. We dropped Mother off at Grandpa's, and then we went on down to Earl's folks and visited with them for a couple of weeks. Just before we were going to leave to go home, Mama rode the bus down and came out to Earl's folks for a while before we started on back to California. Mother was very heavy at that time. She was always immaculate and had to have a bath every day. I don't care if she had to go out in a snow storm and stand there and have a bath, she would have done it. Earl's folks didn't have a bathroom, so we had to either take baths in the number 2 wash tub, or go down to the horse tank to take a bath, which is what most of the men did. But the women generally used the number 2 wash tub.

Well, what you'd have to do is, go down to the windmill with your tub and fill it full of water and let it set out until it warmed up a little bit. Then, you'd pull it back up to the house. Well, they lived up on a little hill, and the windmill was down the hill a ways, and out behind the barn. The windmill was on a little knoll. So Mother usually would draw her water early in the morning and wait until all the men were gone to town or out in the field working. As soon as they would leave, she would go out there and take a bath, instead of bringing the heavy tub up the hill. Well, one day she had drawn her water and it was warming out by the windmill. She made sure all the men were gone to town and just Earl's mother and sister and me at the house. She went down there and got all soaped up--she was standing up in the tub, because she was too big to sit in it. There was a railroad track near the windmill, and we had forgotten that there could be a handcar on the tracks. I heard the noise of the handcar and I knew Mama was going to start and, before I could even get out the door, I heard her screaming, 'Lily Ferrrrn! Lily Ferrrrrn! Come help me!' Well, I don't know what she thought I could do, but I headed down the hill and the sight that I saw was the funniest thing! I laughed 'til I could not breathe. She was in this tub, all soaped up, and she'd danced practically all the water out, jumping up and down. This little handcar was coming down the railroad track, which was only about ten or fifteen yards from the windmill, so the men on the handcar had quite a view. And what Mother was doing, was, she had grabbed the towel and she'd put it in front of her, but she turned around, with her back toward them, and then she'd realize that she was exposing herself that way, so she'd put the towel around her back, and then turn around facing them, which exposed her in the front. She was so panicky that she did that several times before I got to her. By the time I got to her, she had gotten out of the tub and had started up the hill. Now, Oklahoma is red clay, and she'd slide and sit and fall down and by the time I got her back to the house, she was one red clay-ball. I mean, it was absolutely the funniest thing I have ever seen. And the last thing I saw out there was those three guys on that handcar, absolutely rolling, laughing, and that little handcar was just going crazy, with the handles they used to pump it just flying up and down on their own, back and forth, back and forth, and those men were dying laughing! I know that if they're still living today, they never forgot that sight and must have told it many times.

The next story involves Lily Fern, and probably, out there somewhere, some folks are still sharing a story about the time they went to hear The Weatherfords sing in a furniture store:

LFW: Along in 1947 or 1948, we were working on the radio in Long Beach and we had a sponsor, Folsum's Furniture Store. We had a kid by the name of Jack Bryson singing baritone for us at that time, and Ann Keel was the pianist. Scranton Hall was singing bass. Every Saturday, we did an hour broadcast from one to two o'clock in the afternoon, from the furniture store showroom. The showroom would be set up with, oh, about one hundred and fifty chairs, back behind where the furniture was displayed. Back in this corner, they had a little stage set up, and that's where we would do our radio broadcasts, by remote control with the radio station. Right behind the stage, there was a rest room. It wasn't a men's and it wasn't a women's; it was just a rest room. But when you opened the door to the rest room, you could see the sink, the commode and everything.

So this one Saturday, we went there to do our live show. I heard someone announce, 'Ladies, don't use the rest room without holding the door. The lock is broken.' When they said, 'Ladies,' I assumed they meant the ladies rest room upstairs, so I made it a point not to use the ladies room upstairs. I didn't want anybody walking in on me. I decided to just use the one downstairs by the stage. Well, what I found out too late was that the one by the stage was the one the lock was broken on! Just before we did the broadcast, while the people were gathered out in front, ready for us to go on the air, I decided I better run in and go to the bathroom. I just got set down good, and the door burst open. It was Jack Bryson, and he'd decided the same thing I did, only he didn't know I was in there. When he saw me, I was sitting there, and all these people out there saw me, because he hollered and they all looked. I said, 'Shut the door, Jack!' Well, he ran away and didn't even shut the door. Finally, he came back and shut the door, but I was there, exposed to the whole audience, trying to shut the door with my foot, which probably was worse than just sitting there!

Lily Fern tells of memories of living with her parents after she and Earl were married, including one story where Lily Fern attempted to bluff an intruder, with little help from Lillie.

One night, Lon went with Earl's group to preach. They left the piano player's thirteen year old wife with Lily and her mother. The previous evening, Lily Fern had heard a Peeping Tom at her window. The window had been open and she heard breathing and leaves rustling. This night, Lily Fern was ironing and the piano player's wife was getting ready for bed, when she said she heard something. The front door had a little "peep door" in it, and suddenly a hand came through it. It scared all of them. Lily Fern ran and locked the door. She yelled, "Get the shotgun, Mother!" Lillie said, "But, we don't have any shells!" Lily Fern tried again, "Get out or I'll knock you in the head with this iron!" Lillie said, "Oh, but that's my good iron!" Desperately trying to scare the intruder away, Lily Fern tried one more ploy, "Mother, call Uncle Henry quick!" Lillie looked puzzled, and replied, "Why, Lily Fern, he's not even home!" Fortunately, the intruder left, no thanks to Lillie's responses to Lily

Fern's quick thinking.

In 1948, the family was shattered by the death of the uniting force, Lon Goble. Lillie Goble was devastated, and Lily Fern tells how the family dealt with this blow:

> LFW: On March the 11th, my father went home to be with the Lord. Earl had a regular service that he and his group did every Thursday night in Compton at a little Baptist church. Earl and I were still living with Mom and Daddy, and Dad had come home a little bit late from work that day. Mom had warmed him some food, and he went into the bathroom to clean up to go to the singing. We heard a strange noise, and I was the only one who could get in the bathroom, because he had fallen against the door and was lodged against it. I went in and I felt sure that he was gone, but we called the ambulance and they pronounced him dead. We lost the best friend we ever had, all of us kids and Mother. He was just our rock, and it was hard to realize how we were ever going to be able to survive without Daddy, but God always provides a way.

Before Lon Goble left the world, however, he had created a beautiful memory that his daughter carries with her to this day. It was the last time they talked alone before his death. Lily Fern had a wonderful 'good-bye' from him:

> LFW: Dad always thought I was just the greatest singer in the world. He loved to hear me sing, and the night before he died, he came home early enough to go to the concert with us. At this time, I was singing in the quartet again. I hardly ever sang a solo, but that night, Earl asked me to sing a solo, so I did. While I was singing, my dad sat there and cried. I rode home with Dad in his car, and on the way home, he told me how much he loved me and how much he enjoyed my solo that night, and he told me, 'Never let anybody tell you that you can't sing. First of all, when you're up there singing and you feel that you're not doing your best, just say to yourself that you're doing better than any of them out there are doing--you're singing, they're not!' I never will forget that.

For such a good businessman, Lon had not prepared for the possibility of leaving his family. Lily Fern remembers the worry and the coordinated effort of the children to care for Lillie:

> LFW: Mother really did think she could not make it without Dad. She

couldn't think of anything else and she wouldn't eat and she'd have all these crying spells. She did some wild, bizarre things that about drove us all crazy. Dad had not taken care of things the way he should have as far as business was concerned, and everything they had--the home, the business, and everything--had to go through probate. He had not put anything in Mother's name, so in order to make ends meet for Mother, since she had no income at all, Meekly and Martha moved back in with Mom and Earl and me. The four of us shared expenses until Mom could get all her property and so forth straightened out. Mama went to work at the Broadway store selling linens. We were all living there with her when my brother's first child was born.

Lillie seemed unable to recover from Lon's death, so the children had to keep an eye on her. Lily Fern finally got her to pull herself together:

LFW: I was working at the restaurant, and we'd call home two or three times during the day to make sure Mother was O.K., because she was acting rather strange. This was before Martha had her baby, so she had gone to work, also. So, Mother was there by herself through the day. One day I called and called and there was no answer. It frightened me, so I said, 'I've got to go home,' and left a little bit early. I lived about eight blocks from where I worked, and ran, literally ran as fast as I could, all the way home. I found Mother, lying prostrate across a bed, bawling and squalling, and she said, 'I just willed myself to die. I want to die. I don't want to live here any longer!' I was so scared and when I found out she was O.K., I was so relieved that it really got to me. I pulled her up off that bed and I shook her and I said, 'You have got to stop doing this, because you're driving us all crazy. You scared me to death! Does it make you feel good to make us feel sorry for you, or what? Why are you acting this way?' And she said, 'Oh, I just can't live without Daddy.' I said, 'Well, you are! You are living. You're not dead; you're living, and if God had wanted you to die, he'd have taken you instead of Daddy, or with him! And what would happen to us kids if you died, too?' She sort of straightened up and she said, 'I never really thought of it that way.' And after that, she began to get back on her feet and start living again.

During this time, Earl was driving a truck carrying pipe, and was usually gone all day. One time he came home during the day. His truck was too big to park on their street, so he left it down at the corner and walked to the house. Lily Fern was home alone and had just taken a bath, washed her hair, put it up in curlers and was in the process of cleaning the bath tub. She had sprinkled cleanser all over the tub, and was leaning over the edge to scrub the tub. Earl couldn't resist. She didn't hear him and was leaning over the tub, so he "goosed" her. She fell head first into the tub and came up with her hair totally full of cleanser. She had to wash it and curl it all over. Earl thought it was funny. Lily Fern didn't.

Earl didn't have the last laugh, though. When he left, she washed and curled her hair, and then she went to his underwear drawer, took five pair of shorts and sewed them shut. She got revenge. Later, when he stopped to relieve himself, he wet himself because he couldn't get the fly open. She says the same thing happened three times, because he didn't realize she had sewn that many!

From the beginning of the marriage, Lily Fern held her own, perhaps in preparation for what she would face in the next stage of their lives. With her father gone and her mother not coping well, Lily Fern had to confront another challenge. She and Earl had to make some decisions and face the world without the safety net provided by Lon Goble. They still had the love of their families and the love for each other, and more talent than they probably realized. It was almost time to leave the nest and strike out on their own.

Earl, Bill Wagner, Roy Trimble, Lily Fern, Fulton Nash

Chapter Five

 Building the Dream

At this point in Lily Fern's life, she began to realize her childhood dream of a gospel singing career. She and Earl decided to leave California in 1949, but they had already gained experience with their group and with all the personnel decisions and problems involved. They had decided that they wanted to go full time, and that they would have to be more centrally located to accomplish that. They began working toward that goal. Earl loved Kansas, where they had done a revival in Wichita, and when they actually left, that was where Earl thought they would head, but they wound up in Illinois.

But before they left, they worked on their group in California. As she and Earl built their musical ministry, they had a lot of work to do and many decisions to make. They carried on the Goble tradition of taking major decisions to the Lord.

Developing the group was an adventure for Lily Fern, because she didn't recognize her own ability. She knew that she could hear harmony really well, but about the only thing she knew that she had going for herself was a good ear for harmony. She says, "I just sang."

It was a busy time, an exciting time, as Lily Fern recalls:

LFW: We had two radio programs a day for a while, one on KGER and one on KFOX, and later we went on to a Catalina station, where we had two radio programs a day that reached out a little bit farther. At WKGR in Long Beach, we had fifteen minutes every day. We bought our time, which we paid for by everyone having jobs. Sometimes we had to transcribe them, because of our jobs. The money from personal appearances helped to support the group. We got sponsors as we got more popular. Then we added the Catalina station, KBIG. Basically, we had one program a day for a while, then about six months we had

With All My Heart

twice a day, then we had three programs a day, over that period of about five years.

But it was also a time of funny happenings and strange personalities. Lily Fern tells of an incident involving her pianist, Ann Keel, and, of all things, a funeral:

LFW: Ann Keel was playing the piano for us, and Ann was a really funny person. I mean, she was just a lot of fun. This was still out in California, and I hadn't learned to drive yet.

I got a phone call one morning from this man--I had no idea who he was or about the family. He had heard our concerts and had heard us on the radio, and he was determined that I was going to sing for his brother's funeral. I have never liked to sing for funerals. I have never liked to sing for weddings. Especially back then. I was fine, as long as somebody was singing with me, but when it came to singing by myself, I just didn't want any part of that. But he was absolutely determined that I was going to sing for this funeral. He called me the morning of the funeral to ask if I could sing, and of course, I said absolutely not. There was no way I could sing for this funeral, because it was going to be about fifty miles from where I lived. I said, 'I have no way to get over there. I don't drive.' He said, 'We'll pick you up and bring you back home.' Since that hadn't worked as an excuse, I said, 'Well, I can't sing without someone transposing, and my piano player doesn't live close by here. She lives farther away than I do.' He said, 'Don't worry about it. We have an organist here and she can transpose.' As it happened, he discovered the woman was not able to transpose, so I thought I was really off the hook for sure. Then he said, 'We've just got to have you, and time is getting away from us.' So I said, 'Well, let me see if I can get in touch with Ann Keel, my pianist.' I called her and she had just washed and rolled her hair. Now, this was back in the days of the little metal rollers with the rubber tips on the end. We washed and rolled our hair and left it up all day for it to dry. We couldn't sit under a hair dryer with those things--you'd have blistered your head! So, she had just finished rolling her hair, and she said, 'I can't go. I just got my hair rolled up and I can't take it out--it would be awful.' So I called him back, and I said, 'She just washed her hair, so there's no way I can do it.' 'Oh,' he said, 'That won't matter. We have a big screen. She'll be behind a screen. She doesn't have to worry about her hair. She can just wrap it up in a turban or something and she'll be O.K.' So I knew there was no way we could get out of that funeral.

I called her back and she wrapped her head up and came by and got me. I think she found the *ugliest* scarf that she could possibly find. It was an ugly, ugly brown and yellow plaid scarf, and she tied it around her head and we went to that funeral.

We got there early enough to talk to the funeral director and decide what we were going to do. I was supposed to sing three songs. The first one was 'The Highest Hill.' While we were waiting, he said to Ann, 'I'd like you to go out and play while the people are coming in.' So she went out and, sure enough, the screen was right there and nobody could see her. Well, between the time that Ann started playing for the people to come in and the time I went out to sing, there had been more people than they expected, and they had pulled that screen down to make more room, without Ann knowing it. Her back was to the people. When I walked out there, I saw that ugly head scarf around her head and she was sitting up there in all her glory, and everybody in the audience at that funeral could see her! She still was not aware of it. Well, the longer I stood there and looked at it, the funnier it got to me, and, of course, being at a funeral, it was worse than ever. I did everything--I tried to think of my mother dying; I tried to think of myself dying, or anything to keep me from laughing.

Then they gave her the signal to play the introduction to 'The Highest Hill,' and I walked out there very sedately, and I got to the last part of the verse, just before I went into the chorus, and my voice started shaking with laughter, and I sang, 'And we shall go to dwellllllll....' I couldn't help it. I couldn't control it. When she heard my voice shaking and all over the place, she thought I was crying. She said she was thinking, 'Lily Fern doesn't even know these people--what's the matter with her?' She glanced around to look at me and saw that the whole audience could see her. All her hands and feet together went on the keyboard and the pedals, and she let out one screech--and that was the end of my singing. Everyone, even the *family*, practically rolled in the floor.

To me that was one of the funniest incidents that I ever went through in my life. Ann never did forgive me for that. The last time I saw her, she said, 'I'll never forgive you!' But it wasn't my fault. I couldn't help it. Nonetheless, it was a funny situation. Ann played with us for quite a while. We had her come back and play for us a couple of different times.

In another case, it was Ann Keel who "lost it," and reacted to a funny situation:

LFW: J.B. Watson was only about eighteen years old when he came to us. The group consisted of Earl and me, a young man named Jack Bryson, and J.B., and Ann Keel playing the piano. We had a regular singing we did at a church in Compton, California, and we always had that little church just packed. In those days, we didn't have television, and people would come out any day of the week and just pack about anything you did. This particular group had a song called, 'Stand Together,' in which we would all sing together on the verse, and on the chorus we would go into an 'oooh,' and the bass singer did a recitation of the 'Lord's Prayer.' I don't know what ever made Earl do this, but he just opened the concert by saying, 'Stand Together.' He didn't even say the title of the song was, 'Stand Together,' or that we were glad to be there and would be opening our concert with 'Stand Together.' All he said was, 'Stand Together.' Well, everybody in the audience stood up, which was funny in itself. We all thought that was funny, but we started singing. One by one, the audience members realized that they weren't supposed to be standing and they all sat down, except two people on the very first row. They just kept standing there, with their heads bowed, unaware that they were the only ones standing. It's funny even when I think of it today!

So, when J.B. Watson got down to the next verse, he was supposed to do this recitation. He was trying to be so serious, saying, in his low bass voice, 'Our Father, which art in heaven....' Well, we were all supposed to 'oooh' in the background. Ann Keel started laughing first, but she could go ahead and play the piano and laugh. We couldn't 'oooh' and laugh! So, we started laughing, and we laughed and laughed, and it made J.B. mad. He started over again, and, when we finally got through laughing, he got through his 'Lord's Prayer' recitation and those two people finally sat down.

Forming the various versions of The Weatherfords was always an adventure. Lily Fern describes one of the most stable Weatherford groups:

LFW: We had that group together for a while, and then we needed to make some more changes. That was when we got Armond Morales to sing bass, and a young man by the name of Les Roberson joined us. We had a girl named Camilla Raye Smith, from Oklahoma, to play for us. That was the group that was together for quite a while, before we moved

Building the Dream

to Akron, Ohio. It was a good group and we did very well with that group. Armond Morales started with us when he was barely sixteen, and he sang with us for fourteen years all together. I just feel like Armond was part mine, and I think he kind of feels that way, too. There's a really close bond of friendship there between Armond and me, just almost like a mother and son relationship.

Both Earl and Lily Fern were forming friendships that would last for decades, as well as exploring their own goals and talents.

Lily Fern reveals how the gospel world almost lost Earl Weatherford to another love:

LFW: When Armond came to sing with us, he was out of high school and had enrolled in Compton Junior College. Earl had been thinking about the future, and he decided he was going to go back to school to get a degree in sports. He loved athletics and wanted to be a basketball coach. He made up his mind he was really going to do that. Then he went to college. It must have been around 1948. I don't really know how long--probably a semester--and was doing very well, until he realized that he would either have to be a basketball coach or sing; he couldn't do both. He was really torn as to what to do. So, he and Armond went to school together for a little while, and then Earl decided that singing meant more to him than being a basketball coach, so he dropped out of college. But Armond went on to school. He left the quartet for a while, and we got another bass singer. Armond went to the Assembly of God Bible School. Then, when he got out of college was when he came back into the group. He had married and, during that time, the group consisted of Armond, Les Roberson, Raye Smith, Earl and me. Armond was so easy to sing with. In fact, that whole group was easy to sing with. Les Roberson gave us a good blend. He was a very easy lead singer to sing with, and had a very good voice. That group hadn't been together very long before Les Roberson and Raye Smith were married, and we traveled that way for a while, before we left California in 1949.

When discussing the various singers and musicians who have performed with The Weatherfords, Lily Fern points out that some of the people who say they sang with The Weatherfords didn't really sing with them or didn't sing with them very long:

LFW: They came and tried out and didn't stay very long, because they didn't work out. When Earl first started his group, he needed a bass singer. I was singing alto and we had Harold Turman singing lead, and Earl was singing baritone, so we needed a bass singer. We had a piano player named Roy Jones, who came to us from Oklahoma City. Anyway, we called this guy. I think he was from Mississippi--I'm not sure--to come and try out to sing bass. We got together the first night he was there and started practicing, and the guy didn't know bass from a crow's calling, really! Back in those days, the singing was a lot of alto leads, bass leads, or baritone leads. That's how gospel music was back then. Now we have more of a middle of the road type thing. But every time anybody's lead came along, I don't care what it was, if it was alto or what it was, he'd take that and say that was his part. He would say, 'I know that's my part.' So, we kept trying to work with him, and I think he was there about five days. Finally, Earl gave him his bus fare and sent him back home.

Then Earl needed a lead singer pretty bad. That was when we were working with the Stamps-Baxter Music Company. Somebody recommended this guy, who had been to the Stamps-Baxter School of Music. So Earl called him. He rode a bus to California, all the way from Mississippi or Alabama or somewhere, to try out to sing for us, and he was a pretty good singer. We'll call him 'Melvin Bartlett.' We thought he talked so funny, because he came from the deep south. I had never been around too many people from the South, and we like to never got used to his accent! On the way home from a concert one night, he said, 'Do you know that down home, everybody has their own holler?' And I said, 'What are you talking about?' I kind of thought he had a screw loose. He said, 'We have our own holler. We can be out and start to come home, and within two miles of home, I would holler.' He said his mama would say, 'Well, there's Melvin Bartlett! He's hollerin'. He'll be home. He's down the hill about two miles.' And I said, 'Why'd you do such a silly thing as that?' And he said, 'That's just the way it was. We just all had a different holler.' So I said, 'Well, what was your holler?' And he let out with some kind of a war whoop that I thought and I still think was one of the most idiotic things that ever was! But the guy could really sing well. He worked really well with us, but he didn't bother to tell us that he had some kind of 'spells.'

One night we were singing and right in the middle of a concert, he just flattened out on his back in the middle of the floor and scared us to death. We thought he was dying! It scared everybody. The audience got up and started running around, and it disrupted the whole service.

We had no service that night! He still didn't tell us that he had problems. He said he probably just fainted. And, so, after while, when he kind of revived and told us that he'd be alright, he said that this had happened before and he would be alright. We didn't think anything about it, then, until he passed out in our living room one day. When he started to come around, he kept saying something that sounded like, 'Eyes, eyes.' We thought he was wanting someone to rub his eyes, but he said, 'No, no, no! Ice!' What he was asking for was ice, but he wasn't making it very plain, and there I was trying to rub his eyes! We told him later that we thought he better go back home and get some medical attention. We were worried about him and kind of concerned about having a death on our hands. So, Earl gave him his bus fare and sent him back home.

Usually, though, they were able to find good singers, many of whom became great friends and admirers of The Weatherfords. Sometimes, in those early years, they were making an impression on future "Weatherfords" without even knowing it. An example would be Bill Wagner, who sang lead for The Weatherfords in 1968 and 1969. This young man came prepared to be a Weatherford! Here is his story as he recalls it:

BW: When I was a boy of fourteen, my mother took me to a concert to hear for the first time some gospel quartets. I will never forget the excitement of that night. There were to be three groups that night, the Blackwoods, the Statesmen and the Weatherford Quartet.

As a boy, I enjoyed the fast songs from the Statesmen, and the low bass singing from the Blackwood Brothers bass singer. But the group I remember the most was the Weatherfords. When they took to the stage, they were different. They had class and sang wonderfully. They had a beautiful lady singing with them, who had on a light blue dress with a white flowing netting of some kind. She sang with a lacy handkerchief in her right hand. When she sang, the whole place stood still and listened. Even some of the other singers came back in and sat in the front row to listen and watch as she lit the house with her beauty, grace and that wonderful, wonderful voice of hers! Now you must remember I was only a fourteen year old boy, but I fell in love that night with that lady. I didn't know her and didn't get a chance to meet her, because there were too many grown-ups around her after the concert. I stood in line to buy a record. I had mowed grass and saved up enough money to buy one album that night. I bought the Weatherfords. A man sold me the record, even though I wanted to meet Lily. He patted me on my head and said, 'Thank you, little boy.' I never got close to Lily. I wish I could remember who the guy was who patted my head. I am six foot, nine inches tall now and would like to pat his head!

On the way home that night, I told my Mom, 'When I grow up, I am going to sing with the Weatherford Quartet.' Every day, when I got home from school, I would put that album on and stand in front of a lamp pole in front of the mirror, and pretend I was singing on a big stage with the Weatherfords.

As I got older, I would sing in groups locally at different positions, to get ready for the big day when they would call and offer me a chance to try out for them. I sang all parts in a lot of groups, because I didn't know what position Earl would need if he called. I even took a job with the city bus company for a while, just in case they needed a bus driver.

In 1968, they called. I couldn't believe it. It was 3:00 a.m. My brother handed me the phone and said it was Earl Weatherford. He asked me if I could come out and audition for a part in his quartet. I didn't even ask what part; I just said I would fly there the next day. The next day I found myself in his living room. It was late in the evening, and Lily was not at home, but would be later. My heart was pounding, but I could wait one more day for the try-outs. The next morning came and I was ready to try out. I remember meeting Lily for the first time face to face. I was nervous at first, but she and Earl made me feel like one of their own. I had written some songs for them a few years earlier, and they liked them. Lily sang my songs like an angel. Then I told them this story of how I had waited all these years for this moment. I told of the concert that my Mom took me to and what Lily wore. At last, Earl said I was hired! This was shouting time for me for a dream of many years just came true.

Bill Wagner now has his own ministry in Rockford, Tennessee.

While the membership of gospel groups tends to change frequently, some stay together for quite a while. Lily Fern recalls one Weatherford group that was fairly stable for a while.

LFW: The group that really hung together for a while was myself and Earl and Harold Turman, who sang the lead, and the piano player, Roy Jones. Then, we got a guy by the name of Bob Gillis, singing bass. Roy Jones played piano with us and at one time played the accordion and sang lead.

She points out that one of her most recent group members and pianists, the versatile Kenny Payne, is the son of one of the early pianists for the group, Dorothy Bright. She played for them during the KFOX radio days, and later married Vernon Payne. (For an accurate list of performers who actually were with The Weatherfords for any length of time, see the Appendix.)

When The Weatherfords left California, the group consisted of Earl, Lily Fern, Les and Raye Roberson and Armond Morales. She swears they left California with little or no idea of where they were going:

LFW: We just started out. We stopped in Springfield, Illinois for about three or four months, and we were going to settle there, but there wasn't a really good radio station there.

Earl just wanted to be more centrally located for travel purposes. Central Illinois seemed to be a good possibility. While they were checking it out, they stayed in Springfield:

LFW: While we were in Springfield, we had a lot of time on our hands. We all had separate apartments. Every morning, Earl and I would get up and go fishing somewhere, because Earl loved to fish. One day, we hit upon this pond where they stocked catfish, and we fished all day. And I mean we caught a tub full of catfish! It wasn't until we got away from there that we wondered what in the world we were going to do with all those catfish. We didn't have a freezer and there was no way we could possibly eat all of them--we didn't even know how to skin them or anything. Well, we finally got enough skinned for supper that night, and we gave our landlady some, and she put some in her freezer for us, but we still had all these catfish we didn't know what to do with, so Earl put them in a big box and took them out by the edge of a road, out of town a ways, and dumped them.

Two days later, we were going down that same road to go to a concert and there was this awful, ungodly smell. It was those fish! Everybody said, 'What in the world is that smell?' We didn't tell anybody. We just kept our mouths shut, because we didn't want anybody to know that we had thrown all those fish away at the side of the road. Earl and I considered that our 'fish story.'

After scouting the possibilities in the Springfield area, they heard about a better location--Fort Wayne, Indiana. The difference was that Fort Wayne boasted a strong radio station, so the group moved to Fort Wayne.

One of the strangest events in the history of Southern Gospel occurred while they were in Fort Wayne. The Weatherfords had a morning radio program that was broadcast from an airplane. George Younce tells the story in Bob Terrell's *The Music Men*, but there seems to be some controversy over exactly how that strange program happened. Lily Fern remembers the engine being revved up to start the program, but she doesn't remember it actually taking off from the runway near Winona Lake in Warsaw, Indiana.

Some really dangerous combinations of personnel in the group occurred while they were in Fort Wayne. The combination of Lily Fern and George Younce and Jim Hamill must have aged Earl tremendously:

LFW: In Fort Wayne, we went on the 50,000 watt station, WOWO. While we were there Armond was drafted into the service and I guess that must have been the Korean War. So we called a young guy by the name of George Younce from North Carolina to come up and sing with us. We worked that way for quite a while.

Now, George likes to scare people, and he's easily scared. He and I spent most of our time scaring each other.

We didn't have a bus at the time he joined us--just a big Roadmaster Buick. He got there on a Friday afternoon and that night we were supposed to leave for somewhere in the Charleston and Huntington, West Virginia area. We had a Saturday night concert and a Sunday morning concert, a Sunday afternoon concert and a Sunday night concert. George had never sung a lick with us, but on the way down there, we sang in the car, and that's how we learned our first few songs together.

He had no idea of our methods or habits or anything. For example, when we go into a church to sing, whenever the congregation stands to sing, we never stand. The only time we would stand would be whenever they would have the prayer. We would stand and sit back down. Well, the first concert we had with George, we were all sitting on the platform and the audience stood as the song director led the song--and George stood up. The rest of us stayed seated, so, in a little bit, he sat back down. Well, after the concert that night, we explained to him that we didn't usually stand, except for the prayer, and then we didn't stand again until we got up to sing. The second concert was on Sunday morning. They had the opening song, and we were on the platform again, and George stood up and sat back down, because we just stayed seated. The third one was on Sunday afternoon, and he did the same thing--he stood up again, but he realized that he wasn't supposed to do that, so he just acted like he was straightening his trousers and sat back down. Now, of course, all these things, in a situation where you're not supposed to laugh, get really funny, and we laughed. We couldn't keep from it.

That night, we were so tired, and had done all those concerts and had very little sleep. We just got a motel room for a few hours and had some sleep before we had to get up and get rolling again. So, then we did the concert that Sunday night in some huge church that was packed to the gills. And, when we got up to sing, we saw they were the most sober, conservative bunch of people I have ever seen. We worked on one mike at that time, so we were all wrapped around this microphone trying to sing and trying to be a blessing to people, and Earl put up a sign where we could see it, but nobody else could. It said, 'Smile.' *Mistake!* He never should have done that. We didn't laugh right them, but, I mean, it struck us all funny. When we got through with our first segment of songs and sat down, we started laughing. We were sitting up there on the platform, just kind of hysterical. By then, we were so tired, and when you get really tired, you just kind of lose control. We started laughing and, mainly, it was just George and me. We just thought *everything* was so funny! If somebody had said, 'You're going to die next minute,' we'd just probably have laughed in his face.

Well, we had some dignitaries of the church there. The District Superintendent was there and was supposed to speak that night. He and the pastor and one other big dignitary in the church were on the platform, and I was embarrassed that we had been laughing, so I leaned over across George, and said to the pastor, 'I'm so sorry that we started laughing. We have worked all weekend with very little sleep, and we're so tired and, when we get this tired, we just act like,' and I meant to say, 'silly fools,' but, instead, I said, 'When we get this tired, we just act like filly sools!' When I said that, George Younce just went, 'Huh, huh, huh, huh, huh,' with his loud, low laugh. I mean, he just burst out loud. Now, this is in the middle of a very conservative church service, mind you. Somebody was speaking in the pulpit. Well, when he laughed out loud, I spit all over the pastor, trying to control my laughter. George and I left the platform and went out the door. We went outside and leaned against the building and lost it! I mean, we could not breathe. We were laughing so hard we couldn't even breathe! We finally contained ourselves and went back in to try to finish singing. I think we had two or three more songs we had to sing. Later, we often discussed why that church never did call us back to sing, but they never did!

George became both a target and a perpetrator in pranks off-stage, as well. Lily Fern laughs as she remembers those days:

LFW: We loved to play tricks on George, and he loved to play tricks on me. We had a three bedroom apartment, and one of those bedrooms was made into an office, and in that office, we had a single bed and a chest of drawers, and that was where George stayed and slept when he first started singing with us. He was in there typing a letter to Clara one day, before they got married, and Earl was in the office, messing around and making a little bit of racket. When you sat at the desk in that office, your back was to the door. I went in to do something and realized that George didn't know I was there. I just went over and poked him in the ribs and kind of yelled, and I don't know what he wrote to Clara after that, but it sure wasn't very pretty, because he typed all over the page!

Earl loved a practical joke at times, too, when it was not in front of an audience. He enjoyed teasing George, as Lily recalls:

LFW: Another time, we were doing a revival, and George and Earl and I were staying in the preacher's home. The preacher had a two-story house and a full basement, and the basement was sort of fixed up like an apartment. The preacher and his wife had to go out and make a hospital call one day, so while they were gone, George decided he was going to wash some shirts. That was back in the days of drip-dry shirts, where you had to wash them and hang them up and let them drip dry. George was down in the basement, washing these shirts out, and Earl had gone down there to go to the bathroom. George didn't know Earl was there. He was just whistling and singing and carrying his shirts back and forth, until Earl jumped out and grabbed him on the back and yelled really loud. I never did really find out all the particulars of what George did or said that day, but apparently it was unmentionable! Earl got a kick out of scaring him like that.

George and Lily Fern had a laundry confrontation, also:

LFW: Another time, George really scared me. We had moved to

another apartment, which was upstairs, and we had an outside entrance. When you walked in the entrance, you would immediately go up the stairs to our apartment. I was going to go down and do some laundry in the basement one day, and when I opened the door to go downstairs, George was there and yelled at me, and said, 'Braaagh!' or something like that. I had both arms stacked full of dirty clothes, and it scared me so bad, I threw them and they just flew down on George, and he had dirty clothes hanging all over him.

George Younce got an unexpected result on one of his pranks with Lily Fern:

LFW: They were always scaring me with spiders. I was scared to death of spiders. The one time that George really scared me was when we had been singing in California and we were getting ready to go to a concert. We had been to these people's house to eat and there was a whole lot of people there, and George just walked up to me and said--he had just put a piece of gum in his mouth--and he said, 'Here, take this for me.' I thought it was paper from the gum. I held my hand out, and when he dropped it in my hand, it was this big, old, hairy spider! Well, I didn't do anything. I was just standing there, against the wall, and I started slowly sinking down to the floor. I didn't faint, but I thought I was going to, because I am literally scared to death of spiders. I have overcome it a little bit, in later years, but then I was terrified. I didn't scream. I had just turned completely white and sunk to the floor. George thought I was dying. He thought I was having a heart attack. It scared him. He said, 'I'm sorry, I'm sorry! I didn't mean to scare you like that!'

Even Earl got in on the spider pranks, and one of his back-fired, as well:

LFW: In Fort Wayne, Earl's desk was always a total mess with papers and such all over it, but he didn't like me straightening it. I just couldn't stand it being such a mess, so I would straighten it anyway and tuck away some of the stuff so it looked a little better. Well, one time Earl got this big old rubber spider and stuck it in the top drawer. He even had it fixed somehow to jump when the drawer was opened. I was cleaning and I went to the desk and got all the papers into stacks and then I decided to put one stack of papers in the top drawer. I held the stack in one hand and opened the drawer with the other. That spider jumped out and I yelled and threw that whole stack of papers up in the air and they went everywhere! I never even tried to sort them when I recovered! I just threw them all in a bag and when Earl came I just said, 'You did it; you straighten them out!'

George and Big Jim Hamill formed a lethal combination with their practical jokes. Lily Fern never knew what would happen next:

LFW: George Younce and Jim Hamill scared me with a spider a few times, also. Jim has scared me with fake spiders so many times that it's not even funny, and so has George Younce. I've opened songbooks with spiders in them, and everything else. Both of them have done their share of teasing and scaring me at different times.

There is no more colorful character in The Weatherfords' past than Jim Hamill. Lily Fern can tell chapter and verse about his antics and his attitudes. They contacted Jim to join The Weatherfords while he was living in Shenandoah, Iowa, and the group arranged to meet him at a revival in Wichita, Kansas at the First Nazarene Church. Jim came from Iowa and met them and they did the first night's concert, having never ever sung a note with him. She remembers a few incidents that are typical of Big Jim:

LFW: Jim Hamill came into the group when Les and Raye Roberson left. Raye got pregnant and she quit. Then, shortly after that, Les joined the Oak Ridge Boys. That's when we got Danny Koker to come play the piano for us. When Les left, we got a young man by the name of Norman Wood to sing with us for a while, and then, when he left, we got none other than Big Jim Hamill. Now, Jim Hamill deserves a chapter, maybe even a book to himself. Jim was just a great, big, overgrown kid! I think he was nineteen when he joined us, and just a very slap-happy, lackadaisical kid. He used to provoke me to no end. I would be so exasperated with him, but I really love Jim Hamill.

He used to tell the story on himself that, when he'd call home, his dad would say, 'Jim, don't come home. I'll just send the money. Just please don't come home!'

When he first started singing with us, at that Nazarene Church revival in Wichita, Kansas, he stayed in some people's home and while he was there, he managed to break their stereo. We had to pay to get it fixed. And the first night he worked with us, he was helping set up, and instead of just setting the amplifier down on the floor, he rolled it off his arm and bounced it on the floor. Jim did things like that all the time. We had Jim with us at a different time, also, many years later, and I said many times that Jim Hamill is the only singer we ever had that Earl hired him three times and fired him two times. The last time he quit. Maybe he saw the handwriting on the wall! Jim used to just nearly aggravate me to death, but I love him. I love him to this day, and I told him how aggravating he was to me. He knew he was.

Hamill's antics extended from Fort Wayne to Akron, Ohio. He had a capacity for making Lily Fern lose her temper:

LFW: When we moved to Akron, we had a great arranger--Danny Koker--and he had arranged a song for us that Mosie Lister wrote, 'Where No One Stands Alone.' It was a beautiful song, and it's still one of the best songs that's ever been written. Danny had an arrangement on that that would knock your hat in the creek! We were working at the Cathedral of Tomorrow, but then it was Old Calvary Temple, before they moved into the new Cathedral of Tomorrow. The stage was very high. We worked two mikes at that time, and Jim got excited on 'Where No One Stands Alone,' and jumped off that high stage and took the mike with him into the audience. The people were standing on their feet, they were so excited, but what he did was, coming up for the ending, he left the microphone in the audience.

Another time when we were doing 'Where No One Stands Alone,' we had an ending--a modern ending--that Danny had arranged, that was just beautiful. When we got to the ending, we hit it as solid as could be--except for Jim. He got excited again, and instead of staying on the note he was supposed to stay on, he hit every note in the scale. 'Where no one stands alooooone!' and he slid up and down the scale. Well, if you know something about harmony, you know you can't blend something like that--especially modern harmony--and that was the last song we were singing that night. It made me so mad! Of course, at that time I was in my early twenties--hot-headed--had a high temper, and hadn't learned that I needed to control myself as yet. I followed him off the stage and back through the prayer room, and I said, 'Jim Hamill, you make me so mad, I'd just like to choke you! What in the world, after we worked all that time on that ending, what in the world would make you go off and hit all those notes like that? You ruined it. You just ruined the whole thing for everybody!' He just shrugged his shoulders and said, 'That's the way the old mop flops,' and walked out. It didn't bother him a bit, but, like I said, I really love him. I hold no malice toward him at all. He was just Jim Hamill.

The experience of The Weatherfords in Akron was a turning point in Lily Fern's life. She speaks with love and enthusiasm of that important time in her life, and for two institutions that were significant to the change in their ministry:

LFW: What really took us to Akron was a call to sing at Akron Baptist Temple. We got the call because they got our radio program from Fort Wayne. At that time, The Akron Baptist Temple was one of the largest Independent Baptist churches going. This was around 1950. They wanted us to come for Saturday night and all day Sunday.

That was when we had 78 RPM records, and we loaded up all our records and went. The place seated about 4,000, and it was packed to the gills when we sang there Saturday night. We just didn't know how to act around so many people. The church had a choir that sang this kind of gospel music, and the church choir was full and they sang--oh, they sang pretty! They called us to get up and sing, and we turned around to sing to the choir, too, because there wasn't any place for them to sit out in the audience, and we turned around and all those women with their beautiful furs on and fancy jewelry and everything were standing there crying, mascara running down their cheeks, because they were so blessed by our singing. We were just elated. We were thrilled to death. That was probably the highlight of our entire ministry up to that point, because it's what really pushed us up to where we really wanted to do better and better, because of our reception at that church at that time, and that it was such a big, well-to-do church. It was well established and well known all over the United States, and it was really something to be able to get in there to sing.

We sold every record we had that weekend. It was really quite a place to sing. The pastor of that church was Dr. Dallas Billington.

Also in Akron at that time, Rex Humbard had just come in to start The Cathedral of Tomorrow. He first had a big tent revival at the Akron airport with the entire Humbard family, and it was such a successful meeting that Rex decided that he was going to leave the family ministry and stay. His sister, Leona, and her husband, Wayne Jones, stayed with him in Akron, and together they started The Cathedral of Tomorrow. It started out as Calvary Temple, and they rented this little theater building in Cuyahoga Falls. That's where they were having their services the first time they called us to sing for them.

Earl always felt that he should be loyal to the people in an area before he agreed to sing for another group in that area, so when Rex called us to sing, Earl called Dr. Billington. The Akron Baptist Temple was the first church we went to in Akron. We knew there was a conflict between Dallas Billington and Rex Humbard, based on the fact that Rex had brought Katherine Kuhlmann in for that tent revival. That was before we really knew Rex. We knew about Rex Humbard, because we had heard him before in California. We knew he was there starting a church, but we didn't have any contact with him at the time of his tent revival. The meeting with Katherine Kuhlmann was so successful that cars lined up for two miles to try to get into the airport, where they had the tent set up. They had some fabulous meetings and some wonderful miracles and healings happened during that meeting. Dr. Billington did not believe in healing in that way. He felt that this was a Pentecostal thing, and, of course, Baptists didn't believe in that, and so he began fighting it--through the newspapers and everything and it was headlines for weeks and weeks and weeks. Now, I love Dr. Billington and I love Rex Humbard, so I'm not too happy about the way it all happened. Rex never did retaliate or fight back. The whole thing just built Rex's congregation. A lot of people from the Akron Baptist Temple left there and went over to Calvary Temple, which turned out to be The Cathedral of Tomorrow.

It was during this time that Rex called us to come and sing for him one weekend--like Wednesday through Sunday, at a revival. So, Earl got on the phone and called Dr. Billington and said, 'One of your rivals across town has asked me to come and sing for him on such and such a weekend.' We found out later that Dr. Billington thought Earl meant one of the fellows who had left his church to start a church across town. Evidently he didn't even dream it was Rex Humbard, so he said, 'Well, Earl, I can't use you that weekend, so go ahead, and I hope you have some good services!'

Earl just took him at his word and we booked in with Rex Humbard at Calvary Temple, and, of course, Rex put it on the television, on radio and in the newspaper, because he always did everything in the biggest way possible. Immediately, we began to get calls from Akron, that we couldn't go there, that we couldn't do that, or we'd never get back in the Akron Baptist Temple. Well, Earl was just stubborn enough that he said, 'Nobody tells me where I can and cannot sing. I asked if it was O.K. and Dr. Billington told me to go ahead, so I'm not changing. It would be wrong for me to say that we can't come over there, because they've already put the advertising out.' To us, it would have just made the situation worse, so we went ahead and sang with Rex Humbard, and we were blackballed with the Akron Baptist Temple for years and years after that, and from any Independent Baptist church for many, many months. But we still felt like we were right, because we didn't change our ministry; we didn't change our message; we just went to that church to sing.

Rex had told Earl, 'If you ever decide to make a move, I wish you'd call me. I've been interested in hiring a group to come and work with us at the church here.' So, when we got ready to leave Fort Wayne and WOWO, Earl called Rex, which led to us moving to Akron.

That ministry was one of the greatest things I have ever seen. We had such wonderful services in the old theater building, and in The Cathedral of Tomorrow, too, but in the old theater building, we couldn't wait to get to church every service. We just dreaded the times that we would have to sing somewhere on Wednesday night and would miss our church at Calvary Temple. We hated to miss church any time there. But many times we were called out to sing on Wednesday evening, and lots of times we were called out to sing for a revival Wednesday through Sunday, but we were always back on Sunday night to be at The Cathedral and to do Monday television. I, and I'm sure the whole group would say the same thing, learned more about faith in Christ, faith in God, at The Cathedral than I would have ever learned anywhere else in my life. I believe with all my heart that if I hadn't been at The Cathedral, I would not be able to believe and have the faith that I have today.

And now there's no way anyone can convince me that if I'm doing everything that I can to live for the Lord and to do what I feel that he wants me to do, and live above sin, I believe with all my heart that God is going to take care of me under any circumstances. He's proven that. I believe that God is obligated to take care of his own children when they give over everything they have to him--every ounce of energy, anything that might come into their lives, over to Christ--I believe God is obligated to take care of them and it's been proven, because he's taken care of me and my family time and time again. I can tell you of stories where impossible situations happened, where we received answers that had to come from the Lord, to prove all this. I learned faith in Christ, faith in God. I knew that God was capable of doing anything, but I learned how to rely in faith and on faith from Rex Humbard's ministry at The Cathedral of Tomorrow.

The Humbard family is obviously the strongest influence on Lily Fern since Lon and Lillie Goble. The warmth and enthusiasm she still feels for the Humbards is evident whenever she discusses this period of her life:

LFW: One of the greatest stories I've ever heard on faith was from Wayne and Leona Jones. I've heard many stories from all of the Humbards, from Rex and from when he'd have Mom and Dad Humbard come and preach. I've heard Mom Humbard speak on faith, and some of the stories, I just couldn't fathom. But one of the greatest stories was from Wayne and Leona. When the Humbards were traveling as a family, they had Mom and Dad Humbard, Rex and Maude Aimee, Ruth and Lewis Davidson--Ruth was Rex's sister--and Wayne and Leona Jones. He also had two younger sisters, Juanita and Mary, and a brother, Clem and Priscilla Humbard. They all traveled in their own trailer homes, and would go all across the United States and hold tent revivals. Or, if the church was large enough, they'd go into the churches and hold these big campaigns.

Wayne and Leona told of one time when they were someplace in California, and they were tearing the tent down at the revival they had just had, and they had to go to someplace like Virginia. So Wayne came in and said, 'There is no way we can get to that revival, because the transmission is gone--it's just not going to pull our trailer.' Wayne said that Leona got down on her knees and said, 'We're just going to pray about it.' And he said, 'There's no need to pray about it. That transmission is gone. God can't do anything about that transmission!' Leona said, 'Well, we're going to pray anyway.' So she just prayed a simple prayer, and said, 'Lord, you know we need to be at that meeting. You know our financial situation. We don't have the money to get the car fixed. You know we need the money from that revival to live on. You know where we have to go. We don't know how we're going to get there, but you're going to have to provide the way.' Then she said to Wayne, 'Go out and hook that car up to the trailer and we're going to start out.' He said he went out and hooked it up, and they started out. They never did have to change the transmission in their car. So, you tell me what happened. God answered prayer. Now, how He did it, I don't know, but God took care of that transmission.

I heard Mom Humbard preach one time, and she said many times they would sit down to eat, and there would not be food on the table. She'd set the table, put the water on the table, call them all in, and they'd thank God for the food they were going to have. And every time, before they would get through praying, somebody would knock on the door with their supper. Now, that's faith. They needed clothes one year to start school. Rex said that she called the kids in and said, 'We're going to pray. Now, Lord, my kids need to go to school, and they need clothes.' And she named off the clothes that each of them needed. And they all needed shoes. Before they said, 'Amen,' from that prayer, somebody knocked on the door and brought her money to buy clothes for the kids and brought shoes for every kid in the family.

Now, you talk about faith in God? After sitting in on that kind of ministry, you believe that God can do anything and would do anything, if you're living for him. But people have to know that they have to obey God. You don't just go out there and do anything you want to do and decide all of a sudden that you have a need in your life and you'll ask God to help you through this. I think God's going to remind you, 'Well, how have you been living?' But it sure has caused me to really live close to the Lord and to rely and trust on his promises for the needs in our lives.

The time spent with the Humbard ministry was inspirational for Lily Fern. She and Earl were growing in their profession, gaining respect and learning from the Humbard ministry.

When they joined the Humbards, they were featured in the newest medium, television. At first they did a Saturday morning show, then they were on every morning. They would go on Mondays and tape shows. The daily shows were thirty minutes and the Sunday show was an hour. Rex didn't do a lot of preaching, but he would put in a little sermonette with each program. He was wise enough to know that the music drew a lot of people to the ministry. Over the years, The Weatherfords and Henry and Hazel Slaughter performed along with a trio of ladies, consisting of Maude Aimee Humbard, Lily Fern Weatherford and Rex's sister, Leona. They worked in television from 1953 to 1963. This was an exciting and special time for Lily Fern and The Weatherfords.

Even Earl's sisters remember the Akron years as special. Bobbie Sue remembers the excitement and the people they met:

BSL: They moved to Akron when I was sixteen years old. My sister and I rode the bus to Akron the summer before my Senior year in High

School and spent six weeks with them. That was a fun time, and they did everything they could to make it a memorable visit. We went on a picnic with Bill and Danny Gaither and their sister. Of course, at that time, they weren't the famous Gaithers like they are now. So it really didn't make a big impression on me until later years. We also had the privilege of meeting Stuart Hamblin, which was exciting.

Bette Jo has good memories of the Akron years, also:

BJW: My husband and I had two sons who were extremely fond of their Uncle Earl. There were always little private jokes between them. Our older son, Jim spent one summer in Akron with Earl and Lily. While on the road to a concert, Earl was stopped by a Highway Patrolman for speeding. When Earl was talking to the officer, Jim reminded him, 'Uncle Earl, you were just going eighty-five miles per hour.' That cost him! I remember making a trip to Akron, traveling on the Weatherford bus, on the Pennsylvania turnpike. I was trying to sleep. The bus had stopped and I heard all this talking and laughing, etc. Well, they had met up with the Speer Family on the turnpike, and it was like a family reunion.

Bette Jo also remembers happy Christmases as they all came home to Oklahoma during those years and later:

BJW: My husband, also named Earl, and Earl were close as any brothers. Christmas was a very special time. Mom and Dad looked forward to everyone being home. During those years, there were six of us kids. We had two younger sisters. Earl had a nickname for each of us, mine being 'Bunson,' which he never let me forget. No matter what the two 'Earls' were given for Christmas, they never went home with that gift. They called it their 'trading material.' Lots of new shirts never worn!

So, the Akron years were a high point in so many ways for Lily Fern and Earl. But, in Akron, the group was to change again. Lily Fern explains how a new Weatherford group came to be:

LFW: It was about this time that we had George and Jim and Danny and Earl and me, when George, Jim and Danny decided to leave the Cathedral and start their own group, which they did. Earl and I were kind of hanging in limbo there for a while, so we just worked with Rex Humbard on the TV programs and so forth until we could get the group back together. We were waiting for Armond to get out of the service, which was going to be in a couple of months, and in that length of time, Earl got the group together, consisting of Earl and me, Glen Payne, and Armond. For a while, we had a young man named George Houston playing the piano. When he left, we got Henry Slaughter, which completed a really phenomenal group. Henry, Glen, Armond, Earl and I worked together from probably about 1954 to at least 1962. That was probably our best group, in the sense that we worked well together professionally and personality-wise. In 1963, I dropped out to deal with children.

During the years with the "classic" Weatherford Quartet (Lily Fern, Earl, Armond, Glen and Henry), the pranks continued, with Armond and Earl constantly teasing Glen Payne.

For example, Lily Fern recalls a revival in Bemis Point, New York in a little country church:

LFW: Earl was always aggravating Glen. There was a cemetery next to this little church, and Earl got the notion to do something and he talked Armond into it. He said, 'After the program tonight, you get Goob.' Earl always gave people nicknames and he always called Glen 'Goober.' He said, 'You get him to come out there in front of that big tombstone.' After church that night, Armond got Glen out there. He said, 'Glen, I was out here before church tonight an I saw some tomb stones for some Paynes. Come out here and look at this--This will be interesting to you.' He took him out there in the dark and said, 'Look real close down there at that stone. It has your dad's name and everything.' Glen got down real close to try to see in the dark, and Earl jumped out from behind that tombstone and scared the life out of him!

Another time, while on the road, Earl got some firecrackers. He was driving and he slipped an aluminum pie pan out the window and held it down by the door and tapped it on the car. He pretended something was wrong with the car and pulled over. He asked Glen to get out and check the tires. When Glen leaned over to look at the back of the car, Earl threw a firecracker back in that direction and when it went off, Glen jumped like he was shot. Life wasn't easy for Glen around Earl.

Glen had enough to deal with in everyday occurrences without the antics of his co-workers. One time he was driving a Weatherford bus that had the gear shift next to the door handle. In an attempt to down-shift, he opened the door by mistake. As Lily Fern remembers, "He cut his eyes at us quickly to see if anyone had noticed. Of course, we were all laughing. He just closed the door and drove on."

Despite all the horseplay, Lily Fern designates this group as probably the best in terms of personality and compatibility in sound, and it was a great period in Weatherford history. They produced some of their finest work, including the critically acclaimed "In the Garden" album.

This group was together for quite a while, until Lily Fern left to take care of the children and work on the staff at The Cathedral. Shortly after that, Rex Humbard had decided to have a quartet work full time at The Cathedral, which did not fit with Earl's feeling about the mission of The Weatherfords as a traveling group. Consequently, Earl, Lily Fern and Armond chose to leave and the remainder of the group stayed at the Cathedral and formed the basis of the group known today as "The Cathedrals." Lily Fern explains her reaction to leaving her happy relationship with the Humbard family:

> LFW: That move was like starting over again, because we had been in Akron so long, and it was a kind of rough thing to do, but Earl decided he had better make the break, because he wanted to keep going with his own group. He didn't think he would be able to do that and still work at The Cathedral. We loved Rex and Maude Aimee Humbard and all the Humbards. Under the ministry there, I learned more about how to be a strong Christian and how to put my prayer to work by praying and then having faith and trying to live a better life than I would have ever done anywhere else. I really owe a lot to Rex Humbard and studying under his ministry.

The Akron years were spectacular for The Weatherfords in terms of professional growth, increase in popularity and, as Lily Fern mentioned, spiritual awakening, but another fulfilling and important facet of Lily Fern's life began in Akron, as well. This was the beginning of new roles for her and Earl, and a joy that her life had not known up to this point.

Chapter Six

 Filling the Void

Both Earl and Lily Fern came from loving families. It was only natural that they would want to begin their own.

Life was going well for them. They were successful, busy and employed in meaningful ministries, both at The Cathedral of Tomorrow and with their traveling quartet. But they were ready for what would be another significant development in Akron--the adoption of their children. This proved to be the most joyous, yet most heart-rending adventure they had faced.

Lily Fern remembers it as though it were yesterday, including the emotions she felt:

LFW: Earl and I had been married for fourteen years. We had no children, and we both desperately wanted children. Every so often, we'd talk about maybe adopting, but then we would just sort of let it drop and wouldn't do anything about it. But then a foster mother came to The Cathedral with this darling little boy, and we fell in love with that baby. She brought him to Sunday School and church at The Cathedral. We began to try to adopt that baby, but it just wasn't possible, because of the situation with the family. It caused us to really start investigating adoption, and we applied for adoption at the Family Service in Akron.

I can hardly even talk about my children and adopting them, because it was such a beautiful time. Susan was our first. From the time we applied until they called us to come get her, we waited nine months to the day. I said, 'You couldn't get much closer than that, could you?' They called us on a Thursday and told us they had a baby to show us, and it was a little girl, and she was two and a half months old. They wanted us to come in on Monday afternoon. I said, 'There's no way we can live a weekend! Can't we come and see her now and then come back and get her?' No, there was no way; she was in a foster home and they were making all the arrangements and we could see her on Monday afternoon. We had to go off to Pennsylvania and sing that weekend. I hardly remember singing. The only thing I could think about was seeing that baby on Monday.

At that time, Rex Humbard had a daily television program. Sunday was done live from The Cathedral. The week-day shows were all taped once a week, which was done on Monday mornings in Cleveland, Ohio. Usually, Earl and I would ride with someone to Cleveland, but we had an important date that particular Monday afternoon. We were going to see our baby girl *for the first time*.

As soon as the taping was finished that day, Earl and I were out of there and made record time back to Akron and to the Family Service Center. We were early and had to wait. Finally our case worker came into the room. We were sitting there talking to her, and I said, 'Well, when are they going to bring the baby in?' And she said, 'She's through that door right there.' I said, 'You mean to tell me that we've been sitting here all this time and that baby has been right through that door?' I mean, I could have reached over and opened it, and she was there, lying in a crib. The case-worker kind of grinned, and she said, 'Yes, but she just woke up and they're changing her and everything.' I hadn't heard a peep out of her. Finally, they opened the door and they told us to come in, and there she was, lying in the crib. To me, she was the most beautiful little girl I had ever seen in my life, and I realized right then what it meant to be a mother. And I hadn't even touched her. But Earl and I fell in love with her. She was just a precious, precious child and filled a void in our lives that we had no idea we even had.

We got to see her that day, but we couldn't get her until the following Wednesday, so I went home and I got the nursery all ready. We had already bought a lot of things for her and Maude Aimee Humbard, one of the most generous people I've ever known in my life, was so excited about us getting Susan, that what I didn't have, Maude Aimee got for her. She went out and bought Susan a complete bedroom set, with a double bed we didn't use until Susan grew out of her baby bed, which Maude Aimee got, as well. It was a white French Provincial canopy bed, plus a complete lay-out.

The day before we were to go pick up Susan, I was running up and down the basement steps, doing some last minute things, and suddenly I got real sick to my stomach, and I thought, 'What's wrong with me?' I went upstairs and went to the bathroom and just threw up my toenails. I said, 'Well, I even had the morning sickness with this pregnancy!'

We brought Susan home when she was two and a half months old. I've never known a baby that was as good as Susan was, ever, at any time. She just never cried. She was perfectly happy and content. The only time she would really get fussy was if we held her too long. She had been taken care of wonderfully in the foster home, but they didn't have time to cuddle and hold a baby all the time, because this foster mother probably had three or four other children to look after. But Susan's needs were taken care of very well. We were so thrilled with her!

I didn't stop singing. I'd take her with us and put her in a bassinet right off the stage and have somebody sitting with her. I would go off stage and see about her often. I never did put her in a nursery until she was a pretty big size girl. We were just so enthralled with her. We'd come home in the middle of the night and get ready for bed and put her in bed between us. I started putting a little curler on the top of her head, and I would do it while she was asleep, so she wouldn't wiggle. I think I had that curler in there so much that she thought it was part of her head, because she never did try to pull it out or anything. We'd pick her up and hold her just because we wanted to hold her, and when we'd be holding her for just a little bit, she'd start squirming and kind of fussing, and she wanted to be laid down. She'd just lie there and play in her bassinet by herself. She was a beautiful, wonderful, precious, good little girl--a good little baby. I continued to sing until Susan was almost two years old.

Susan was very intelligent and very alert. She was just quick to catch on to things. In fact, she talked very young. She started talking at seven months old. She said words like 'go' and 'go bye-bye' and 'Daddy' and 'doggie' and 'car' and several others.

When we adopted the children, we would have them for six months and then, if we were ready, we could sign the final papers. Just as soon as that six months rolled around, we were ready to sign, because we didn't want to lose that little girl!

One thing I will never forget. We went to the court house and to the judge's private chambers, just the case-worker, the judge, Earl and me and Susan. Susan could just barely walk by holding on to chairs. By holding on to something, she could walk around the room. She got restless and wanted to get down while the judge was looking over all the papers. She held on to the desk and walked over to a bookcase where pictures of his grand-children were, and she turned around to me and said, 'Mama, see baby?' The judge looked out over his glasses and said, 'Did she say that?' I said, 'She sure did!' And, boy, I think Earl and I popped ten buttons off our shirts that day, we were so proud of her. We had her dressed up so cute. Of course, we changed her clothes probably about every four hours, because we were so thrilled to have her, and we treated her just like a great big baby doll.

She was really a good child. We'd take her to concerts when she was just very small. I would have somebody hold her while I was up singing, and then, as soon as I got through, I'd go back and get her. As she got a little bit older and began to understand, even when she was just a few months old, I would tell her, 'Mama has to leave you for a little bit, but these people are going to take care of you and they're going to watch you, and as soon as Mama gets through, I'll be right back.' I just felt like it was important to tell her those things, so that she would be secure and not feel like I was running off and leaving her.

She was probably about nine months old when we did a concert out in Harrisburg, Pennsylvania, with The Couriers at the Forum Auditorium. I needed someone to watch her that night, and the wife of one of The Couriers asked a doctor and his wife to hold Susan while I was up singing. He was a psychologist. Usually, I left Susan a little cloth book to read, but that night I had forgotten to take her book in, and somebody in front of them had a magazine, so they gave her that magazine. She looked at it all the time we were up singing, they said. The psychologist came to me later and said, 'You know, you have a very intelligent child there.' I said, 'Well, of course, I know that.' I thought she was just perfect in every way. He said, 'No, you think I'm just saying that, but I'm a child psychologist, and when a child that size follows her finger along the lines, like she is reading, that's one of the first signs of real intelligence in a child.'

I always told Susan, and I told her that night, 'Now, you watch the stage up there. See that stage up there? And when Mama comes out, you'll see Daddy and Mama singing, and as soon as we go off that stage, I'll be right back to get you.' And I always did. I always told the kids where to be and what I would be doing and, even when they got older. I just felt it was very important that they knew I'd be back to get them, no matter what.

Lily Fern experienced the worries of motherhood early on with Susan. She and Earl seemed to know instinctively how to handle Susan's need for security, especially when dealing with Susan's childhood medical problem:

LFW: Susan had been born with ptosis of the eyelid, where the eyelid drooped quite heavily over the iris of the eye. So, when she was a little over a year old, we had to have surgery done. They went in and clipped the skin and then clipped the muscle of the eye that lifted and raised the eyelid, and then sewed them up. Of course, when she had this surgery, she had to have her eyes bandaged for several days. We tried to prepare her the night before, when she went to the hospital. One of us was allowed to stay with her twenty-four hours a day, because she was really just a baby. She understood so well, so we talked to her, Earl and I, and said, 'Now, you're going to go to sleep tonight, and in the morning, when you wake up, everything's going to be really dark, because they're going to work on your eyes. It's going to be dark for a few days, but you don't need to fear, because Mama and Daddy will be right by your side, and all you have to do, if you need anything, is just say what you need and we'll be right there.'

Sure enough, when she came to, she didn't make a fuss. She didn't complain about her eyes being covered or anything. Of course, people had brought her toys--mainly Maude Aimee. She just doted on Susan like she was her own child. Susan had this autograph hound--she hadn't seen it, but she just loved it--and it was almost taller than she was. They'd let me walk around the halls, holding her hand, with the bandages on her eyes. I saw more parents crying when I'd walk by with her than you can shake a stick at, because she looked so cute, walking around that hallway, little, tiny thing with her eyes bandaged, dragging that autograph hound and not complaining. She had to have the bandages on her eyes for about three days after she came home. When I first brought her home, I led her around through the house two or three times, to show her where the doors were and everything. I said, 'Now, when you want to go someplace, just call Mama, and I'll come and lead you to where you want to go.' Well, she didn't even do that. She just started feeling her way around by herself. She was such an unusual child and just accepted everything so well.

But I'll never forget the day we went to have the stitches out! She wasn't a very good child that day. She screamed every breath, but she got over all that just fine. We could never explain the insight that it seemed Susan had on that eye surgery, even though we did take three or four days to explain to her that she should not be afraid, that we would be right with her and that Jesus would be with her, and, no matter what happened, it wouldn't be long before she would be able to see again. We just worked so hard to reassure her and pray with her, and I guess it worked, because the child was absolutely marvelous. She didn't seem the least bit frightened or concerned at the fact that she could not see.

After she woke up the morning after surgery, the only thing that she said that was in any way a complaint, was, 'Mama, turn the television this way. I can't see it.' We were watching television, and the thing that drew her attention was that our television program, which had been taped earlier, came on. It was The Cathedral of Tomorrow, and she heard the familiar singing and the familiar talking--Rex's voice and the quartet singing. She couldn't figure out why she couldn't see that, since she could hear the music. I just reached over and turned it off, and I said, 'Baby, we can't see it either,' because I didn't want to confuse her. I said, 'Mama and Daddy are right here with you,' and, at that point, Earl had to leave the room, crying, because he could hardly stand it.

She was just an amazing girl through all of that. She sat in that little rocker in front of the television, and she had pulled the rocker over right where she always sat to watch it. It was just like she knew how to measure that distance, and she would sit there and rock by the hour, just like she could see it. Maude Aimee broke down and cried, saying, 'I do believe that Jesus has given her sight through those bandages.' The only bad part about the whole thing was when the stitches had to be removed and they wouldn't let me stay with her. I think, if they had let me stay with her, she would have been O.K., but I heard her scream with every breath, 'Mama, Mama, Mama!' I thought I was going to go out of my mind before they finally finished.

Lily Fern had been able to spend this time with Susan, since she had stopped singing with the quartet several months earlier, after the adoption of their second child. Earl was working with a male quartet at the time.

Filling the Void

Adopting Susan was a pure joy to Earl and Lily Fern, but their second attempt was quite different. Lily Fern recalls the painful experience of the second adoption:

> LFW: Earl decided he wanted a boy, so we went down and applied for a little boy. When they called us about the boy, we had again been doing television all day. We got home that evening and were broiling some steaks outside and the phone rang. Earl answered, and he said, 'You're kidding! Really? When can we see him?' And I knew that they were calling us about a little boy. When Earl got off the phone, he came into the kitchen, picked me up, and threw me in the air until my head hit the ceiling! I mean, just lifted me up in the air and said, 'We've got a boy! We've got a boy!' We went down the next morning to see him. He was probably the most beautiful baby I have ever seen in my life. He had the most beautiful big, brown eyes, and just black, black hair, and very fair, sort of transparent skin. Just a beautiful child. We named him Randall Wayne. Randy was only three weeks old when we got him, and he was not well. I sang the first six weeks we had Randy, and he was fine.

They broke with tradition at this point, and Lily Fern explains how they neglected the practice they had learned from Lon and Lillie:

> LFW: We had decided I would quit singing as soon as we could get somebody to replace me in the quartet. I have to confess, and I'm sure Earl would, too, that while we talked about it many times, we didn't bother to pray about it. We just decided that was what we would do--that I would stay home and take care of the children and we would get someone to take my place in the quartet.
>
> As long as I sang, Randy was fine. We had to be up with him a lot at night, just like you would with any other child, but the day that I quit singing, we started having problems with him. And I feel now that I was out of the will of God. I didn't realize it then. There was nothing wrong with wanting a little boy. That was just perfectly normal. There was nothing wrong with me quitting singing to stay home and raise a family, but that wasn't what God had planned for me to do. I feel that God wanted me to keep on singing.
>
> But I did quit, and immediately he started having ear infections and giving us a lot of problems. It got to where he cried so much, he

would never sleep more than fifteen minutes at a time, and he'd be awake most of the time, crying. It got so bad that Maude Aimee hired a girl, full time, to come in and stay with him at night, so I could get some sleep, because Earl was gone, singing, and I had Susan to take care of, also. Maude Aimee paid the girl to stay with Randy at night, while I slept, and then, through the day, I would take care of the children. But he cried so much, and I took him back to the doctor repeatedly. We'd never had any problems with adjustment or anything with Susan. She was just a perfectly normal baby, but Randy was not a normal baby.

We first thought he was deaf, because he didn't respond to hardly anything, and we'd clap our hands and make noises, but every time Susan would walk up to him, he would turn and look. He just never responded to anything except his needs. When he was hungry, when he was hurting, or when he needed to be changed, he responded, but most of the time he was crying. So, we had his hearing tested, and then, we thought maybe he was blind and we discovered he wasn't blind. We had so many troubles that, when it came time to sign the final papers for him, the case-worker said, 'I think we need to take him and have him tested before you sign these papers.'

Well, Earl and I told her they didn't need to do that. We wanted to keep him, no matter what. Of course, they would not do that, so they took him to Children's Hospital in Akron. The Head of Children's Hospital examined Randy himself, and told us that he was about eighty per cent retarded, which made him far, far below normal, and that he would never be able to go to school or work, or do anything. So, they would not let us keep him. They took Randy and put him back into a foster home, until he was sent to Columbus, Ohio to the state hospital.

That was a very sad time. It was just very hard for Earl and me to accept. It seemed like it was worse than death. I have looked back over this many, many times and I was totally convinced, even then, that I was not in the will of God when I quit singing. There was nothing wrong with us wanting children. When we adopted Susan, He made a way for us to travel with her, and everything was going just fine. I've heard Rex Humbard say, many times, that there's a perfect will of God and the permissive will of God in your life. God was not condemning us for wanting children, but we didn't take it to God for guidance. I look back now and I know that God would have made a way for me to sing and have the children both, because later in life we did that very thing. I believe that I was out of the perfect will of the Lord. It taught me a lesson. I knew that I had to keep singing, and that God would work things out for me and the children and Earl and allow us to keep going that way.

Lily Fern was torn between her feeling that she was called by God to sing the gospel and her desire to be with her children. Whether or not her feelings about the perfect will of God were valid, she felt strongly that she had to follow her instincts:

LFW: There were times when I thought I just couldn't possibly leave those children and go off on another tour, but I knew I had to go, and I would explain to them over and over that I wasn't going because I was trying to be mean or didn't care about them. I told them I was doing it because I felt that this was what God wanted me to do and I would have to do it. The children seemed to understand that.

It was shortly after they lost Randy that Susan had her surgery:

LFW: We'd already scheduled the surgery, so, to keep my mind off Randy, I said, 'Just keep the schedule going,' and we went ahead and had the surgery. It was probably for the best, because I could spend all my time with Susan.

The loss of Randy was especially difficult for Lily Fern, since she was left at home to deal with it while Earl was on the road:

LFW: I remember Earl left to go on another tour, and I was trying to clean up Randy's room. I wanted to try to get rid of all of Randy's things while Earl was gone, because it really crushed Earl to have to lose him. But I thought, 'Well, maybe if I call them, they'll let me see Randy one more time.' I called Family Service and talked to my case-worker, and those case-workers were so gentle and kind--they were very wise people. She said she didn't think she ought to do that unless Earl was home, where we could talk together. Of course, she was just putting me off, because she knew it would be harder on me to have to part with Randy a second time.

Then, when Earl came home, he said, 'I think it's best that we not try to see him again.' So, we didn't see Randy after that. When they took Randy from us, it wasn't that they wanted to take him back. They wanted him to be in our home, but they knew that he was going to be a hindrance to us, and they knew that it would probably be a hindrance even to Susan. When I begged to be able to keep him anyway, the case-worker finally said to me, 'What if we let you keep him? These children tend to live a long, long time. They usually outlive their parents. What if you kept him, and you died? Who would take care of him? Would you want that burden on Susan?' And, naturally, I said, 'Of course not. I don't want that.' And that made me see that they were doing the best, but it was still very hard. When they took him away from us, it was very hard--just like they ripped part of our bodies away from us.

Earl was wise enough not to leave Lily Fern alone to ponder the loss of Randy any more than absolutely necessary. Lily Fern tells of a turn of events that led to a very satisfying new chapter in their lives:

LFW: Shortly after Susan had the bandages off her eyes, the male quartet was going to California on tour, so Earl said, 'I want you to come out there while we're there.' That was my home. My family was all there and my mother was still living in California. So we decided that Susan and I would get on the train and take a sleeper car out to L.A. We should have flown, but we decided to take the train, which was Susan's first train ride, and she thought that was just something. I didn't! She was still too young to walk by herself, and it was a lot of problems for me, but we managed. While we were on the train, some child had the three day measles, so Susan had measles when we got to California, but she got over them O.K. We visited with my family. Then, Susan and I were going to meet Earl back in Oklahoma, where his family lived. This was before we moved to Oklahoma--we were still living in Akron. So, we got on a plane and flew to Oklahoma City, and Earl met us at the airport.

Earl's baby sister was expecting her first child at the time. She was visiting with Earl's mother and her doctor was still in Pauls Valley. While she was visiting, she started having labor pains. Earl was gone singing and Susan and I were just visiting with Earl's family. Then we were going to fly home from Oklahoma City. Another of Earl's sisters was there, and I said to her, 'If you'll stay with Susan, I want to go to the hospital with them.' She said she would stay, and I went to the hospital.

Pauls Valley Hospital was just a little, tiny thing at the time, and the rules and regulations weren't too strict. We were allowed to be in there with Mary all during her labor. She kept saying, 'This baby's coming. You've got to do something!' For three or four hours we were thinking she was going to have that baby, and we'd run get the doctors and the nurses. They'd just come and look disgusted and say, 'She's got all night yet--she's not about to have that baby.' She called me over, finally, and said, 'Lily Fern, please call the doctor. I know I'm having this baby!' So I went and got the nurse again. She looked, and I was standing right there, and I saw the baby's head. The nurse said, 'My God, she's having this baby!' And she said to me, 'Get out of here!' She ran me out and I ran and got her husband, and we were standing right outside the door within five minutes of when that baby was born, before the doctor even got there. They brought the baby out and uncovered him. He was still not cleaned up at all, and when I saw that baby boy lying there, I said to myself, 'I want another boy.'

So, when I got back home, Earl and I got to talking again, and I said, 'Earl, let's try for another boy.' What I didn't know, was that Steve was already born. He was six weeks older than Gary, the baby that was born that night in Pauls Valley. So, as soon as we got home to Akron, we went down to the Family Service and told them. They knew they had Steve to show, but they couldn't show him to us until the mother signed the final papers. That was the law in Ohio. Once the biological mother signed the final papers, she had no rights to that child at all any more, but they would not even show them until that was signed. He was five months old before they called and told us they had a little boy to show us. We told them we didn't want an infant. We were afraid to get an infant again. So, we set up an appointment to go see Steve.

When we had gone to see Randy with Susan, they encouraged us to bring the first child along. Well, I went down and I bought her a little doll, and I said, 'This is your baby, and we're getting another baby, but you can hold this baby while Mama's holding the new baby.' And, oh, she thought that was something, until she saw the baby. Then she didn't want the play baby any more. We did that with Randy, and it worked out just fine, but when we went to get Steve, she was a little bit older. We got her a doll and, of course, when she saw Steve, she didn't want that doll. Steve was much older than Randy was.

On the way down there, Earl stopped the car and said, 'I think we need to pray that God would direct us to the right child. We certainly don't want to go through what we went through before.'

So we sat there, about two blocks from Family Service, and we prayed that the Lord would direct our paths and help us. If this was the right boy, we asked that He would give us a sign--some kind of a sign--so that we would know that he was alert and he was the boy that He wanted us to have.

Steve was five months old the day we saw him, and he was the funniest looking little guy you ever saw. He was cute as a button, but he was skinny. He had a long, slender face and his hair was so wild, it didn't look like they'd ever put anything on it to tame it down. And he had great, big blue eyes, that if you didn't love him before, you had to love him when you saw them. They gave him to me, and he was just all over me in no time. I mean, just wiggling and twisting and wanting down. Earl said, 'Please let me hold him.' And when Earl reached for him, his sleeve came up and showed his watch band. Steve grabbed for that watch band and pulled that watch clear off his arm. That was the sign that we were looking for.

We took him home a couple of days later and he was our boy. He fulfilled what a little boy should in the life of a father and mother. And let me tell you, he was and is all boy. Susan was always such a little dainty thing when she would eat. She couldn't stand anything on her face, and if I got anything on her face, I'd have to wipe it off immediately, or she'd fuss. And Randy had been too sick to care. But Steve wanted everything before he could get it. I couldn't feed him fast enough. Before I'd get the spoon out of his mouth, he would be saying, 'More! More!' I had to take his bottle away from him early, because when he would get finished with his bottle, he'd take it and sling it around and hit it against the wall and break it, because he wanted more. That's just the kind of child he was.

We took the lace canopy off that beautiful bed that Maude Aimee got Susan, and put a red and white striped canopy on top for Steve. Steve shook that bed, when he woke up, until he shook all the slats out of it. I finally had to take him out of that and put him in a regular bed and hope he didn't roll off! Steve did not walk; he did not ever hardly crawl. He started running at seven months old, and, I mean literally, he started running. Because he knew he couldn't quite make it to the next destination, he'd turn loose of a chair and run for the divan, but he'd generally fall just before he'd get there. But that didn't slow him down. He just kept right on going. He never stopped and hasn't since! He was always a very hyper child. In fact, at times I didn't know what I was going to do with him.

People would say, 'Oh, you better take him to the doctor and let him give him something for that.' I said, 'No way. No way! I'm not giving this child any kind of dope or anything like that to slow him down. He's just a normal boy.' And he was.

But Steve has always been a good child. He minded well. He was just busy. Both of my children minded very well. I think they knew better than not to mind. And I could take them into anybody's home. I've seen children tear into people's drawers and their pots and pans in the kitchen, and pull out magazines and have their house looking like a tornado struck it in less than five minutes. My children never did that. I just didn't allow them to do that. They were both very good children. Steve was very active and it was a little difficult to set him on the front row and keep him still in church, but we did.

While Lily Fern was dealing with the children and helping out at The Cathedral, Earl was working with his group. When Lily Fern quit singing to deal with Randy, Earl hired James Hopkins to sing in her place. After about a year, Hopkins returned to Marietta, Georgia with his family, and Earl hired Bobby Clark, who stayed until the group split up in 1963. The Cathedrals were formed and The Weatherfords went back out on their own again.

Just before The Weatherfords left Akron, Lily Fern had to confront a question that she had anticipated and dreaded, and it came from four-year-old Susan. Lily Fern tells the story:

LFW: Before I had started singing again, I had a lady named Ruth living with us and helping to take care of the children, because, even though I wasn't on the road, I was working with the Humbards at The Cathedral of Tomorrow. I was working on all of their television shows. I was on the staff and I had to be there for all the church functions and every time the church doors opened. I'd do the television rallies with them, and everything, so there were lots of times that I really needed a babysitter. Rex hired Ruth to come and live with us and watch the children so that I could be free to go when they needed me.

Earl was gone on a trip with the male quartet, and Steve was sick one Sunday morning and we didn't want to take him out, so Ruth stayed home with him, and Susan and I went to Sunday School and church alone. On the way home, out of the clear blue sky, Susan said, 'Mama, what does adopted mean?' I thought, 'Dear Lord in Heaven, how am I going to answer this child?' I knew this question was going to come some time, and I had already talked to the children, from even before they could understand what was going on. We told them stories about how this mom and daddy wanted a child and they couldn't have one of their own, so they went down and adopted a little girl, and that little girl was Susan, and we'd say how much she meant to us and how happy she made this mama and daddy. Then we'd tell Steve the same thing about how happy he made us when he came into our home, so they had heard the story over and over, but the word, 'adopted!'

I don't know what prompted her to ask that. I don't know whether somebody in Sunday School, some of the children, had said, 'You're adopted,' or how it came about, but she wanted to know what adopted meant. I just quickly, under my breath, said, 'Jesus, help me.' Then I said, 'Well, Susan, adoption means this. You know before Christmas last year we took you to the store and we took you to where all the dolls were, and told you to pick out any doll on the shelf that you wanted and it would be your Christmas doll? And who did you get?' She said, 'I got Sam.' She had picked out this ugly little boy doll and she named him 'Sam.' She carried Sam everywhere she went. I'd have to fight her to keep her from taking him to Sunday School and church. We'd put him at the table in the high chair, ready to eat dinner when we came home from church to get her to leave him. We'd say, 'Now, Sam's going to be waiting here when you come back. He'll be right here.' Otherwise, she would have taken him everywhere. She loved Sam. Then I said, 'O.K., you picked out Sam. And who does Sam belong to?' And she said, 'Sam is my doll, my baby.' I said, 'That's right! But before Sam was your baby, who did he belong to?' She said, 'He belonged to that lady at the store.' I said, 'That's right. But we bought Sam for you and said this is your doll, and now nobody can do anything with Sam. He's yours. If you want to take his clothes off and put on new clothes, you can. You can put him to bed, you can play with him, you can hold him. Nobody else can do anything for Sam or with Sam, unless you say they can. Do you understand what I'm saying?' She said, 'Yes.' And I said, 'Well, that's what adopted means. Before Sam was yours, he belonged to the lady in the store, but now he's *yours*. Before you came to Mama and Daddy, to live with us, you belonged to somebody else, but now you belong to Daddy and me and you're ours forever and ever and ever.'

Then I went on and told her about how Jesus died on the cross, and I said, 'He shed His blood and He bought and paid for our sins and gave us life. He died on the cross so we could become His someday and be adopted into His family by accepting Him. Do you understand what Mama's saying?' She said, 'Yes.' And I said, 'Well, is it O.K.?' She said, 'It's O.K.!' That was the last time she ever mentioned it. But you could always tell Susan almost anything, and she seemed to understand it so quickly. I thought it was the most fitting story for adoption that I had ever heard of, and I know where it came from! I know that immediately God gave me that answer, because I hadn't really thought about it enough to know what I would say when the children asked me what it meant. But they don't question it any more! They know exactly what it means. And she knew then.

Now that Lily Fern and Earl had their family and had made their decision to leave the security of The Cathedral of Tomorrow to return to a traveling music ministry, they faced a whole new set of adventures. It was not easy for Lily Fern to leave Rex and Maude Aimee, but she joined Earl in the search for a headquarters from which to travel. And traveling became a really different experience with children to consider.

Chapter Seven
The Young and the Restless

Transitions are always a challenge, but the move from Akron to Johnstown, Pennsylvania was especially so due to two factors: the pain of leaving the Humbards, and the stress of dealing with two children in a gospel evangelistic life style.

The Weatherfords moved to Johnstown, where they had connections which they thought would create a good base of operations. They were well known in the area, due to their association with The Cathedral and their concert exposure. They had been promised a television program, which would form a solid basis for their ministry.

That did not soften the loss Lily Fern felt in leaving The Cathedral. To this day, Lily Fern expresses her love and appreciation for Rex and Maude Aimee for all they taught her and for all they did for her family. But the Humbards needed a full-time group, willing to stay at The Cathedral and do staff work, and The Weatherfords felt that they were called to a traveling ministry. Both the Humbards and the Weatherfords had to follow God's call as manifested in their lives, so a long and effective working relationship ended. Perhaps it was time to spread the influence that had been concentrated in Akron by sending The Weatherfords on the road.

Traveling with children is not easy, as any parent who has ever traveled cross country with the family can attest. Imagine dealing with the squabbles and lively curiosity of children on the road, not for a few days or a week or two, but as a life-style. It was not easy for Lily Fern and Earl, especially with a lively young Steve Weatherford setting out to explore the world, including every nook and cranny! Susan preferred to stay at home or in the bus and avoid crowds. Their attitudes were certainly a contrast. Lily explains how they attempted to handle the situation:

LFW: In 1963, when I started singing with Earl again, we left The Cathedral to move to Johnstown and we had hired the full-time baby-sitter. I could seat Susan on the front row where we were singing, and she would be fine. But we couldn't do that with Steve. He was probably around two by this time, and somebody had to hold him or he'd be clear on top of the church! When we got to a church, Steve could tell us where the rest rooms were before anybody ever asked, and if we missed him, the first place we would look would be up in the balcony, and next, down in the basement. He could get away from us that fast! So we had to hire Ruth.

Steve was probably the wildest experience facing the Weatherfords. Lily Fern lists examples of Steve's "adventures" as he grew up on the road:

LFW: When Ruth was working for us and Steve was about four, we were on a summer tour in Greeley, Colorado. We were getting ready to do a concert on a Sunday night at a church. We'd been sitting in the bus at the church all afternoon, and the kids had taken their naps, so I got up and I got Susan ready, and I told Ruth to get Steve ready. She got him dressed and, since Earl was about ready to go into the church, I told Ruth to send Steve with Earl when he goes in the church, and I'd bring Susan with me. Then Ruth went to get ready.

I took Susan in and seated her on the front row. I saw Ruth come in the back. Steve wasn't with her. We started singing, and I kept looking back at Ruth and mouthing, 'Where's Steve?' When she finally understood me, she shrugged and mouthed back, 'I don't know!' We sang two songs, and finally I said to Earl, 'I'm sorry, I'm outta here! I have to find that boy!' The boys just went ahead and sang without me. I don't know what they sang, but I had to find Steve.

We looked everywhere. I had the ushers looking. I looked in the bus, and Ruth was out looking for him. We looked in the balcony, in the radio room, in the rest rooms, down in the basement, then back out on the bus. We couldn't find him. Finally, I didn't know what in the world I was going to do. I was getting ready to go back in the church and call the police, when I looked up the street and about half a block away, I saw a lady coming, walking hand in hand with Steve. He had his little suit and tie on, and his little ol' burr haircut. What had happened was that Ruth and Earl had mis-communicated and Earl didn't take him in the church; he thought Ruth had him. Ruth thought

Earl had him. I thought they had him. Well, he just got off the bus and went down the street and started playing with a little boy. The little boy took him in his house and they were playing there. His mother realized that this boy seemed a little unusual, all dressed up, so she asked him where he belonged. He said, 'My Mama and Daddy's singing at that church.' So she brought him back.

Needless to say, he got his fanny spanked and he never wandered off like that again! However, it was partly our fault, because we weren't being careful enough. He knew better than to do what he did, and he never really wandered off like that again. But it taught me a lesson, and I began preaching at the children again. We had even gone off and left some of the quartet members at restaurants, thinking they were somewhere on the bus. We had to go back and get them. So, I began telling Susan and Steve, 'If ever anything happens and you're left someplace, wherever it is, if it's a motel or church, whatever, it would be an accident. You just stay right where you are and don't go anywhere with anybody. Just stay where you are. Tell them your name and what you're doing there, and as soon as we miss you, we'll be back to get you.'

Not long after that, we went to a church--I don't know where this was. Steve was probably five by then. We left the motel, went to eat, and then went to the church. Everybody was busy setting up, and Steve got off the bus to play with an airplane. They got everything all set up and we got ready to go back in the bus to another motel, to check in for that night. I thought Steve was in the back of the bus, because I had told the kids to go to the back and pick up their toys, and I heard Susan back there. I thought Steve was back there, too. We got clear to the motel, and when we started to get off, I missed Steve. Well, I went all to pieces. I said, 'We don't have Steve!' I had no idea what he would do, because, knowing the way he was--he never met a stranger, never was frightened of anything in his life. Susan said the last thing she knew, he was running down the street flying that little toy airplane. To save time, I called the church and asked the secretary if she had seen my little boy. She said, 'I sure have! He's sitting out on the front steps.' She had tried to get him to come in, but he said, 'Hunh-uhhh! My mama told me that if they ever left me to sit right where I was and they'd be right back to get me. It may be four or five hours, but they're going to come back and get me.'

Of course, it wasn't four or five hours before we got him. I sent a cab after him and pretty soon he was at the motel. He thought that was big time stuff, because he was left and he did what he was supposed to do and got to ride in a cab. A frightening experience, believe me. We never did leave the children anywhere after that!

Earl and Lily Fern became experienced at keeping one eye out for Steve, no matter what they were doing on stage. One adventure with Steve involved his constant curiosity about how things work. The inquisitiveness and urge to learn is what made him a good mechanic and sound man, but it got him into trouble as a little boy. Even on the front row, Steve could get into mischief:

LFW: One Sunday morning, we had Susan and Steve sitting on the front row, but not next to each other. I never worried about Susan cutting up in church. She was always the best thing, really. I think a lot was because she was timid and she didn't want anything to draw attention to her. We never let them sit together, because we knew Steve would aggravate her to death. So we had her at one end and Steve at the other and that was just fine until this little girl came in. She was just about the age of Susan. Steve was a couple of years younger. This was when girls wore those nylon dresses that had crinoline underskirts that made the skirts stand way out. She came in and she was so prim and proper and so cute. And she sat down in the middle of the front row between them.

I know what must have been going through Steve's mind. He must have been thinking, 'I wonder what's under that skirt that makes it stand up that way.' He kept looking at her and we were singing and I saw him keep looking at her and I thought, 'Oh, surely he's not going to do something.'

He got up in the middle of our song and got right in front of her and pulled those slips up and ducked his head way up underneath. He wanted to see what was underneath there! This poor little girl was saying, 'Oh, oh, oh!' and wiggling around, trying to get him out! We just kept on singing until he got his head out of that mess of crinoline.

Lily Fern laughs as she recalls that sight. She says that the lady they hired to look after the children spoiled Steve so much that he could get away with murder, so they always had to put him where they could watch him. He was usually fine until another child would come and sit with him. Then the trouble began.

Another incident during Steve's front row years had worse results for Steve, as Lily remembers:

LFW: One time we were singing and Steve was doing something he shouldn't have been doing and wouldn't pay attention to Earl, so Earl said to the audience, 'Now Lily Fern is going to sing a solo, while I go out and take care of my boy.' And he took Steve outside, but the audience could hear the result! And I was trying to sing, 'He'll understand and say well done!' The audience had to laugh, but Steve didn't think it was so funny.

Steve had a number of ways of dealing with his escapades, not the least of which was "playing innocent:"

LFW: When we were singing, Earl had a habit of snapping his fingers in time to the music to get Steve's attention when he would be too close or too involved with another child. Then he'd signal Steve to move over. This one time, Steve put on a wide-eyed innocent look and mouthed back to Earl, 'Me?' Now, who else in that big audience would Earl be telling to move over?

Steve had another way of getting out of difficulty--by some quick thinking. In one situation, he used a little game to try to distract Lily Fern from a potential spanking:

LFW: When Steve was little--Susan hadn't even started to school yet, I believe--he had one of those pens that has three points, all different colors. Somehow he managed to get all three points down at once. I looked out the window to where he was playing in the yard and I thought he had some awful disease! He had taken that pen and drawn all over himself with all the points down. I mean, every inch of his flesh that I could see was covered with colored ink lines. I brought him inside and set him up where I could try to scrub it off. I said, 'Steven Earl, what ever possessed you to do something like that to yourself?' I held him up to a mirror and said, 'See how ugly you look?' I saw those blue eyes get big, and I said, 'You know I'm going to have to spank you now, don't you?' He thought quickly, then he turned those big blue eyes up at me--with that ol' burr haircut--and he tilted his head and smiled sweetly through all the ink. Then he started walking his fingers up my arm, clear over my head and down the other arm, saying, 'Moutsey, moutsey, moutsey,' in a little sing-song voice. Do you know how hard it was to spank him after that?

But Steve had a stubborn streak, too, and it showed up just after they had moved to Johnstown. Lily Fern relates Earl's method of dealing with it:

LFW: Steve hadn't started kindergarten yet, but Susan had, so we had started making the children go to bed a little earlier. Steve just wasn't quite used to that regimen. One night, we came off of a tour and it was our habit, when we were home, to always read *Bible* stories to the kids at night and pray with them before they went to sleep.

Well, Steve was mad and pouting, because we told him he had to go to bed. We didn't think it was fair for him to be up if Susan had to be in bed. We were ready to read *Bible* stories to them and Earl said, 'What story do you want us to read tonight? Do you want us to read this story about Jesus?' Steve frowned and said, 'I don't want to hear no Jesus stories!' Earl said, 'Oh, Steven, that is not the thing to say! I just want to remind you of something.' We just had the little bed light on, and Earl went over and turned the big light on. Steve was angry and pouting and he had tears in his big, ol' blue eyes. Earl said, 'Pull the cover back.' Steve pulled it back. Earl said, 'Pull your pajamas down.' Steve did. Earl said, 'Look at that fat tummy! What makes that tummy fat like that?' Steve said, 'My supper.' Earl said, 'Steve, do you know there's a lot of little boys and girls that went to bed tonight hungry and they don't have a fat tummy from supper? Now, I want you to put your hands over your eyes, both of them.' Steve did. 'What do you see?' 'Nothin'!' Earl said, 'There are a lot of little boys and girls who can't ever see anything, because they're blind.' Then he made him put his hands over his ears and asked him what he could hear, and then said, 'There are some little boys and girls today who are deaf. They can't ever hear. Mama and Daddy, we love you and want you to know that Jesus loves you, but there are thousands and thousands of little boys and girls who go to bed with no mother or daddy to tell them that they love them and nobody to tell them about Jesus.' By this time, Steve was completely torn up. He sniffed and said, 'Read me a story about Jesus!' He was glad to hear about Jesus by the time Earl got through with all those illustrations.

The promised television program did not materialize and a former member of the group had caused problems with some bookings, but Lily Fern has warm memories of that period, including some that involve her neighbors. Both Steve and Lily Fern had adventures involving them, as Lily Fern recalls:

Lillie and Lon Goble, Lily Fern's parents

Cowgirl Lily Fern

Lily Fern, Lillie, Meekly, Lon and Florence

Lily Fern ready for church

Teen-age Lily Fern

Young love: Lily Fern and Earl Weatherford

The wedding party.

Mrs. Earl Weatherford

Mr. And Mrs. Earl H. Weatherford

Bob Jones and His Harmony Boys, 1944; Rev. M.P. Smith, Billy Jo Hall, Earl, Lee Jones, Rady Weston, Bob Jones

Weatherford Stamps Quartet, 1945; Ray Jones, Lily Fern, Bob Gillis, Earl, Harold Turman

Lily Fern, Earl, J.B. Watson, Jack Bryson, Ann Keel

Armond Morales, Raye Roberson, Earl and Lily Fern, Les Roberson (1950)

George Younce, Lily Fern, Norman Wood, Earl, Danny Koker (1951)

Glen Payne, George Houston, Lily Fern, Armond Morales, Earl

The "classic" Weatherfords; Henry Slaughter, Armond Morales, Earl and Lily Fern, Glen Payne

Proud parents: Earl and Lily Fern with baby Susan

Susan and Steve Weatherford

Danny Larson, Lily Fern and Earl, Fulton Nash, Roy Tremble

Fulton Nash, Earl and Lily Fern, Betty Jean Reynolds, Gayle Tackett

Fulton Nash, Jim Holbrook, Lily Fern and Earl

Cloid Baker, Debbie Baker, Earl and Lily Fern, Steve Weatherford

Haskell Cooley, Tracy Dartt, Lily Fern and Earl, Ken Williams

At the Grand Ole Gospel Reunion; Glen Payne, Lily Fern and Earl

Cathedral of Tomorrow reunion at National Quartet Convention; Van Payne, Lily Fern, Rex Humbard, Glen Payne

Lily Fern, Wayne and Leona (Humbard) Jones, and Steve

Earl and granddaughter, Megan

Lily Fern and Megan

Tim, Susan and Megan Cunningham

Susan Cunningham and daughter, Megan

Earl and Florence Squier (Lily Fern's sister)

Meekly and Martha Goble (Lily Fern's brother)

Lily Fern and Maggeline Miles

Standalee and Steve Weatherford

Lily Fern, Jake Hess, Mickey Vaughn

Lily Fern, Brock Speer

Jake Hess, Lily Fern, Hovie Lister

Lily Fern, Faye Speer

Lily Fern and Tim Lovelace

LaBreeska Hemphill and Lily Fern

Lily Fern and Wally Varner

Wynema (Nema) King and Lily Fern

Lily Fern and Gloria Gaither

Lily Fern and George Younce

Great Western Quartet Convention reunion, 1997; D. Ellis, T. Dartt, B. Brisendine, G. Younce, C. Baker, Lily Fern, D. Baker, Steve, G. Payne, J.B. Watson, F. Nash

Old friends and colleagues; H. Slaughter, G. Payne, D. Holm, E. Terry, G. Younce, Steve, Lily Fern, E. Curtis, S. Pratt, L. Orris, R. Wiles

National Quartet Convention reunion, 1997; J. Holbrook, G. Tackett, D. Baker, C. Baker, B. Jones, Sr., J. Caldwell, B. Brisendine, Steve, Lily Fern, V. Clay, B. Clark

Lily Fern and Lillie Knauls

Lily Fern and Vestal Goodman

Amy Pauley and Lily Fern

Two "Strangemen" with George Younce

Lily Fern and Carolyn Branham

Damian Derrick and Lily Fern

Fulton Nash, Steve, Earl and Lily Fern.

Steve and Standalee Weatherford, Roy Pauley, Lily Fern

Lily Fern, Larry Gatlin, Kenny Payne, Steve.

Mr. And Mrs. Mosie Lister and Lily Fern

Lily Fern's original female quartet (assisted by Kenny Payne); Dorothy Payne, Martha Goble, Kenny, Lily Fern, Bette Jo Williams

Grand Ole Gospel Reunion; Living Legend Award Presentation to Lily Fern by Charlie Waller.

1998 Weatherfords—Steve, Lily Fern, Jamie Caldwell

LFW: When we were living in Johnstown, we had some of the best neighbors, the Kepplers. Mrs. Keppler absolutely adored Steve. He would go over and play in her yard and, one day, she came out on the porch and found him digging in her flower bed. She said, 'Steve, I wish you wouldn't dig in my flower bed. Why don't you go home and dig in your mama's flower bed?' He said, 'Oh, no. My mama doesn't allow me to dig in *her* flower bed!' Mrs. Keppler had to laugh as she told me later.

She always had three or four mama cats hanging around her house. Therefore, she had litter after litter of kittens. Steve used to go over there and play with those kittens. One day, we called Steve home to eat lunch. Mrs. Keppler always kept an eye on him, and, when we called him home, she happened to see him put a cat in each pocket and carry one in his hand. She thought, 'I wonder what he's going to do with those three little kittens?' So, she followed him, without him seeing her, and when he got to our house, he put them in the trash barrel outside and put the lid on it. She waited until he got in the house, and she went and got them out, because they could suffocate in there. She came in and was talking to the lady that was working for us at the time, and Steve was sitting there eating lunch. Mrs. Keppler said, 'Steven, you put those little kitties in your trash barrel. Why did you do that?' He said, 'I just put them there, 'cause I wanted to play with them when I got through, and I knew if I didn't put them there, they'd run away.' She thought he was really something else.

The other story involving her neighbors reveals not only Lily Fern's compassion for others, but her ability to get into silly situations:

LFW: Mrs. Keppler's mother died while we were living in Johnstown. Mrs. Keppler called me and told me about it and that a lot of the family members would be coming. She said there would be eighteen or twenty people there for two or three days, in and out. I said, 'Well, I'll tell you what. Tomorrow night, I'll fix your dinner for you and bring it over. You won't have to worry about anything. It'll all be prepared--the meat, the salad, the dessert--everything will be prepared for you.'

The next morning, I got up and made sixty-five meatballs with spaghetti sauce. I did the whole bit. I had a tossed salad and a fruit salad, and fixed green beans for a vegetable, and went and got some French bread and made garlic bread. I baked two pies and two cakes. I had dinner rolling really well. Just before I made the meatballs and put them on to cook, I had broken a fingernail, so I had one really short nail and all the rest were long. Well, anybody who knows me knows that I am very meticulous about my fingernails. I want them looking just right all the time. So, I had put on a false fingernail. Later, I missed the false fingernail. I looked everywhere. I had a bunch of garbage from making the salads, so I even sifted through the garbage. Finally, I realized that the only things I had used my hands in after applying that nail were mixing the meatballs and making the pie crust. Well, I knew it was not in the pie crust, because I could have seen it. I knew that the fingernail had to be in one of those meatballs, which were already cooking. I didn't want to have to cook something instead of the meatballs and spaghetti, but since I couldn't find that nail, I thought, 'Well, I'm just going to have to do something else.'

I decided I'd just go down to a fast food place and get some fried chicken and some mashed potatoes and gravy to take over there. By then, I was running out of time, so I was really in a hurry. I ran in and took a shower and got dressed and was going out the door, when I thought I'd better check those meatballs, to make sure they weren't going to boil over while I was gone. I wasn't going to throw them away. I was going to freeze them and we would eat them. We would understand what it was all about, if we ran across a fingernail. I lifted the lid, and right on top was this one meatball that had this funny-looking thing sticking up. At first I thought it was an onion, but then I realized that it could be that fingernail. I took the meatball out, and, sure enough, it was. Right on top! So, I didn't have to go buy the chicken. I went ahead and took the dinner over.

A couple of days after the funeral, I told Mrs. Keppler the story, and she really, really laughed. She said, 'I'd have given anything if you had just left it there and let one of us find it! We would have died laughing!' I said, 'It would have turned your stomach!' She answered, 'Oh, no! That food was so good that nothing would have turned our stomachs, and we appreciated it so much.' I had gone around to other neighbors and had them handle the other meals, so she didn't have to cook for three or four days. She was just so grateful that somebody would take the time to do that for them.

When the Weatherfords realized that the promised television program was not going to materialize, they knew that being well known in that area was not enough to hold them. They made plans to leave, but, since Susan had just started kindergarten, they decided to stay long enough for her to finish the school year.

When school was over, they left Johnstown and headed for their old territory, Southern California, where they had been offered a good position with a sponsor. They worked there for a year, and that position did not work out, so they moved up to Sacramento for a year, which also fell through in terms of what they needed.

Southern California was not without its adventures, though. Lily Fern recounts another frightening experience:

LFW: It was Steve's kindergarten year, and when we moved to Southern California. When school started, I wanted to take the kids to school, but they would not have that, no way, because they wanted to ride the bus to school. They had to go down to the corner and then to another corner two blocks away to catch the school bus. They didn't even want me to walk with them! What they didn't know, was that I went another way, where I could watch to make sure they got there and on the school bus. And I watched them to make sure they got off the bus at the same corner, and then I'd beat them home.

The first day of school, Susan didn't get off the bus when she was supposed to. Well, of course, I was panic-stricken. I went back home and began to call the school and to run things down to find out where she was. The problem turned out to be that the bus passed the street she was supposed to get off and then came back the other way, and she was supposed to get off at the second stop on 'Ivy' street. She just saw 'Ivy Street' and got off with other kids. She didn't know and I didn't know about this first and second stop. Well, I was just frantic, when the phone rang. There was a little service station down on the corner where she got off, and the service station attendant called and said, 'Do you have a little girl named Susan?' I said, 'Yes!' I was terrified that somebody had kidnapped her. He said, 'Well, don't worry. She's right here and she's safe. She got off at the wrong stop at the school bus, and she came and told me what her phone number was and what her name was, and so I told her I'd call you for her.' I asked to talk to her and when she answered, I said, 'Are you alright?' She said, 'Yes. I got off on the wrong street.' The service station man was very nice and, fortunately, she was alright. Today, you might not be so lucky, would you?

Anyway, I took them back around again so they knew exactly where to go. The very next day, Steven didn't get off the school bus. He was in kindergarten and had a name tag that he had to put on every morning. During school that day, he had gotten into a scuffle with a little boy and they got their name tags mixed up. The teacher was kind of old and decrepit, and she not only put the wrong name tag on him, she put him on the wrong bus. He told me later, 'I kept telling the teacher that wasn't the bus I was supposed to get on, but she wouldn't pay any attention to me.' Well, I went through the same fiasco of getting information from the school. Finally, they said, 'He has gotten on the bus that picks up the high school kids. Go to the high school and maybe you'll find him there.' So, Susan and I went to the high school and all the buses were lined up to pick up the high school kids. Susan said, 'Mama, he's on that bus right there.' I said, 'How do you know? There's not a soul in there.' She said, 'Yes, he is. I just saw a paper airplane go out the window.' And, sure enough, Steve was in that bus. He was so disappointed when I found him, because he was having a ball. He thought he was going to get to ride on the high school bus route, before the driver was going to take him back home, but Susan found him by the airplane.

The children got a good start in school in California. Susan was a perfect student, with straight "A's," even as a small child.

LFW: In the second grade, Susan was given and I.Q. test. Her teacher said, 'I'm not supposed to tell you about her test, but I will tell you that her I.Q. is somewhere over 150. I don't know if you know what that means.' I said, 'No, I don't.' She said, 'Well, that's genius.' Now, Susan acted like a normal child. She was always very good in her school work and would get it completed first. In fact, they always had a problem keeping her busy and occupied. She was the one who was running errands for the teacher and cleaning off the blackboards and doing things like that, because she would finish her work before the other children did.

When she was in third grade, they wanted to let her skip the third and put her in the fourth grade. When we discussed it with Susan, she said, 'No, no! I don't want to do that. I don't know that fifth grade work.' We tried to explain to her that we knew she didn't know it, but that she would be able to learn it pretty fast. She was so against it that Earl and I would not allow them to put her up in the next grade. But she was in an accelerated class, where she got to do extra-curricular things that most children never got to take advantage of. There were about six or eight students that had special classes. They had so many weeks of journalism, so many weeks of art, and so many weeks of music--I forget what all they had now.

Lily Fern explains why life in California didn't work out and why they had to look for another base of operation:

LFW: While we were in California, we were sponsored by an industrial chemical company that paid us high, high salaries to do concerts for them, and they had what they called Brush Arbor Jubilee. We had a big concert for them once a month. It was us and The Song Fellows and a couple of other groups that worked for this company. They did pay high salaries, but it got to where the checks bounced, and then we all began to starve, and we knew that we had to do something else. It was quite a fiasco.

Fulton Nash explains some of the problems they faced during this period and how Lily Fern coped with them:

FN: Unfortunately, I didn't get to be with them through what I feel were their best years, but I was with them through some lean times. Those lean times were very precious, because they brought people together, so I'm thankful for them.

Some decisions that we thought would be the best for the group turned out to be near-disaster. Lily and Earl lost their car and their piano and a lot of stuff. We lost some people. Sometimes it was just the three of us. We had to settle for second best in some cases, and Earl and Lily didn't deserve second best.

There were times in the quartet when personalities conflicted. Sometimes Lily would take it for as long as she could, then she'd have to put her two cents worth in to kind of calm things down and straighten things out. She was a peacemaker with a lot of the fellows we had in the group.

Fulton listed a number of "disasters," including booking problems, health problems, talent agent problems, bus break-downs and vandalism of the bus. Lily Fern had the strength and patience to cope with all of them.

One of the health problems involved Lily Fern's headaches. Fulton was amazed at her ability to perform through bouts with fierce migraines:

FN: I've seen the time when we traveled all day and all night, going to a concert, and she would be so sick she couldn't hold her head up or open her eyes, but she'd walk out on that platform and sing, with her head up and her eyes open, just singing praises to the Lord, and not make a bobble. I always marveled at her.

He recalls overwhelming responsibilities that Lily Fern handled constantly:

FN: You have to stop to analyze just what all Lily did--not just singing, but what happened after she got off the platform.

One thing I can say about Lily, she's an excellent cook! I've eaten just about all her different kinds of cooking down through the years and her Mexican food really stood out. I wish I had a dollar for every meal!

I remember one time when we were having a rough time financially out in Los Angeles. I had to move out of my apartment because I couldn't pay my rent. I was going to move on the bus, but Earl and Lily said they didn't want me to have to do that. They had me move in with them. They couldn't afford another mouth to feed, because they had Susan and Steve. I had to stay with them for a period of time, and Lily didn't complain. It was a difficult time for her, and she had her housework and getting the kids off to school.

She did all that, and then, when Earl decided we had to practice, why, we had to stop and Lily stopped what she was doing. We might be at it for several hours--most of the time it was a few hours--and she had to stop what she was doing. But in order for us to keep the group going, we had to learn new songs and everything. Sometimes we'd have trouble--I know in the early years, we'd work several hours just maybe on one or two chords. Lily worked at it just as hard and feverishly as the rest of us, and then, instead of relaxing and taking it easy, she'd have to get back to her housework. Nobody realizes all the work and the stress and the time involved for her just to keep her head above water, just so the quartet could keep going. And a lot of times, she'd fix a meal for the whole group.

After the financial problems with the Brush Arbor Jubilee, The Weatherfords moved on to Sacramento. Lily Fern explains their last effort to make it in California:

LFW: In Sacramento, we were on the staff with Reverend Clyde Henson at the Assembly of God Church and Bethel Temple for a year. Then he passed away, so we left there and moved back to Oklahoma, since it is more centrally located and we had family in the area.

Lily Fern tends to gloss over this California stage in the career of The Weatherfords, since it involves some disappointments in both sponsors and group members. About the only thing that was consistent during that phase was the children. Steve was still all boy. Susan still preferred her own company to crowds.

Steve thrived on tour. He was never at a loss for something to do, whether good or bad. Lily Fern gives an example of his industrious nature as a child:

LFW: We were at a church in a program with several groups. The kids were seated in front, as usual. When we were finished and the next group was on, I came out and sat behind Steve. The church didn't have pews; it had individual seats with arms. Eventually, I noticed that Steve seemed to be doing something. He was hunched forward on one of the chair arms and seemed to be hiding what he was doing under a book. When we stood to sing, I saw what he had been doing. He had carved "S.W." into the chair arm. He was probably around kindergarten age. As we stood to be dismissed, I stuck my finger down his collar. The minute the minister was through, Steve started to leave. I pulled him back and said, 'Stay where you are.' I made him stay until everyone was out, then I said, 'I want to show you something. Look on that chair arm. Look what someone did.' His blue eyes got bigger as he looked carefully at the chair arm. I said, 'Someone scratched something into a chair in God's house. This chair belongs to God and somebody has scratched His chair! Now, what would make someone do that?' Steve solemnly answered that he didn't know. I said, 'Let's look closer and see what it says. Why, it says S.W. Isn't that what it says?' His eyes got bigger. I said, 'Isn't that the seat you were sitting in? Steven, did you do that?' He swallowed and answered, 'Yes.' I said, 'Oh, Steven! Now we have to go tell the pastor and we'll have to tell God.' We went to the pastor's office. I told the pastor what happened and I said, 'He gets a little allowance and he'll have to pay. You just tell us how much and we'll pay it.' The pastor got the idea right away. He said, 'This is God's house, Steve. Are you sorry for what you did?' Steve said he didn't mean to do anything wrong. The pastor said, 'Well, Steve, I was just going to get new seats here and give these to someone else. Maybe it will be O.K. if I just tell God and you say you're sorry?' Steve said,

'Yes, yes!' The preacher said, 'O.K. It's settled, but promise you won't ever do this in any other church.' Steve promised. He was feeling pretty relieved by the time we got out of that office, but he still had to deal with me when he got back to the bus!

Even while they were in Fontana, California, Steve had gotten into trouble--this time with Earl. Steve was recovering from chicken pox, but he wasn't allowed back in school yet. The Weatherfords had a recording date and nobody to look after Steve, so he had to go along. The sound engineer at the studio graciously offered to keep Steve busy in the booth. The group crowded around one microphone, facing the window of the booth while they sang. For a while, the engineer used Steve's curiosity to keep him busy with the instruments, so Lily Fern relaxed and concentrated on the recording, glancing at the booth occasionally to check on Steve. She looked up once just in time to see Steve, in true little boy fashion, put his finger in his nose and then in his mouth. She says, "There was nothing I could do at that point, and I hoped no one else had been looking!" But someone else *was* looking--Earl. Nothing was said in the studio, but on the way home in the car, Earl scolded and berated such behavior. Steve got very quiet and very small.

At that time, the Weatherfords had a couple of poodles who had the run of the yard. Arriving home, Earl took Steve into the yard and made him look at the dog droppings. He told Steve he might as well eat "dog dirty" as to do what he did. Apparently Steve didn't seem adequately responsive, so Earl took a piece of an old shingle and scooped up some dog droppings. "I'd rather see you eat this. Go ahead!" Steve's eyes got big as he contemplated this turn of events. Just then, the droppings fell off the shingle and the ever-alert boy saw his way out. "I can't eat that. It fell in the dirt!" Lily Fern laughs at Steve's ability to find a defense, no matter how unlikely. Earl may not have been so amused at his son's logic.

The California years were good in terms of the children, but another cloud was forming over their heads throughout this transitional period. This problem involved events spanning the point of leaving Akron through the brief stay in California and into Oklahoma. Lily Fern cannot speak of this experience without a tinge of bitterness:

LFW: One of the biggest cases I can remember of God answering prayer has a rather complicated history. When we left Akron in 1963, a guy who had been singing with us got mad because the guys--I mean the whole group--decided to let him go. And when he got mad, he called the IRS and told a lot of things that were not true, which caused the IRS to investigate everybody in that group. Now, we had always been really faithful to do our income taxes and so forth. When they began to investigate us, we had moved to Johnstown. It was 1963 when this boy left the group, but by the time they got around to investigating our taxes for that year, a couple of years had rolled by and we had already left Johnstown and moved to California.

When we moved, we took what we could and left the rest in storage. Some things, special important papers, like income tax and important books and so forth, we left at a friend's house. These people were really sweet elderly people, and they had a big attic. They said we could leave anything we wanted there. Earl felt it was best, until we found a place to live and got settled again, to leave all the important papers there. We left a few books, all the income tax papers, records for seven or eight years back, and albums and recordings.

When the IRS notified us that they were investigating our '63 returns, Earl called Johnstown and told them to send the box marked, 'Important Papers.' He said to send them to us in California by way of UPS, but to send the tapes and recordings by railroad. I suppose they got confused, perhaps because they were elderly, and they did just the opposite. They sent our important papers by rail and somehow or another they got lost. We never did find them, but we got proof that they had sent them by rail, and the shipment just got lost. I guess it kind of helped with the IRS that we had the receipt, proving they had been shipped, but when they found out the papers were lost, they knew they really had us over a barrel. So, they went after us as much as they possibly could.

At this point, Earl and Lily really needed God to answer their prayers, as this situation became intense. Their transitions from Akron to Johnstown, and then to Southern California involved some humor, some excitement and some worry, but the worst was yet to come as Earl and Lily took their family from California to Oklahoma, with the hope of peace and prosperity that Lon and Lillie Goble must have felt as they left Oklahoma for California.

Chapter Eight

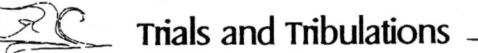 Trials and Tribulations

Ironically, the final move for Lily Fern and Earl was back to the same area of Oklahoma they left, separately, so many years before. In 1967, they moved to Yukon, where Lily's father had once pastored a church. They stayed there for two years and then made their final move to Paoli, Oklahoma, just south of Oklahoma City.

They had moved so much in the years before moving to Oklahoma that long-time Weatherford member, Fulton Nash, jokes to this day about the moves:

FN: There were lots of times when I had the privilege of helping them move, from Johnstown to Los Angeles, to Fontana, and from Fontana we moved to Sacramento, and after Sacramento, we moved back to L.A. for a little while--about three months. We just stored our stuff, then we moved to Yukon, Oklahoma. And then, even after I left the group, after being in Yukon for four and a half years, I think, it just happened that Brenda and I were pretty close at hand at the time when they were ready to move to Paoli. So we moved there, and through all of that time, there were a lot of exasperating moments but Lily kept her sense of humor through all of it.

The sense of humor was hard to maintain, though, when the stress of the IRS investigation hung over their heads as they tried to get re-established in Oklahoma. They were to have more tense moments there:

LFW: The IRS gave us problems for seven solid years, to the point of coming with papers to take us to court. They came one time while we were gone and my mother was visiting at our house. We had told my mother what was going on, and that day the IRS people came to the door and told her that we were crooks and that we had not paid our income tax. Well, that made Mother mad. Now, I never heard Mother say a bad word in my whole life, but this time, she said, 'You're a bunch of liars and you can just go to Hell! That's exactly where you belong!' When Mama told me she told them that, I nearly fainted. I couldn't believe it! But she was so mad, because they were talking about her children that way. She said they told her we'd been hiding from them for fifteen years. She said, 'I don't know how in the world they could hide from you, when they travel in a bus with their name plastered all over the side. A great, big, forty-foot bus, and they sing at churches all over America! How could they hide from you and advertise everywhere they go on television and in newspapers? That's proof enough that they're not trying to hide from you!' But they took our van that day anyway, right out of our driveway, and they notified us that it was going to be sold at auction. Earl's dad went to Yukon and bought the van back at the auction.

They actually harassed us for seven years. I mean, I know what harassment from the IRS is! It finally got so bad that Earl told our attorney, 'We have to stop this somehow or another, and I want to meet with them and their attorneys.' He met with them and said, 'I'm going to open my heart to you and I'm going to tell you the truth. Then, you can just do what you want to with me. I have never been anything but totally honest with you. You know that I have filed income tax, and you know that my papers were lost. You know that I don't owe you all this money, and I know that! Now, you've taken my word on the offerings that I get, and I gave you the names of the pastors and the names of the churches, and you've taken my word for that. But you won't take my word for anything else! So, I challenge you to send somebody to spot-check me. I'll give you my dates. You can spot-check me anyplace I go, to see if I'm telling you the truth, or, you can take my date book and double check with me. I'll give you the records and you can double check. But, somehow or another, you've got to get off my back, because you are killing me! You can come and take everything I've got and I'll start over completely, but you've got to leave me alone!'

Earl's plea and challenge must have done the job, at least for a while, since the IRS cleared their names. The lien on their personal property was finally lifted and they were able to buy a house. Lily Fern considers this another miracle situation. They had been given notice that they had to move out of their rental house by a certain time, because the owners were selling the house. Earl and Lily Fern didn't want to buy it, even if they could have, because it was such a small house. So, they had been packing up and getting ready to move into an apartment or something. But, then, this house in Paoli became available. Even though all this IRS business had been abated, the financing had to wait until it was completely clear.

When they saw the house, they went ahead and made the down-payment and trusted the Lord to work out everything, so that they could move into it. They had to be out of the rental house on a Saturday, and at four o'clock on that Friday, the bank called and said the records had been cleared. They were informed that the house was theirs and they could move in. Earl loaded his truck. His parents brought their vehicles and they loaded everything else into them, and they headed for Paoli. Lily Fern stayed behind with the children to clean the house. She remembers the realization that came over her as she and the children left for their new home:

LFW: As we were driving toward Paoli, a rain storm came up, and it rained so hard that we had to stop. While we were sitting there, I was just going over in my mind what had happened. I said to the children, 'Do you realize what has transpired in this last twenty-four hours?' Steve was almost ten and Susan was about twelve, and they understood. Those children knew. They knew all the bad things we'd had with the IRS and everything. I said, 'I think while we're stopped here, it's time for us to really thank the Lord for giving us a home and just be really thankful that he's made this possible, because it truly is a miracle.' We praised the Lord and thanked him for what he'd done for us. Finally, the rain let up and we went on to Paoli. At four o'clock that afternoon we had gotten the call that we could move, and at ten o'clock that night, we were sleeping in our own beds in our new home in Paoli. That's the way God works miracles.

But the IRS was not finished with the Weatherfords yet. Lily Fern still had to face another confrontation:

LFW: About three or four years later, a man came to our door. I was standing at the kitchen sink when I saw him open our front gate. Something told me that this was an IRS man. We hadn't had any problems with the IRS for a while, but I just knew he was an IRS man. We had opened a little gospel record shop in Pauls Valley and Susan was helping Earl at the shop that day. I was the only one home. I went to the front door and I didn't even open the screen. I just talked to him through the screen door. He said, 'I'm so and so, and I'm an IRS agent.' When we went through all that problem before with the IRS, our attorney had said that if any of them ever come to our door, no matter what they say, I should never acknowledge anything they said.

123

He said, just say, 'It's beautiful weather today,' or just say anything, but don't acknowledge anything they say. Just change the subject or whatever. He said it irritates them no end and they're nothing but corrupt people anyway. So, when the man said, 'I'm an agent from the IRS, and I have this paper here that shows that you owe us fifteen thousand dollars,' I forgot all about what the lawyer said. I said, 'You are the biggest liar that ever walked! And you are the most corrupt people in the whole government.' He said, 'But Ma'am, you don't understand.' I said, 'I do understand. I understand we went through seven years with you stupid, ignorant people and you're not going to intimidate me again!' He said, 'I just need to talk to your husband.' I said, 'My husband isn't here.' He said, 'Do you know where he is?' And I said, 'Yes, but I'm not going to tell you where he is.' So, we stood there and argued, and I said something like, 'I'm not giving you the sweat off my armpit! You might just as well turn around and walk back out that gate, because you're not getting any help from me at all. I am not going to cooperate with you. I don't care what you do. You can throw me in jail! I'm not going to cooperate with you!' I was getting madder and madder and talking louder and louder. He said, 'Well, would you please call your husband and tell him I need to talk to him?'" I said, 'O.K. I'll do that.'

I turned and went to the phone. I was talking to Earl on the phone and, when I turned around, this man was standing in the middle of my living room! Well, I went crazy! I told Earl, 'This crazy, stupid man is in my living room and I'm going to knock him in the head.' The man must have believed me, because he sort of backed off, and I said, 'I want you out of here!' Oh, I was just so mad, and Earl was on the phone, trying to calm me down. He said, 'I'll be right there!' He just hung up and started home. When I hung up, I said, 'I want you out of here. Get out of my house! You have come into my home and intruded on my privacy! I didn't invite you in--you just were brazen and bold enough to come right in anyway!' And the more I said, the more he backed toward the door. I said, 'And I want you to know, we are God's anointed people, and you are touching God's anointed, and I can show you scripture in the *Bible* that you should not touch God's anointed people!' Well, I finally got him out of the house, and by that time, Earl was pretty close to home. He ended up talking to him.

Eventually, the Weatherfords learned that their local agent in Ardmore was a Christian man, who had been fighting for them and had probably helped clear up the problem. This agent told them that he had been replaced temporarily by an atheist, because the IRS officials seem to think he would be more likely to go after the Weatherfords. The Christian agent said he had seen the atheist agent get angry and stomp at the mention of church or God or salvation, or commitment to Christ, so he seemed to be put on the case to go after the Weatherford ministry. Lily Fern summarizes the outcome when the Christian agent returned to their district:

> LFW: He said, 'I guarantee you that this will be taken care of, because you don't owe this.' Well, he did get it taken care of, but, in the meantime, they still gave us all kind of problems. During the time that we were still being threatened, we were on tour. Susan called us and told us we had a letter from the IRS. Earl told her to read it. Basically, it said they were going to find us wherever we were on the road and force us to pay this money. If we had owed it, it would be another thing, but we didn't owe it and we knew it. And we didn't have it, to begin with! So, finally, they said, 'If you will admit to owing this much of this withholding tax for this one man, we'll forget the rest, and it won't be that much money.' It was for the guy who had turned us in and said we had collected withholding tax and hadn't paid it, which wasn't true. So, Earl said, 'No, I won't admit to anything that isn't right. I don't owe it. And if I agreed to this, you would accuse me of all of it and more, and I'll have to go through all this stuff again.' This was before we found out that this agent was transferred to another territory, so that day of the letter, we were all concerned and worried and we all, Steve and Earl and I, gathered together and placed our hands on the *Bible* and said, 'On the authority of God, we claim victory over this thing and we believe that it is going to be resolved and our name is going to be cleared in some way.' Then, the older agent contacted us again. He said, 'This is going to be taken care of in a few weeks.' We finally got the word that they had taken care of it and we were clear again. Since that time, we have not had any problems at all from the IRS, and I pray that we never have another problem with them!

The tremendous relief of getting out from under the long and stressful battle with the IRS was short-lived, since the lawyer bills and expenses left them in financial difficulties. Lily Fern believes this was resolved by another miracle:

> LFW: We were still in a big mess financially. Almost every week we thought we couldn't go another week, and we didn't know what we were going to do. We owed so many debts and couldn't get them paid off fast enough. There were two bills that we owed that came to twelve hundred dollars, and we knew we had to have that money by the

following Monday morning. Earl had written a letter and had it printed up, and we put it on our table at concerts to explain to people what was happening, to see if they could or would help. We were in Tucson, Arizona on a Saturday night and, before the concert, Steve and Earl and I were standing around the record table, when this scruffy-looking man came in. He looked pretty rough. He took one of those letters and came in and listened to the concert. Later, he came back to Earl and he said, 'I listened to your concert and I read one of these letters. A few weeks ago, I had a tape of The Weatherfords and I went up into the mountains. I just took that tape. I had some things I really needed to pray about, and I played that tape over and over again. The name of the tape was 'Because of Yesterday.' I was really down and out as far as my self-esteem and I was just really down. I heard that tape and I thought surely, surely God does love me. If that story can be true, God still loves me. I made up my mind right there that I was going to ask God to change my life.' He was a Christian, but he just had all these things piling on top of him. He said, 'God changed my life that day, through listening to that tape. I took this letter and I read it during your concert. I've got this check and I want you to have it to help with your needs.' We opened the check as soon as we could, and it was for eight hundred dollars! Earl said, 'Well, it's not twelve, but maybe it will satisfy the creditors until we can get the rest of it.' When we got back to the motel that night, we started to doubt. This man looked like he didn't have a cent to his name and maybe he didn't know what he was doing. Earl said, 'Well, the check may not be good.' We could hardly wait for Monday morning to go to the bank to try to cash it.

On Sunday night, we sang at a different church and, lo and behold, while we were sitting on the bus, waiting to go into the church for the concert, this same man drove up, and he had his wife and two children with him. He came and knocked on the door and, when Earl went to the door, he said, 'Earl, can I have that check back?' I knew what Earl was thinking, and I thought, 'That check that we needed so much is not any good.' Earl got the check and gave it back to him. The man said, 'My wife and I have been praying and talking, and we decided that we need to do something else. I'm going to trade that check for this one.' Well, we couldn't look at the check right then, but we just knew that it was for fifty dollars or a hundred dollars--something like that. When the man went on into the church with his family, Earl opened the check. Yes, you guessed it! The check was for twelve hundred dollars! We were elated, but we still couldn't believe the check was good. I mean, we were up before the banks opened. We were waiting at the phone to call. Earl called the bank and asked if the account would cover the check and if we could get a money order for the check. They took the man's name and number and they came back and said it was good and that we could come cash it. So, that was another miracle that only God could've performed, because the man gave us eight hundred first, and only God could have said, 'They need twelve hundred dollars.' From that day on, things began to get better for the Weatherfords. It wasn't a bed of roses for a long time. We still had problems and disappointments, but we had victories, because we really trusted the Lord for every need in our life and he took care of them. And I believe he always will! We were always grateful to that man and wife for what they did for us.

With the IRS out of their way and their financial crisis under control, Lily Fern and Earl were able to concentrate on their ministry and on their children. Lily Fern lists two of the major problems she and Earl faced in their singing careers: bus break-downs and dealing with the children's needs while traveling. The bus break-downs were occasional, but the problems of caring for the children were on-going. Lily Fern had so much to do between tours, and she had to work in all the normal "mother" tasks. Sometimes she may have tried to move a little too fast, as in the case of a trip to the orthodontist with Susan:

LFW: I was driving Susan to the orthodontist in Norman, Oklahoma. We didn't get to leave until 3:30 and our appointment was at 4 p.m. Well, I was running late, and of all things, I sailed right past our exit. I was speeding up I-35, when Susan said, 'Mama, there's a Highway Patrol car behind you flashing his lights.' He pulled us over, and I didn't even give him time to say a word. He was standing there with his ticket book out and Susan was sliding down in her seat in embarrassment. I said, 'Sir, I think I missed my turn,' and I asked him how to get back to it, since I was late for this appointment. He said, 'You passed it alright!' He told me how to get back and then he said, 'I was all set to give you a ticket, but if you'll do something for me, I won't. Just promise to slow down and be fifteen minutes late for that appointment.' I promised really quick. I didn't have the money to pay for a ticket!

When they had someone living with them to care for the children when they were small, life was a little simpler, but as they soon discovered, Steve got pretty spoiled. During the summers, they could take the children with them on tour, but during the school year, they tried to be home through the week and travel on the weekends.

After they moved to Oklahoma, they were able to have Brenda Nash stay with the children. Brenda, wife of former Weatherford bass, Fulton Nash, testifies to how Lily Fern balanced her life between the duties of her career and those as a mother:

> BN: She's an exceedingly strong person. This is where her perseverance shines. When she would have to leave and I kept Susan and Steve, she'd call often, inquiring about what they ate, what they needed for school, just making sure their needs were met while she was gone--mothering. I know she was so torn between mothering and the call that was upon her life, and she did them both so well. That's hard on a mother, to leave your children. She loved having those kids with her and took them most of the time and home-schooled them. But there were times that she didn't. The kids were wanting to stay home and that was hard to do. The first time I was in Earl and Lily's home, Earl was booking dates and Lily was taking the kids to an amusement park in Oklahoma City for the day. They'd just gotten in off tour and the quartet always ran themselves ragged between the tours with so much to do, but, even though a lot had been accomplished, there was still plenty to do. She still had to clean the interior of the bus, but she took the time. She stopped what she was doing in quartet business and took Susan and Steve to Frontier City and just dedicated the day and focused on them.

No matter how Lily Fern tried to give "quality time" to her children, she could not make the life of a singing evangelist one that her daughter, Susan, now Mrs. Tim Cunningham, could enjoy. Susan responded to the question, "How would you describe life on tour?" in her own direct style:

> SC: Well, you asked for it, you got it. Always waking up in a different place, very rarely getting anything good to eat, never knowing when the bus might break down, no heat sometimes, no air conditioning until about 1972 or so. I won't even mention school on the road, people always asking you questions that you didn't want to answer, up too late, and just when you thought you couldn't stand it any more, you would meet some people who would take you home and feed you a good meal and generally be very nice to you. I will never forget meeting Brenda Nash. We were traveling in vans and for some reason we were late. We got there and she was standing in the foyer of the church--one of the nicest people you could ever meet--her family, also.

So in the Oklahoma years, having Brenda Nash was certainly a great help to Earl and Lily, as they tried to maintain a secure and happy life for their children, while following their call to sing. Lily Fern says of Susan, "She's just a precious girl and she loves being home, so she didn't like traveling on the bus." One of Lily Fern's major fears was that the children might not feel secure. Susan seems to put that fear at rest:

> SC: I think I felt like everybody else does when they are children, but things were a little more complicated because of the kind of life we led. I don't think I ever felt insecure as far as my parents loving me. I always knew that they did and would no matter what.

Having come through their troubled times with the IRS and the resulting financial difficulties, Earl and Lily Fern faced their mature years on the road. As with most human beings, they faced more trouble ahead, but of a different kind. Lily Fern speaks often of miracles, and the next few years contained some.

The nucleus of The Weatherfords—Steve, Earl, Lily Fern

Chapter Nine

 Music and Miracles

Lily Fern treasures memories of her children, but as they became young adults, she began to have to deal with them and their "grown-up" personalities and problems. Singing and traveling were the base elements of their lives from that point on. Fortunately, the miracles counter-balanced the difficulties, especially in the case of the children.

Like any mother, Lily Fern went through trying times when her children were ill or troubled. She remembers the painful experience of Susan's illnesses, reliving the emotions as she traces the story from Susan's childhood:

LFW: We never really had many major catastrophes. Of course, we lost Randy. We've lost other members of the family, and we've had some illnesses. There was one time, when Susan was eleven and the children were traveling with us. I don't remember where we were coming from, but we were headed for Ottumwa, Iowa. At that time, Ottumwa was sort of a little, one horse town, and had one hospital. We pulled in there some time in the middle of the night. Earl went into the Holiday Inn and got a room. The kids and I just stayed on the bus and slept until it was time to get up the next morning, and were going to go up to the room. Earl had driven all night, so he needed to get some sleep. When we woke up, I got the children cleaned up and dressed.

To let Earl sleep a little longer, I took the children to the restaurant to have lunch before we went up to the room. We were standing in line for the buffet and, suddenly, Susan got sick. She said she felt like she was going to faint. She was very nauseated, so I was trying to get out of the line to get her downstairs to the rest room, and she passed out and scared me to death. Of course, we didn't eat anything, we just went right up to the room and I took her temperature. It was very high. I put her to bed, and she stayed in bed all that day. That night, her temperature broke and I thought she just had the flu or something. We put her back on the bus and went to do this concert. She stayed in bed while we were in singing, but I'd go check on her about every fifteen minutes. When we got through with the concert and back to the motel, her temperature was very high again. In the middle of the night, we had to call a cab and take her to the hospital. They never did really determine what was wrong with her, but the doctor said he thought she had walking pneumonia and that we should take her to our doctor when we got home. He gave her some antibiotics and she got better, but really she wasn't strong enough to walk. We'd just take her food to her and she'd eat on the bus.

We were home in a few days and I took her to the doctor and he agreed that she had walking pneumonia, but I believe with all my heart that it was the beginning of Susan's physical problems. I may be wrong, but I think she kind of thinks the same thing. Every year after that she would get the same thing over again. The next time she had it, the doctor said she had mono. I just know she wasn't very healthy from the time she was eleven. She would have recurring spells of weakness and flu symptoms. She had her tonsils removed, but it didn't help.

While Susan's health during her teen years was a concern for Lily Fern and Earl, it was all but devastating as Susan grew older and married. Lily Fern finds it hard to talk about it, but she finds in it another miracle:

LFW: Susan got married and got pregnant. She did very well and had an easy delivery. My grand-daughter, Megan, was perfectly normal and healthy. Megan was not quite two when Susan and Tim had to move to Kansas, from Yukon. After they moved up there, Susan got really bad. Tim had to go out of town for a week on his job, and when he got home, he said he realized how ill she was. He didn't know if it was because he was away from her for a week, or whether she just looked so much worse, but he told her, 'You're going to the doctor, whether you want to or not.' They hadn't gotten their medical insurance with the new company yet, so she didn't want to go until they had insurance. He said, 'You're going anyway.' After all the tests, they told her she had Lymphoma Hodgkins Disease.

Tim called me around 9:30 on a Saturday night, and he said, 'Can you come up? Susan's in the hospital and there's something wrong with her lungs.' We just threw things in the car and started out. It is three and a half hours from where we were, so we stopped half way and called him at the hospital. He'd been there all day with Megan and Susan. He said, 'She has cancer.' I can't begin to tell you what that did to Earl and me. Earl had diabetes, which was pretty well under control, but from that day on, they couldn't get his sugar down to normal again. He was so concerned about Susan, and stress and worry is hard on a diabetic. It did come down after his last heart attack, but the doctor doesn't know how or why.

Anyway, we got there about two o'clock on Sunday morning. Tim had just gotten home with Megan. It was such a pitiful situation, it just broke my heart. When something is wrong with your children, you would give anything you own if you could just go through it for them. But, there's some things you can't do, and some things they have to go through on their own to learn some things of their own. I think both Susan and Tim learned a valuable lesson in all this. I know Susan immediately learned what it was to really trust in the Lord. Susan had always been a very negative person, and all the way from home until after we talked to Tim and found out she had cancer, I said, 'Earl, what are we going to do? How are we going to keep her morale up and keep her going through all of this?' We prayed that God would help us to be able to encourage her--but we were so discouraged ourselves, I didn't know how we were going to possibly even keep ourselves going, much less raise her morale.

When we got there, Tim was worn out from being at the hospital taking care of Megan all day and being upset about Susan. Megan just ran and grabbed me around the neck, and the baby knew that there was something wrong. She always called me 'Nania.' She clung to me and kept saying, 'Nania, Nania, my Nania.' I knew that the child was just wanting some security and some kind of reassurance that everything was alright. And, of course, I did that. I whispered to her, 'Grandma's here and everything's going to be alright.' Soon after that, she fell asleep. She was such a good little girl. We went to see Susan the next day in Intensive Care. She had an emergency chemo treatment on Sunday morning and was still doing some of the IV when we got there. When we walked in, and I saw her lying in that bed and she'd lost so much weight--she went down five jean sizes--that's how much weight she had lost. She was so pale and looked so pitiful with all those tubes running in and out of her body. I know now that God can perform miracles, because I'm not a strong person when it comes to my children and their problems and illnesses. I just kept praying, 'Dear Lord, please don't let me break down.' I walked over and started talking to her, and she said, 'Mama, I know you're scared and I know you're worried, but, when Tim called you, I started to tell him to ask you to pray, but I realized I didn't have to do that, because I knew you were praying for me.' I said, 'Baby, we have been. We've been praying so much, and we know that God is on our side, so we're just going to have to trust him through this. You're going to have to trust him, and you're going to have to pray for me, too, because I need God's help now more than any time in my whole life.' She said, 'Mother, I'm going to tell you something....' Usually she said 'Mama.' This time she said, 'Mother, I'm going to tell you something. I already feel God right here on my pillow by me. I know everything's going to be alright. I've asked God to let me live to see Megan raised, and I know he's going to do that.' You know, I never had to encourage that girl one time! I'd go to see her and she would be in such high spirits, which was so completely opposite of what she ever was, and I knew that was God working. They didn't let me stay long when I saw her in Intensive Care that first day, and when I walked out, I barely got outside the door and I just collapsed on the floor. The nurses carried me out. I didn't do that for attention. I just didn't think I could make it, seeing my daughter sick like that.

It was just the most frightening time of my whole life--even more than when Earl passed away, because my child was sick with something that was incurable unless God intervened. But, immediately she began getting better. I started calling people all over the United States and I had twenty-seven twenty-four hour prayer chains going for Susan in less than twenty-four hours. When we talked to the doctor, he said, 'She has just responded to everything. She's a miracle!' Her doctor, who did not even believe in God, calls her his miracle patient to this day, because she responded to everything faster than any patient he'd ever had. I said, 'Can we bring her food? She has asked for things.' He answered, 'If she asks for anything and you can get it, you get it here! Her body has to be built back up again.' They fed her well at the hospital, but I took food or sent it with Tim. Later, I told the doctor about all the prayer chains, and he said, 'I don't know what you're doing, but just keep it up, because whatever you're doing, it's working!'

Earl and Lily Fern stayed until the end of that week, but they had to go home because of some concerts and other obligations, and they had been told that Susan would be in the hospital for another six weeks. Lily Fern and Earl were torn at the prospect of leaving Susan, but thought they could free Tim to deal with her by taking Megan with them. Lily Fern was surprised by what happened that week:

LFW: On Thursday we went back home. On Monday, Susan called me. She was home! She said, 'I've done so well that they let me come home, and we'll be there this weekend to celebrate Megan's second birthday, and I'm going to bring her back home.' Now, she didn't have an easy road, but God worked a miracle in that girl's life, and I believe with all my heart that He healed her. She's gone her seventh year now with no problems, and I believe it's going to continue to be that way. They came that weekend and we had Megan's birthday party. It was more like a celebration for all of us, because we had our girl back and felt like she was going to be O.K. She went through several weeks of chemo and the illnesses that you have with that. I tried my best to get her to let me keep Megan at my house, but she said, 'Mama, if I don't have that baby, I have nothing to live for.' So, she took her back and somehow they survived. She has a wonderful husband, who helped, and Megan was a good baby, so they survived very well.

Lily Fern worried about Susan through the chemo treatments, when she was so ill, but Susan learned how to deal with them and steadily improved. At the end of the treatments, although the tumor in her lungs had not gone away, it had shrunk considerably. On the advice of the head oncologist at Mayo Clinic, she was given radiation, just to be sure. Now she goes back once a year for a check up, but as Lily Fern says, "Praise the Lord, everything's been O.K. since!"

Another complication of dealing with the children when they were younger was that Susan hated the traveling life, while Steve seemed uniquely qualified for it, and they were different in how they dealt with school. Lily Fern defines their differences:

LFW: When Susan was in high school, she wanted to take geometry and trigonometry at the same time. The teacher advised her not to do that, and Susan said, 'I think I can handle it.' So she took them and she passed both with straight 'A's.' She was always a straight 'A' student. While she was in high school, they did occupational testing on all the kids. They got the tests back and a man from the local vo-tech school brought them and explained them. He passed out the papers and said, 'You'll know by the marks on your paper what your best ability is.' Susan's paper had no marks on it. She thought they failed to grade it. She raised her hand and said, 'I don't have any marks on my paper.' The man said, 'Are you Susan Weatherford?' She said, 'Yes.' He said, 'We didn't put anything on yours because you could do anything on there. We didn't feel it was necessary to instruct you in any way. You could do any occupation that was on there.' I said, 'Well, Susan, there was a diesel mechanic program on there. Your dad needs one pretty bad.' She didn't think she wanted to do that!

I knew that our life was not the life that Susan really liked. She was always a very quiet person. We would be in a group of people and I'd miss her, and I'd find her on the bus, lying on the bed reading. She's just completely opposite of Steve. Steve has always been a very outgoing people person. Susan is not, and that is not to fault her. That's just the way she is. Then, when she got older, she said, 'When I become eighteen, I'm not traveling anywhere ever again. I'm getting off that bus and I'm staying off of it!' And she did exactly that. We tried to get Susan to sing with us several times, because Susan has a beautiful voice and she hears the floating harmony that is hard to hear. Most people can't hear it. She could have worked in with us very, very well, but we never believed it was right to force her to do that. We just made up our minds that if that isn't what she wanted to do, we weren't going to force her, and, sure enough, when she became eighteen, she stayed home. She didn't want to go to college and she didn't want to travel, so she stayed home and worked.

We had a few problems with Susan during that time, but really, all in all, we didn't have any major problems with either of our children. But it was enough back then that she gave me a few headaches and a few gray hairs, I'll say that! She went through quite a period of rebellion, but she's a wonderful, wonderful girl now, and has a lovely family and a great husband. She and Tim have my only grand-child, Megan. Tim is a wonderful father, husband, and son-in-law, as well as a great provider. Tim and Steve describe everything you could ask in a son. They are both very fine sons. I love Tim with all my heart, and so did Earl.

Steve was a totally different kind of person. He liked the travel and thrived on the people contact. During one summer, he took a page out of his mother's book and made his bid to be a permanent member of the quartet.

LFW: Our lead singer got sick and had to quit, and he left pretty suddenly. We didn't know what we were going to do. We had a bass, Earl was the baritone, and I was the alto, and we needed someone to sing lead. Steve kept saying, 'I could sing that part. I could sing that.' We just didn't pay any attention to him. We knew he could sing a little bit, but we didn't dream that he could really sing with the group and sound as good as he did. So we talked about who we could get, and

Music and Miracles

Steve kept saying, 'I could do that.' One day, Earl got tired of hearing him say that, so he said, real gruffly, 'O.K! Just show me what you can do.' Steve did, and he handled the part pretty well. Of course, his voice has matured a great deal since then, and he has learned a lot. He wasn't the greatest singer in the world right off the bat, but we realized that he could do it if we worked with him. We did that, and I think sometimes that Steve may be sorry he said he could do it. But, not really. I think he's really glad to be able to sing. I believe that God has called him to do what he is doing.

Anyone who has known Lily Fern for a while knows that she believes that her children are a miracle, in themselves. While they were very different, each has contributed something special to the family. She is proud of each for different reasons. She sees God's hand in the way the children came to her and in their different contributions. Her voice is filled with awe as she speaks of the miracle of Steve's gift for contributing to the Weatherford ministry:

LFW: There's one thing I want to say, and I hope I can get across the way I really, really feel it, because it is so true and so very close to my heart. The circumstances by which Steve came to us overwhelm me. We had lost Randy, and I felt that I was not in the perfect will of the Lord when I quit singing. I went back to California and then to Oklahoma, where Earl's sister's baby was born, and I was there when it happened. That was when I knew that I wanted another little boy. And up to that point, I was really frightened and afraid to give in to those feelings. Then, when I came home and discussed it with Earl, he was just waiting for me to say that I was ready to adopt another boy. And all this time, Steve was already born! I believe with all of my heart that all of this worked in God's plan. I believe Randy was not the child that he meant for us to have. Not just everybody would be able to do what Steve does. I believe that God put him in our life and in our hearts and in our home to do what he is doing.

Steve looks so much like my own father--his hairline, his coloring, the blue eyes, the shape of his lips, his nose--everything is so much like my dad, even though there is no blood relation at all. He acts a lot like my dad--his habits, the way he dresses, the way he carries himself. Everything is so much like my own father.

The thing that is amazing to me is that we went through all that with Randy, and thought that this was the boy for us, and we found out we couldn't keep him. Then, while we were trying to make up our minds what we wanted to do, God had Steve waiting for us all this time! My heart tells me that God gave him to us to help me in the day and time I'm living in right now. I believe that He looked into the future and saw my need. It's just amazing that Steve has the talent and the disposition to sing.

Susan never wanted to follow this kind of life, but it just seems that Steve was meant to do this. Susan would be very discouraged and get upset with pastors when they took advantage of us, or with singers when they would do her daddy wrong. She would get bitter and hard, and she still holds quite a bit of resentment in her heart against different people. But Steve always just accepted it as life. Susan doesn't have the disposition to take the things that Steve has had to take in traveling--the knocks that we've had to go through--any more than Steve could have settled down the way Susan has done. They have different qualities. I've often thought and worked this back over in my mind about how God looked down and knew that this was the boy that I would need. And I believe he was born to be in my home, in my arms, in my family, and to be in this group. I believe God placed him there to help me in this day and time, after Earl went to be with the Lord. He came to help me carry the load of the group, and carry the load he certainly has. He is just an unusual boy in the fact that he has the dedication to do what we do. It takes perseverance, dedication, sacrifice. Susan was not made for that kind of life. It does not take away from her at all. I love them both the same. They are just different people.

I think you have to be a special breed to do what we do. Steve can do it. Most people couldn't cope with bus break-downs and not knowing if we were going to make it to the next date or not, or meeting a deadline and staying up all night, or maybe two or three days, and working on a bus, and then getting in and driving on and making the next engagement. They couldn't take getting to a date where we were supposed to be making a certain amount of money and have them come up with excuses, such as they couldn't get the word out, or they've had sickness in the church. So many times they use the weather as an excuse. It is one of the favorite excuses. It just comes a little drop of rain and they say, 'Well, we just couldn't get the people out because the weather was so bad.' That happens to us all the time. We have expenses, and many times we have been disappointed with the offerings that we were supposed to get, or the flat rates that we were supposed to get, and they would come up with some kind of excuse and we wouldn't get what we were told we would get. But, all in all, the Lord has really taken care of us, and Steve is able to cope with the life. He has seen the miracles that have happened. For instance, buses would break down and there just seemed no way at all to get them repaired. You couldn't get the parts or something, but always the Lord would work out some way and always give us the answer or a reason why we should go on and keep trying. But, I believe God brought Steve into the world for us to have, that he might help with this group, and he has proved to be a fine singer, a fine son and a fine, dedicated Christian.

Because she knows that other people have trouble understanding this kind of life, Lily Fern was careful to explain it when Steve's girlfriend, now his wife, Standalee, questioned her:

LFW: When Steve started going with Standalee Smith, I know she didn't understand why he had to be gone all the time. They went together for about five or maybe six years before they got married. But soon after she started going with him, she came to talk to me one day, and she wanted to know if they got married, if he was ever going to be able to stay home and be with her. I told her, 'Standalee, I can't answer that for you. I can't answer anything for Steve's life. He has to do what God has called him to do, or what God has laid on his heart to do. But I can tell you one thing, and I have taught my children this. If it's God's will that they do something, and they don't follow through with that, they will never be completely happy. They will never be really happy unless they're doing what God wants them to do.' Again, this is the permissive will of God and the perfect will of God. It would have been alright for Steve to marry Standalee, or anybody, and stay at home and be a husband and father, like normal people usually do, but apparently that isn't what God called him to do. I said, 'I can't tell you what's right for his life and what's wrong. I never told Steve he had to sing, and neither has Earl. We never said, you have to do this, we need you, we have to have you. We never threatened him or anything. We just told him that if this is what he wanted to do, we were glad he was there to do it. I'll tell you one thing for sure. I believe with all my heart that God has called Steve to do something special for him, whether it's with The Weatherfords, whether it's to preach, whether it's to sing, whatever it is. I don't know what it is, but if it's something that God calls him to do that takes him away from home, you're going to have to pray for that dedication, or neither one of you will be happy. You could get married and you might talk him into getting off the road, and he would quit, but you will never be completely happy as a married couple unless he is in the will of God and you are in the will of God. And you must understand that this might be what God wants him to do.'

What I was trying to tell her was that they both had to put God first or they'd never be completely happy. She said she understood, and if there ever was a dedicated girl, I believe it's Standalee. She has been behind Steve whole-heartedly all the way, and there have been times when she and I have talked, when we knew that Steve was discouraged, and she'd tell me, 'I told him he couldn't quit, that he had to keep singing--that this was just a down time for him,' and she told him that together they were going to make it and we were all going to pull out of the problems we were facing at that time. She's been a great encouragement to him and a great help to this group. She does all our photo shots for albums and advertising, and she gets our posters made and gets them out. She's just a great, great help to this group, and she's been a wonderful wife to Steve. I've often said I'm glad she's living with him, and not me! He's just not a real easy person to live with. His life style--he stays up half the night and sleeps half the day, and now she lives about the same life style.

Lily Fern cites only one time when she was concerned about the decision to take Steve on the road:

LFW: One summer after Steve had started singing with us, it came time for him to go back to school. We decided to have him travel with us rather than stay with the baby-sitter any longer. We tried that for a couple of years, and he just wasn't doing as well in school as he should have. We kept telling him, 'If you don't apply yourself a little bit more and work a little harder, we're going to have to take you out of school and go back to home schooling and traveling with us.' He just never did take that to heart. By then he was in junior high school and into football, and his peers were most important. He wanted to be popular with the kids, and studying and doing things like that weren't very important to him. So, finally, I told him that if he didn't make a certain average, the next year we'd have to take him with us. Now, I do believe that Steve was bitter about that for a while and he may still hold a little bitterness in his heart, but I felt that we were doing what was right, because later most of those kids that he was running around with got into serious trouble with dope and drinking and all kinds of things--even some robberies. So, I really feel like we did what was right in making him go with us.

Lily Fern never tires of telling stories about her children, and stories about miracles. One she tells involves the period when Steve started singing with them:

LFW: We started on a tour and we were going to Houston, Texas. For ever so long, Earl had been saying he didn't know whether the tires on the bus would make another trip or not. We knew they were threadbare, but we just kept going. We got to a church in Houston and the pastor met us at the bus and looked at the tires. He said, 'Man, those tires are threadbare! How in the world are you traveling on them?' He didn't offer to find any help for us. He gave us our offering, but that didn't take care of expensive things like tires. We went from there to Ottumwa, Iowa, and there was a man in the church who had a tire dealership. He said, 'I want you to come down tomorrow and get some tires for that bus!' Earl said, 'We don't have the money to buy tires for that bus!' The man said, 'You come down and we'll work something out.' He let us buy the tires on credit. We went down and they were changing the tires and Steve was standing out there talking to them. He was about sixteen and just like he is now. He was trying to see everything and learn everything he could by watching what the mechanics did. So, he was just standing there talking to the guys, when one of them said, 'Look at this tire! There's a big hole in it. I mean you can see clear through it! How did you get here?' Steve turned to him and he said, 'Well, I reckon God had his thumb in that hole, and that's how we got here!' I laugh when I think of his answer, but it must have been, because we got there and we got new tires and we got them paid for. It was another miracle!

She remembers still another miracle involving a bus:

LFW: One time we were just desperate to get from Martinsville, Virginia to Charlotte, North Carolina to begin a revival. Something happened to the bus. It must have been a radiator hose or something-- but we were in the middle of nowhere! We had to stop and we needed water. We looked around and there was an old rickety house right behind us, and a bunch of people were lounging around on the porch. Earl and Steve took buckets and went to see if they could get some water. Well, the guy they talked to must have seen an opportunity to make a few bucks. He tried to charge them something awful, like a dollar a gallon or something. Just as they were talking, it started to rain. And I mean, it really rained! Earl just looked up at the man and said, 'Never mind. I think we've got our source.' By the time they got back to the bus, they had collected some water in their buckets. There was a groove down off the roof of that bus, and the water started pouring a solid stream, just like it was out of a spigot. They put the buckets under that stream and got enough water to fill the radiator, and we went on to our revival.

Despite all the miles traveled in Weatherford buses, they had comparatively few mishaps and probably several more miracles. Fulton and Brenda Nash shared some memories of "bus problems:"

FN: We had bus fires. One was in Minneapolis when the whole dash caught on fire, and we were on snow and ice! That was a bad time. James Clark and Glen Couch were with us at that time. Another time, in Illinois, we were driving down the highway with the whole rear-end burning. We had to stop at a main intersection.

BN: Was that the time that you didn't know the bus was on fire?

FN: We didn't know it at the time. We were just driving along and we thought everyone was really friendly in that area, but they were trying to tell us that our bus was on fire. Then we saw smoke and some flames. We stopped and unloaded all our stuff, and I never saw Roy Trimble move so fast! Getting his stuff off was the fastest he's ever moved! We had stuff laid out all over that intersection. A fire truck was right behind us trying to get our attention to put the fire out. But we had other times. The bus broke down once and Bill Wagner and I had to fly back to Oklahoma City to pick up the two vans, and then we drove back in order for us to make the rest of our trip. Back at that time, we were taking three month tours. Those were long, long tours!

BN: You were mentioning the fires, but we also discussed Lily's sense of humor. What was that story that she and Susan always told, that *you* were on fire and they were laughing....

FN: I don't even want to talk about that! Brenda, I wish you hadn't brought that up! Well, it was winter time, and I had a new jacket on and I liked it. The bus didn't have heaters, so we used those big propane heaters--one in front and one in back. I was back there talking to Lily and Susan, and I backed up too close and my jacket caught on fire. You talk about Roy Trimble being fast getting his stuff out of the bus, why, man, I got out of that jacket real quick! Here I was about to burn to death and those girls were just laughing at me. That was really kind of rude of them to do that. They should have felt sorry for me, but they didn't. They just laughed and laughed. They never forgot that!

Traveling on the bus provided both miracles and funny situations, but it became the way of life for the intrepid Weatherford group.

Steve grew up with bus problems and traveling mishaps, so he is sensitive to the problems of others, as well. Lily Fern expresses her pride and love for Steve, even in the midst of frustration:

LFW: Steve was always such a great kid, even though he was always really active. He was not "ornery," or mean. In fact, Steve is a very tender-hearted young man, and always has been. If he thought somebody was in trouble, he would do everything he could to help them. I've gotten aggravated with him at times. We've been riding along in the bus, trying to get someplace, tired and worn out, trying to get to a bed or a motel or something, and somebody would be beside the road with a break-down. He's actually stopped and gotten out of our bus and worked on their vehicle and got them going down the road before we could go on to our destination. Well, you can't really fault anybody who does things like that, can you?

Others have reported Steve's caring nature, such as an incident with the tenor of the Midwestern group, The Bradshaw Brothers and Don. Don Hays tells of Steve's compassion for a stranger:

DH: I went to the National Quartet Convention one September, when I wasn't really able to be there physically. I had a very painful hip, and I had to carry my luggage quite a distance into the hotel. I got into the elevator with a young man and we started up. The bags were heavy and he must have seen that I was in pain and exhausted. He looked familiar. I said, 'Aren't you Steve Weatherford, Lily's boy?' He smiled and said, 'Yes I am!' We chatted a minute, and then he said, 'Could you use some help with that luggage?' I said, 'I sure could!' He took the heavy bags and when the elevator stopped at my floor, he insisted on getting off and carrying them down the hall to my room. I'll always remember that kind act by Steve Weatherford. Lily Fern has a right to be proud of that young man!

And she is, indeed, proud of Steve.

Over the years, The Weatherfords had funny experiences to balance the times of trial. An afternoon with Lily Fern can garner dozens of stories of funny or touching moments with family, friends and co-workers, such as the one she tells about when Armond Morales came to the bus to tell her that he was leaving to join Jake Hess in the new group, The Imperials. Armond was like a son to Lily Fern and she was sorry to lose him, but she was happy for his success. As he sat by her bunk and explained what he planned to do, she wished him well and added, "But I hate your guts, you dirty rat!"

Fulton and Brenda Nash attribute Lily Fern's ability to survive the gospel singer life-style to her marvelous sense of humor--what they call the "gift of laughter."

One of the funniest stories of this lifestyle involves the stress of having to dress on the bus:

> LFW: We were running late for a concert and we knew we wouldn't have time to stop and take showers, so I was in the room Earl and I shared at the back of the bus, trying to get ready. I plugged in my curling iron and got a basin of water for a sponge bath. Earl and the others were up in the front of the bus. I bathed, stark nude, and went to my bunk to get clothing out of the drawer under it. To get at it, I had to sit down and pull it open. I sat down, realizing too late that I sat right on the hot curling iron! Well, I yelled and shifted my weight to one side, which just allowed the curling iron to roll under the other side. By the time I could struggle up off the bunk in the moving bus, that iron had covered a lot of territory! I tried to find something to put on the burns, and I found a bottle with a little aloe, barely enough to cover the burns. Bending over, with my bottom to the mirror, I tried to find the worst areas, so I could use the small amount of aloe to the best advantage. With my tri-focal glasses, I think I saw three bottoms, but I couldn't feel where the worst burns were. I threw on a robe and went to the door and asked Earl to come back. I said, 'I need you.' He came back and I explained the situation. Well, he didn't think much that I did was funny, so he sat down on the bunk, solemnly, and I told him to rub the aloe where the burn was. I turned and presented my bottom. I waited and nothing happened. I looked around and he was sitting there looking through and over his glasses. 'Oh, I can't see anything,' he grumbled. I stood up and said. 'That's it. We should give it up! When you're too old to see anything and I'm to old to feel anything, it's time to quit!' He got up and stomped out and slammed the door.

Another time, they went on a gospel cruise ship and the lock on the door to their room stuck. They got locked in. They yelled and tried to get help, but no one came. They tried to call Steve, but he wasn't in his room. Lily says, "He was out horsing around, as usual!" So his roommate came over to try to get them out. He decided to try to open the porthole over one of the bunks. Earl was in his shorts. He got up on the bunk to pull on the porthole, while the other man pushed from outside, and Lily was holding on to Earl, to balance him. Suddenly the porthole came open and Earl fell on top of Lily. Earl looked down at Lily and said, "Why couldn't this have happened when I felt good?" It must have looked risqué. They agreed that there was a time when they wouldn't want to get that door open!

Lily Fern treasures the moments when Earl was able to laugh and tease in the later years. One of her fondest memories was in a photo shoot. The photographer had posed Lily Fern and Earl with their arms around each other. She ran out of film and had to change rolls. She told them to just hold it for a minute. As they stood holding each other, Earl looked down at Lily Fern and said, "Well, if we're going to have to stand here, I'm not going to waste it," and he kissed her. Lily Fern says that he felt so bad in the last years that he wasn't very demonstrative, so this was a special moment for her. The picture that is on the back of the dust cover of this book is the one taken immediately after that kiss. Earl's handsome face betrays a touch of mischief in that photo, and anyone can see on Lily Fern's face the glow of a woman still in love after all the years.

In the following chapter, the events of the last few years, stories of pivotal moments, such as the loss of Earl, and the wit and wisdom of Lily Fern round out her life.

Lily Fern, Earl, and Steve Weatherford

Chapter Ten
One of God's Singers Goes home

With Steve traveling and singing with them, Susan's health restored and her family secure, Lily Fern's major worries were behind her for a while. The Weatherfords continued to have adventures as they traveled, such as accidents and near-accidents.

They had a brush with disaster one time when Earl, Steve and Lily Fern were touring in California. They had just had Thanksgiving dinner with a pastor in Valejo and were on the freeway to go to another location. A car passed them and then cut right in front of the bus. Earl had to swerve all over the road to keep from hitting the old couple in the car. Just a few months later, in Tucson, Arizona, a city bus side-swiped the Weatherford bus and put it out of commission for a while. She cites as one of the closest calls the time when they were near home, going from Pauls Valley to McAlister to do a concert. Steve was driving through the little town of Allen and the roads were slick due to a recent rain. A man in a little pick-up truck suddenly turned, without giving a signal. In order to keep from hitting him, Steve had to go into the ditch on the far left side of the road. Lily Fern describes the scene from her vantage point:

> LFW: It was frightening, but later we laughed about this. Earl and I were relaxing in our compartment. Fortunately, I had just emptied our portable 'potty,' before settling down to rest. The next thing I knew, I opened my eyes and the potty was flying through the air, along with dog food dishes and our two little dogs! I thought, 'Well, we're goners!' But Steve finally got the bus stopped, and what a mess we had!

Other than changes in personnel and adventures on the road, the ministry was fairly peaceful during this period, allowing for a more "normal" family life. Lily Fern's daughter, Susan, has a special term for such periods. She calls them, "Weatherford normal," which certainly wouldn't fit a national norm. Time at home is spent working on inventory, rehearsing, recording, filling orders, booking dates, changing schedules, repairing vehicles, answering phone calls, and catching up with every-day household duties and family obligations that have been postponed while the group traveled.

During the years after their return to Oklahoma, Earl and Lily Fern were able to keep strong ties with both his and her families. Lily Fern's mother had moved back to Oklahoma in 1973, just after Earl and Lily Fern's move to Paoli in 1971. She and her husband moved to Pauls Valley. When she came back, she wanted to reminisce a bit, so Lillie and Lily Fern took a day and drove up to where Lillie was raised. It was about a hundred miles from Paoli, and they drove all around, while she showed her daughter where the school had stood and where she had lived. They went back through Bethany, and Lillie pointed out where their house had stood when Lily Fern was born, just about a block and a half from the main street.

In a peculiar twist of fate, Lillie's last husband was the man who had traveled with the Gobles to California.

While there were some strange times after Lillie moved to Pauls Valley, Lily Fern was grateful for another period of closeness with her mother. They had been quite close during Lily Fern's childhood. Lily Fern reflects on her deep attachment to her mother as a child:

LFW: I worshipped my mother. Growing up, I was always really close to her. I remember coming home from school and she was always there. There were a few times when she said, 'Today I might not be here because I'll be at a missionary meeting,' or something, but almost every time, she was there. I came home from school one day and it wasn't missionary day and there wasn't anything going on, and I couldn't find her. I thought, 'The Lord's come, and they've left me!' I went outside and I heard her. She used to talk to herself a lot, and she was bringing clothes from off the clothes line. I was never so glad to see her bring in clothes in all my life.

She realizes, however, that Florence's experience with their mother was different, possibly because of Lily Fern's status as "the baby" and Florence's strong personality and oldest child role. They felt that Lillie was a bit manipulative and used her poor health to shift some of her work to the girls, but neither of them felt mistreated.

As happens in so many families, Lily Fern and Lillie seemed to change roles as the years passed. Instead of Lily Fern being dependent on her mother,

her mother became dependent on her:

> LFW: I could talk to Mother, especially the last few years that she was here. After we had to put her in the nursing home, though, it got to be pretty rough, because I'd go off on tour, and I was the only member of her family around. And then Earl's mother was put in the same nursing home, with one room between them.
>
> I remember coming off a tour one time and we got in at about two in the morning. I used to do a lot of my work at night, so I thought, 'Well, I'll get everything done now, so first thing in the morning, I'll just get up and go to the nursing home.' I worked the rest of the night, didn't go to bed, and Earl got out of bed and said, 'I'm going to the nursing home to see Mama.' He was going to see his mother, whose room was close to my mother's. I said, 'Well, go in the front way, so Mother won't see you, because she'll wonder where I am.' I knew I couldn't get down there for about another hour. Well, for whatever reason, she saw him. When I got there, there was a nurse standing behind her, rubbing her back, petting her. They treated my mother like a queen down there.
>
> But when I got there and saw this, I said, 'What's the matter?' Mother was crying. She said, 'Oh, Earl's been here for....' I was just so tired, I said, 'Don't start with me, and I mean it!' I told her just what all I had done since I got home. I said, 'I cannot get down here every time you think I should get down here and, if it's going to be like this, I won't tell you when I'm coming home any more. I'll just come home and get down here as soon as I can.'
>
> And I told the nurse, 'This is not what you should be doing. You should have seen through this. I let her know that I was on to her right away. She knows better and everyone at this nursing home knows that I do everything that I can for her, but I can't tolerate this.' Well, she never did that again.

Lily Fern recognized her mother's manipulation and set boundaries on how much she would tolerate.

Fortunately, Florence and Meekly were supportive of Lily Fern as she cared for their mother. They understood the stress Lily Fern was under through trying to care for her mother, her own family and her ministry with Earl.

Perhaps remembering the difficulties they faced when their father, Lon, died without preparation, the family gathered before Lillie had to go to the nursing home and dealt with all her business:

> LFW: Meekly and Martha and Florence and her husband, Earl, came back here purposely because Mother said, 'I want to get all this business taken care of.' The six of us sat down with her and she told us what she wanted. But--and this is the kind of family I have--they told Mother, 'Whatever you have, you need to get it in Lily Fern's name--every penny of your money, everything--because she's the one who will have to handle all this.' The family knew I wasn't going to spend her money and there wasn't much to spend, anyway. They said, 'By rights, she's the one that should have it anyway,' and that's the way they wanted it. We all went down with her and she picked out her casket and we made arrangements with the funeral director, so we wouldn't have anything to worry about later. I've never known a family quite like this.

Lily Fern was able to look after her mother until she died in 1986. She and Earl looked after both of their mothers, part of the time in the same nursing home. Proximity allowed for much more interaction among the families.

Earl's sister, Bobbie Sue, recalls some of the significant events in his family during the period of his return to Oklahoma:

> BSW: When Earl and Lily moved to Yukon, my younger sister, Mary, lived just a few blocks from them. She was elated when they moved so close to her, but she was diagnosed with breast cancer and had a radical mastectomy. We were all just devastated. Earl just wouldn't accept it. Mary was always special to him, I guess because she was the baby for one thing, and they were just very close. It didn't matter how bad she felt, she never missed one of his concerts when they were home. It was just understood--Mary was going to be there. She also took care of the business affairs while he was away. Later, she had a lung removed with cancer, and then, eighteen months later, she was diagnosed with brain cancer. She refused surgery and passed away December 30, 1971.
>
> My family and I moved to California in 1973, and a few months later, we learned my dad had lung cancer. He passed away in 1974. We moved back to Oklahoma in 1977 and a few months later, our mother was diagnosed with stomach cancer. She recovered from cancer surgery and, a few years later, she had a stroke and the last four years of her life were spent in a nursing home, completely helpless. She passed away September 20, 1986.

One of God's Singers Goes Home

After Mary had passed away, Earl and Lily had moved to Paoli, where our parents lived, so Earl was able to be close to them for the first time since he left home when he was nineteen. He was a very devoted son and loved his 'mama and daddy' dearly. He couldn't do enough for them. The group even sang at Daddy's funeral.

After the death of Mary and our parents, Bonnie and Earl were sort of left to carry on--they were the oldest two. I think they became closer during this period than they had ever been. Bonnie's husband passed away in 1989, so she really leaned on Earl for support. She had heart surgery and Earl pampered and babied her as only he could do, and she mothered him.

Earl was able to spend twenty years back in Oklahoma, near his family, as he and Lily Fern carried on their traveling ministry.

During the late fifties and the sixties there was an element of corruption in the world of Southern Gospel, and Earl would not take the group to the concerts and big "sings." He preferred to concentrate on the church ministry, which occupied the Oklahoma years. By the end of his life, he had reconciled with the major body of Southern Gospel. He was able to take part in the beginning of the Gaither video tape series and to attend Charlie Waller's Grand Ole Gospel Reunion before he died.

Lily Fern has difficulty talking about the last year of Earl's life. Not only was it traumatic to lose her husband of so many years, but it was a very hard period. To this day, she can barely stand to listen to recordings with Earl's voice. Talking about his death was obviously the hardest part of writing this book.

Earl did not relinquish his responsibility lightly as he became more infirm. Lily Fern had difficulty getting him to give up driving, even when he was on oxygen. The final straw was when he was driving in a major congestion area and struck the back of the car ahead of him. Even after the investigating policeman over-looked the oxygen and the fact that Earl had no license with him, he wanted to drive home. Lily Fern had to point out firmly that the policeman knew the situation and was still on the scene. After that, he let her drive.

His insistence on maintaining his usual pace made his final year stressful on everyone who cared for him and for himself. Lily Fern describes that year:

LFW: Earl was very determined to sing, even when he had bouts with the hospital, once with the heart attack and once with pneumonia. When he got out after the pneumonia, he said, 'I will never go to the hospital again. I'll die first. I'll never go again!' He was determined. There were many times when we probably should have had him in the hospital, but he just would not go. I think it was probably about the October before he died in June that he began to need oxygen all the time. For a long time, he had just needed it at night.

We had a concentrator--a portable machine that we carried--and he got more dependent on it as time went on. Of course, I don't know whether he knew it or not. When he began to fail, it was harder and harder to breathe even with oxygen. He began to think there was something wrong with the concentrator. On Saturday, before he died on the following Wednesday, he insisted that I get him another concentrator. He said, 'This one is just not working properly!' Well, I knew what was not working properly--and we had to go through all the red tape to get it from Medicare--but they finally delivered it. We were at Wynema King's house in California. 'Nema' is one of my oldest and best friends. He said, 'There's something wrong with this one, too. It's not working right, either.' I think what really happened was that he wasn't getting enough oxygen and he just wasn't thinking clearly. You could not really reason with him in those last days of his life.

Also, we would have to put him in a wheelchair and wheel him into the churches, and none of us minded doing that. Kenny Payne was with us then, so Steve and Kenny and I cared for him. I soon learned that I would have to allow an extra hour to get him ready, because he was moody. I understand that this happens with a lot of severe heart and diabetes patients and he had both. They may be really high and everything's fine, and then they'll just come off the wall with something. You have no idea why they said it or where it came from.

One day, I might try to help him get ready for a concert and he'd say, 'I can do this myself! Do you think I'm helpless?' But, most of the time, if I didn't offer, he'd say, 'Well, I guess I'm just going to have to do this myself. Nobody's going to help me do it.' I never knew what to do, so I just allowed an extra hour. If he needed me, I was there. Sometimes I could just go over and start doing the things that he was trying to do. He got to where he couldn't even comb his hair. He couldn't raise his arms very high and breathe. He couldn't put his shoes

One of God's Singers Goes Home

and socks on and breathe. He couldn't take care of his personal toilet habits and breathe. Earl was a very modest, proud man. He was too much of a man to easily accept help with things like that, but he knew he had to, especially when he was in the hospital. But I think he soon adapted. You know, it didn't matter any more.

It was the personal things that just he and I went through that really bothered him. One day he would think it was just something to be pushed in the wheelchair by the boys. Steve or Kenny usually pushed him in. I seldom ever pushed him in. Then the next day, he might be ashamed, and he didn't want them to push him in. He was embarrassed, but he would get up on the platform sit on a stool and do the concert. The audience didn't know that maybe he was singing only three words in a phrase, or maybe not at all. They thought he was singing, but we were singing the three harmony parts and it didn't matter. We just covered for him. He couldn't sing and breathe. Especially the last tour, out to California, was really, really miserable, but he insisted on going.

We had just gotten a bus finished with a compartment for Earl and me in the back. He had sold the big Eagle bus to get me out of debt. He got all of my personal bills paid by the time he died. He knew he wasn't going to be there long. He wanted to do that, and that was fine.

The week before he died, we did eight straight concerts. We took him in and he emceed them, except for one that he missed because he was having awful nosebleeds.

Most of the time, up to that point, we could live with it and he was pretty good. He was in a pretty good mood most of the time and he could accept most things. His appetite was completely gone and nothing tasted right to him. Then he would have these really weird cravings. Like, one day, he just wanted salad, and I went out and got stuff and made salad, and he said, 'I love that salad dressing!' For three or four days he ate nothing but salad with that certain kind of salad dressing. He used to love Mexican food and hot Spanish food, but got to where he couldn't eat that at all. He used to love breakfast--big breakfasts--eggs, bacon, sausage, biscuits and gravy. He got to where he couldn't eat anything but maybe a little bit of hot cereal. Food just gagged him. He couldn't swallow it, so, therefore, he lost a lot of weight.

During the eight days he was trying to sing, Earl suffered from nosebleeds that sent him to emergency rooms, where they packed his nostrils with cotton, which was very uncomfortable. After one concert, they went to the home of some friends for dinner, and Earl insisted on removing the packing. Lily Fern prayed that he would not hemorrhage, and, as she said, "The Lord answered my prayer again."

Lily Fern remembers the progression of events after that incident:

LFW: The next night, he missed the concert because his nose started bleeding again. He couldn't get it stopped long enough to go in. He couldn't lift his head off the pillow or it would start again. I was afraid he was going to bleed to death. We went in and did the concert, and I went out and checked on him two or three times. That was on a Friday night, and we got back to Los Angeles, to Wynema's house. Saturday night, we were getting ready to leave to go do a concert, and that's when he started talking about his concentrator and I got him a new one. We did a concert on Saturday night. He was just determined he was going to go! We had a motel that night, and three times during that night he said, 'I think this is it.' I just went over and held him and prayed, and said, 'Lord, just give us strength to carry on and do what we have to do. Just give us strength and the wisdom to know what we need to do.' He wouldn't go to the hospital. He wouldn't let me call the doctor. He would get better each time, fall asleep and be fine.

The next morning, we went to do a concert and I said, 'Why don't you just stay on the bus and rest, and we'll do the concert?' We were doing it, anyway. He said, 'No.' He was determined to go in, and he did. But, it took Steve and Kenny and the preacher about eight or ten minutes just to get him up two little steps about six inches apart and onto that stool, and get the oxygen set for him to sing. That afternoon, the pastor took us to a Mexican restaurant to eat, and Earl ordered a huge meal. He sat in his wheelchair and fell asleep--just kept dozing off. We knew, again, that was lack of oxygen. He never touched his food. Incidentally, that pastor was Reverend Joe Penrod, who was Guy Penrod's father. Rev. Penrod was the last person outside of the family to visit Earl in the hospital. He died a few months after Earl died.

After that concert, I knew in the back of my mind that Earl was going, but I would not let myself acknowledge it. We got him on the bus, and he couldn't make it to the back, so I put him in the chair up in the front and undressed him and he sat there napping and sort of rested. When he insisted on doing the concert that night, I dressed him at the front of the bus. The boys were doing something special at the church. They'd gotten his wheelchair out, and I had to push him in that night.

He had gotten to do the Grand Ole Gospel Reunion in Greenville, South Carolina, but he was really looking forward to doing the National Quartet Convention in Kentucky. As I was pushing him in, we talked. He said, 'Mama, I can't do this any more.' And I said, 'Yes, you can. We're going to help you. We're going to do this and you've got the convention to go to.' He said, 'I can't do it any more. I can't have you pushing me around like this.' And I said, 'Well, what if it was reversed and you were pushing me in? Wouldn't you want to do that for me?' He said, 'That's a different story.' I said, 'No, it's not a different story. The only difference in the story is that it's you and not me.' I stopped and looked him in the eye and put my hand on his shoulder. 'Earl,' I said, 'I am proud to push you in this wheelchair, and I am thrilled to be able to do something for you.' He didn't ask for much in his life. He wouldn't ask favors of people.

We got him up on the platform and he talked like he had never talked before. He introduced each one of us. He introduced Kenny first, and he talked about Kenny and told how much he appreciated Kenny, and how he had known him all of his life, and what a fine young man he was. He had never said those things before. He talked about Steve and he said, 'I'm proud that Steve's my son. He's been a great help to me. Steve, I love you.' Then he said, 'And Lily Fern, she's not only my wife, but she's been my helpmate, she's my best friend, and I don't tell her often enough,' and he turned to me and said, 'Mama, I love you.' I'll never forget that. He was telling us goodbye. And I think maybe the people at that concert might have sensed that.

People throughout that tour would come to us when he was in the wheelchair or on the oxygen and they'd say things like, 'You can't know what that did for me! I've been complaining about this and that. I felt like there was no hope for me, and then I saw him up there and I was determined in my heart that I was going to go on and make it.' It really did help a lot of people.

That night we were supposed to go to Phoenix. It was hot in Phoenix, and he couldn't handle hot weather. We would have been going to my brother's, but I said, 'Earl, I don't think you're able to go anywhere tonight, any further than we have to go.' He said, 'I'm not.' I said,

'Why don't we go back to Nema's and then go on?' He said, 'Maybe we ought to do that.' So, we went back to Nema's and we finally got him in there around midnight or one in the morning. I got him in bed-- he was in the front bedroom and I was in the room right next to him. I could hear him all night. When he would peck on the wall, I would go in and see about him. He would say, 'I can't breathe. I can't breathe.' I begged him to let me take him to the hospital. About six o'clock in the morning, he woke me up, pecking on the wall, and I got up. Wynema was already up. He said, 'I can't breathe.' I said, 'Earl, I'm going to have to call 911. I know you don't want me to, but if you died and I hadn't called, I would never forgive myself, because I don't know what to do for you. But maybe they will do something to help you. If I didn't do everything I could to try to help you, I couldn't live with myself.' He said, 'Well, call them.' I called and we got him to the hospital.

That was on Monday. By Monday afternoon, the doctor said, 'I think we need to put him on a respirator. He is just worn out. He's going to die from just being exhausted from trying to breathe. This way, he can at least breathe.' I said, 'Well, we have to see what he feels about that first.' I didn't really like the word, 'respirator,' but I didn't realize what all that entailed. The doctor told me Earl wouldn't be able to talk to me, but he would get rest. So we went in and explained it to him. The doctor told Earl that I could be with him and talk to him, but that he couldn't talk to me. I said, 'But, if you don't want us to do it, we won't do it.' Earl said, 'I've got to rest.' He hadn't been able to sleep. After they put him on the respirator and gave him something to help him sleep, he went to sleep immediately and slept four straight hours. The doctor said, 'This is helping him more than anything.' I knew they couldn't do anything like surgery to help him, but he just rested completely.

When he would come around after being asleep, it was very frustrating, because he would try to tell us something and he couldn't really write too well, because he was so shaky. Most of the time I think I could guess what he was saying, and I would just talk to him, but they wouldn't let me stay with him very long.

The nurses in the Cardiac Care Unit said, 'You've got to have these people stop calling here.' I said, 'I can't tell people to stop--I don't even know who's calling!' I mean, people got word and they were calling from all over. One nurse said, 'You've got to screen those calls. Who is this man, anyway?' And I said, 'He's my husband!' She said, 'Well, you've got to keep them off this floor.' I said, 'I can't control that. *You* keep them off this floor!' The calls and all were about to drive them crazy.

He did pretty well, but I could tell that he was going down--we could all tell. On Wednesday morning, I went to the hospital early, because Susan was coming in and I was going to the airport to meet her. I had called her and said, 'If you want to see your dad, I think you better get here.' She was coming in at nine o'clock and I think I got to the hospital about seven thirty. I went to tell him that she was coming in. I was going to leave right away to go pick her up.

When I got there, they were bringing him back to his room and a surgeon met me there and said, 'We're just bringing him back from the operating room.' I said, 'From what? Why?' They didn't get my permission, and I don't know whether they got Earl's. Earl was very upset about something and I think maybe he was thinking that I told them to do this. They were trying to get him back on the respirator again and get him adjusted and so on, and he was trying to write me a note. He couldn't even write. I said, 'Earl, I've got to go get Susan and let them get you settled.' I told him that because I didn't want him to think they were running me out, even though they were. They were pulling on me to get out of there. I said, 'As soon as we get back, maybe you can let me know what you wanted to tell me.' Something was bothering him and that's bothered me--to know what it was. I really don't think he gave them permission to do what they did.

I wouldn't have approved what they did. Four heart specialists, two of them surgeons, had told me not to let anyone do surgery. The first one, in Oklahoma City, said, 'I wouldn't touch him with a ten foot pole. He doesn't stand a chance of pulling through surgery.' The one I took him to in California said, 'I don't think he would make it through any kind of surgery, because of the condition of his heart. The walls of his heart are just like a banana peel. They wouldn't hold any pressure--no stitches, nothing.' And the very surgeon that met me that morning had said the same thing! They went through his throat, down into the heart, and put an instrument in to gauge the fluid. I couldn't grasp why they would do that, if he couldn't stand anything else and there was no possible surgery, why gauge the fluid? At this point it was not even important. To me, they saw an opportunity to make a little bit of extra money, and they did this totally useless surgery. If I had been thinking clearly at that point, I would have said to that surgeon, 'You have killed him!' But I wasn't thinking clearly.

While I was in there trying to talk to Earl, they called a 'code blue.' I saw when he died, because his eyes kind of went back. I thought he was watching what this nurse was doing behind him but, all of a sudden, it dawned on me and they pulled me out of the room and that's when he died.

I couldn't believe they had done that. I was within ten minutes of the hospital. They had the number and could have called me. I wanted to stay at the hospital, but they wouldn't let me. They knew how to reach me.

When the surgeon finally came and told me that Earl was gone, I started hitting him on his chest and screaming, 'No! No, he's not! You're lying to me!' I knew very well what I was doing, but I just couldn't seem to control it. Steve jumped up and tried to control me. I didn't pass out; I just collapsed on the floor.

Earl's insurance and Medicare paid for everything except something about that last particular surgery. I was to pay something like three hundred and some dollars or something. I would just send something--a little bit--each month until I paid it. I wish now that I would have said, 'Why did you even have to do that surgery?' I really should have sued them. I know Earl would have died anyway in his condition, but they had no right to put him through that, especially since I didn't give permission. I'm sure he was upset because he thought I told them to go ahead and do it, and I didn't.

Anyway, that was how he died. Really, the last two or three months were pretty miserable for him, for me, for all of us.

When asked how she got through this painful period, Lily Fern described the rough spots and what brought her through it:

LFW: There were some days when I thought, 'I just can't do this any longer.' A couple of times, I really thought I'd lose my mind, because I didn't know how to handle it. I just had to handle it one day at a time, trying to survive my own problems while Earl wasn't himself.

For example, one time we had gone from El Paso to Tucson, and we stopped at a truck stop and finished the night there. Well, we had gotten something to eat at a place on the road, and I ate something off the salad bar that didn't taste quite right. I think I got food poisoning, on top of everything else that was happening. I got Earl all settled for the night, then I went to bed. I barely got in bed when it hit me. I've never been so sick in all my life! I had cramps, nausea, everything! Earl was asleep and didn't know a thing about it. All night long I fought this.

Now, Earl had two pills that he had to take immediately when he woke up in the morning and he always had to turn on the little television at the foot of his bed when he woke up. We had learned to put his pills and a glass of water on the table right by our beds, so he could just reach across and take his pills. He could raise up first thing in the morning and flip on his television, also.

Well, we were at this truck stop and I was still feeling pretty bad. I heard him stirring and I heard him turn the television on, and I thought, 'Oh, maybe if I just lie here for a little bit, he'll sleep a little more.' I had gotten over the worst part after being sick all night, but I still just felt so bad. Pretty soon I heard him say, 'Well, I guess I'm gonna have to take care of it myself. Nobody else's going to take care of it for me!' I didn't even open my eyes. I said, 'What is it? What do you need?' He said, 'I need somebody to give me my pills.' I said, 'They're right there, Earl, just....' He grumbled, 'I can't reach over there and get them.' The day before he had just reached over and gotten them. This morning, he had managed to sit up to turn the television on, which took more effort than reaching the pills, but it was little things like that. So, I got up, got him his pills, got him his water, and went into the truck stop to get him something to eat. Truck stops aren't always the most pleasant places in the world, and the smell of all that food frying just about did me in, but I took him something to eat. He ate about two bites and couldn't eat any more.

It was just things like that all the time, and it was not easy. Unless he was in a rare mood that he was really happy and everything was O.K., he complained about everything. It was hard. That wasn't Earl. I had to listen to it, but I didn't really know what to do with it, so I just lived day to day.

Lily Fern was exhausted from the ordeal of Earl's long illness, but she had to get through even more as she faced life without him. Aside from everything else she was feeling, she had to consider the future of the Weatherford music ministry. She recalls the process by which she decided her next course of action:

> LFW: Of course, right at first I didn't know what in the world I was going to do. I remember thinking--not praying out loud or anything--just thinking, 'Lord, I'm not asking why you took him. I'm just asking you what am I going to do and how am I going to do it?' I had always depended on somebody in my life. Immediately, and I am telling the truth as close as I know how to tell it, immediately I felt the peace of God come over my entire being! I get goose bumps when I think about it even now. It was just like He said, 'That's not your problem; it's mine. I'll take care of that.' It's just like He said, 'My grace is sufficient.' And I realized right then and there, and I've tried to point it out to people in testimonies and at other times, that I didn't ask for God's grace, but it was there for me anyway. When we go through difficult times, and He lets us know that the grace is there, then, even though we may have created some of our own problems by the things we have done. That grace may not be as strong, but it's always there.
>
> After that, I just thought, 'Well, O.K. I'm going to wait.' He died on Wednesday and we had a memorial service in California and his funeral in Oklahoma on Saturday. It was that Friday that Steve and Kenny said they'd like to talk to me about the group. They asked what I felt about going on and singing. I said I had thought about it and I didn't know what to do. I said I certainly would consider it and that I was willing to try it. I think it gave me some hope of something to do, and I'm sure it gave them some hope, too.

For the first time in her life, Lily Fern was on her own. Of course, she had her children, and Steve was there for her in terms of the group, but this was a new way of life for her. She had gone directly from depending on her father to depending on Earl.

While Lily Fern had depended upon both her father and Earl, she was not really dominated by either of them. In her opinion, there was really only one area of their life where Earl was domineering, and that was in their music, but she learned to cope with that very early on:

> LFW: If I didn't sing it just like he thought it ought to be, he didn't mince words in telling me! I was young enough that it hurt my feelings and I cried every time he would look at me wrong. Well, I finally learned. I wouldn't cry. I wouldn't let him see me cry. I'd die first. In

a way that's good and in another way it's bad, but I finally let him know he couldn't treat me that way.

This was the way that Lily Fern learned artistic objectivity. Through this experience, she learned that in order to become a professional, you must forget about relationships as you work. You were not husband and wife, mother and son, but co-workers, who had to be able to take criticism without making it personal.

At first, she did not realize how much she had learned and that she had depended on herself a lot more than even she knew. She had been a hard worker in her home and the family ministry. She had taken responsibility and worked beside Earl for all those years. Her ability and effort would now be more specifically her own.

She thought carefully about her future in singing and decided to reorganize The Weatherfords:

LFW: I told Steve and Kenny that some things would have to change in the financial operations of the group. They agreed to the changes I proposed, and we committed to going on as a group. I may not be a good business woman, but I know that you can only split a pie in so many ways, so I use common sense to run my business affairs and rely on Steve's help to keep the group going. I know God gave him to me to see me through this period of my life and I am so grateful.

Reminiscing about how she had the courage to make this decision and go on, she contrasted her situation with that of her mother:

LFW: I was in a different situation than my mother. I think Mother didn't have the confidence that she could make it on her own. That doesn't take away from her at all; it was just different. I was already established in the gospel ministry. I knew that if I had any credibility at all, I could still go on with that. That was what I was counting on, subconsciously. Mother had nothing to bank on. She could not stand to be alone. I never thought I could stand to be alone, but I soon found out that I could and that I could even enjoy it. I was proud of myself that I was making it on my own. I didn't gloat over it. I was just glad that I could say, 'Hey, I can do this.' It takes a certain confidence in yourself to be able to do anything that's worth while. I think we all felt better about ourselves as we accomplished more. I felt good that I could go on on my own, if I had to. I didn't want to, but I knew I could, with God's help.

Lily Fern believes she is still following God's will, or she would not continue. Losing Earl just brought her to another stage in her life and her career. She says the added responsibility for the group has been good for her, in that it has broadened her mind and let her know what she could accomplish as an individual.

She had to be strong for others, as well. She tells of the first Christmas after Earl's death, when she spent the night with their six-year-old granddaughter, Megan. As they snuggled under the covers, Lily Fern thought Megan was asleep, but she heard a small voice ask, "Will you promise me something?" Lily Fern answered, "Well, I'd have to know what it is before I can promise." After a brief silence, Megan asked, "Is my Capaw happy in Heaven?" Lily Fern set Megan's mind at ease when she whispered, "Yes, I can promise that!"

Earl's death was a great loss for his siblings, as well. His sister, Bette Jo, expressed gratitude for what her big brother meant to her, and stated what many others probably could have said about his contribution to them:

> BJW: The thing Earl taught me the most is the value of our Christian life, and that we live what we sing. He always said that if we couldn't do that, we weren't worthy of singing gospel music. He was an example to me, and when he passed away, I felt my only friend was gone. But I can rejoice to know he is in a much better place, and I have the memories of the sweetest, kindest brother in the world. He passed away on Wednesday, June 26th, ironically, in the same vicinity where he started singing over fifty years earlier.

Earl didn't make it to the National Quartet Convention. That would have completed his reconciliation with Southern Gospel, but he died a loved and respected member of the Southern Gospel family. Lily Fern and Earl were a dynamic team, recognized by fellow singers for their talent, accomplishments and faithfulness to their ideals.

Charlie Waller, the extraordinary showman and promoter responsible for one of the premier events of the year, the Grand Ole Gospel Reunion in South Carolina, quoted Earl and commented about The Weatherfords during the August 8, 1992 program:

> CW: Last year's Grand Ole Gospel Reunion, according to Earl, was the highlight of his career. 'We don't have any sad stories to share with

One of God's Singers Goes Home

you. We're just singing victory in Jesus. Want no sympathy. The Lord's been good. Good to be with you. It's a great honor--the greatest thrill of my life.' The Weatherfords quartet was an institution to gospel music. Their full, rich blend of harmonies made their sound unmistakable.

When recalling the people who helped her after Earl's death, in addition to family, Lily Fern gives credit to her friends and to Southern Gospel colleagues, such as J.D. Sumner, Glen Payne, George Younce, Bill and Gloria Gaither and others. Some churches and The Gospel Music Trust Fund were supportive, as well. She is appreciative that a certain part of the profit from the Gaither videos goes to that trust.

She is grateful, as well, for the love shown to her by her audiences. Following Earl's death, she was embraced by both long-time fans and by the new fans created by the resurgence of Southern Gospel popularity, for which she credits both Bill Gaither and Charlie Waller.

An example of the love of audience members is the gift she received from young Damian Derrick, who has Down's Syndrome. A smile and hug from Damian will brighten anyone's day, but his concern for her heartbreak at the loss of Earl particularly touched her. His ministry is sending a prayer package to someone he feels has suffered a loss. Damian gave her a tiny gift-wrapped package with the following note:

I want to send you
Some of my love today
But I didn't know
How I could
When we're so far away.
So I wrapped my love
In this little box
And sent it on its way.
If you ever feel lonely
Or ever feel blue
Just take this little box
And hold it close to you.
Don't ever unwrap it
Please keep it tied up, too.
And remember it's full
Full, full of love
From me to you.

Damian's mother says the box contains a prayer by Damian wishing her peace, joy and love. Lily Fern has not opened the box, and she treasures it. His sweet ministry of love reminds her of why she sings and it helped to comfort her.

With Earl's death, another phase in Lily Fern's life ended, and brought her to being a woman of the 90's, secure in her own abilities, but supported by the love and assistance of her family and friends and the respect of her peers. Her daughter, Susan, has assumed duties in promoting the group through newsletters, price lists, scheduling and Internet information distribution.

Lily Fern had been so busy living her life that she had some surprises coming in terms of how people would respond to her as "Lily Fern," after all those years of being half of "Earl and Lily Fern."

Lily Fern and tenor Larry Ford

Chapter Eleven

A Life Examined

A conversation with Lily Fern can range from the sublime to the ridiculous. While her focus is on serving Christ and helping her fellow man, and her public image is of dignity and grace, she can tell a joke, pull a prank or appreciate a silly situation with the best of us. She handles the vagabond life of the gospel singer with grace and courage. The losses in her life become gains in her spiritual journey. All of these factors add up to form the personality of this very down-to-earth messenger of Heaven.

Lily Fern's philosophy has been that you must try to build on your failures and disappointments in life in order to make things better, and then they won't be failures. Throughout her life, she has done that by using the special elements in her personality, such as her work ethic, a love of gospel singing, her adaptability, a loving and giving nature, her ever-available sense of humor, her capacity for friendship, devotion to family, a remarkably modern attitude and youthfulness, as well as a sincere commitment to God.

In preparing this book, there has been over a year of interviews and research. Many of the stories and remarks gleaned from these meetings and observations bring out who she really is. This chapter attempts to highlight her personality and philosophy, but perhaps her main characteristic is that whatever she does, she does "with all her heart."

After losing Earl, Lily Fern threw herself into her work. She and Steve continue to travel. For example, they have attended the tapings of the phenomenally successful Gaither videos. Lily Fern has been featured on several of them, coming into her own as a gospel pioneer. They continue to perform at the Grand Ole Gospel Reunion in South Carolina and at the national quartet conventions in both Kentucky and California.

Personnel continues to change, as it does in many gospel groups. The stable element remains. Lily Fern and Steve carry on just as they did when Earl was alive. They have a comfortable working relationship, even after working and living together for all these years. Sometimes Steve's wife, Standalee, travels with them, but usually she is busy working back in Oklahoma while they are on the road. Standalee is very supportive of Steve and Lily Fern.

Whenever possible, and especially in Florida or at the Grand Ole Gospel Reunion, they add Roy Pauley to their group. As one of the best bass singers available, he adds a lot to the "Florida Weatherfords." He and his wife, Amy, provide a home away from home for The Weatherfords during their Florida tours. Steve explains to audiences that The Weatherfords feel a particular burden to minister to Florida during the winter months.

A favorite activity while visiting Florida is a trip to Disney World with friends and family. Lily Fern has become so well known that even a large public place like Disney World does not provide anonymity. Sometimes this constant recognition interferes with the small pleasures of life, as she describes in this story:

LFW: Steve and Standalee wanted to go to an exhibit, but I had seen it and was a little tired. I told them to go on and I would just wait for them on a nearby bench. It was very warm, of course, so I decided to treat myself to an ice cream bar. I sat on the bench and prepared to enjoy my ice cream in peace. I had just started when I saw two older couples stop abruptly in front of my bench. One lady pointed toward my bench and said, 'Look! Look what I see!' I turned and looked over both shoulders to see what she saw. I thought, 'What is back there?' I couldn't see anything, so I turned back toward them. The lady continued, 'I see Lily Fern Weatherford sitting on a bench. And she is eating an ice cream bar!' They just went on and on and one man started about how great the Gaither videos were, and how much he enjoyed my singing. He said, 'To think, I'm seeing Lily Fern Weatherford!'

I was stunned by their reaction. I felt guilty because at first I had rather resented that my private moment was being disturbed. As I talked to them, I said goodbye to my rapidly melting ice cream bar! They were very nice people and I felt terrible for having that initial reaction, so I talked to them and hugged them and they went on their way with smiles. I can always get another ice cream bar, but I can't always make someone feel better!

She still does not understand her "star" status with many fans.

She takes things at face value until she has reason not to do so. When she begins to feel that someone is "not what he or she should be," she becomes quiet and observes. This does not mean that she just lets things slide. When she has an important problem with someone, she prefers to confront it directly.

There is a lot of give and take between her and her fans and friends--literally. An example of this would involve her various collections and her eye for clothing and jewelry, scarcely reminiscent of her strict up-bringing.

Over the years, she has collected pigs, china tea cups, owls, watches and, most recently, jewelry depicting lilies. When people become aware of these collections, they tend to send her gifts relating to one or the other of them. She actually has to be careful mentioning that she likes something.

Earlier this year she sang at a church in Oklahoma, where she visited with her dear friend, Brenda Nash. As they chatted, they noticed a "classy lady" wearing a lovely black and white outfit with black and white polka dot shoes. When Lily Fern spoke to the lady at her sales booth later, she said, "I love those shoes!" They joked about them and the lady made her try them on. When Lily Fern went back to the bus to change clothes, Brenda arrived carrying the black and white polka dot shoes. The lady had gone to her car, changed shoes and sent them to Lily Fern, who was both embarrassed and touched.

On the other hand, when Lee and Kay Campbell attended a Weatherford concert not long after that, Kay spoke with Lily Fern at the sales booth. "I noticed Lily studying the pin I was wearing. Suddenly she said, 'I have some earrings that would match that pin perfectly. If I can locate them, I'll send them to you.' A couple of days later, a package arrived for Kay. Sure enough, it was the earrings, and they matched perfectly. Kay said, "My husband couldn't get over the fact that Lily had such a keen eye. Neither of us could believe that she actually took time out of her busy schedule to find those earrings and send them. I will treasure those earrings the rest of my life!"

Lily Fern's fans and friends recognize that she is a giving, loving person and they respond in kind. She is welcome in homes throughout the country.

When she gets a break from life on the road with all its "people contact," Lily Fern is very happy at home. She loves her home and she enjoys "letting her hair down," which she can't do much on the road. For example, in Paoli, she rarely wears make-up. She says she hates putting on make-up and that she usually doesn't have "a drop of make-up" on at home. She loves to wear casual clothes, instead of having to "dress up."

She doesn't have enough time at home. While she likes people and is usually happy to deal with them, she admits a very common feeling: "When I'm tired, or if I'm sort of melancholy or something, I feel like I need to be alone." She loves what privacy she has left. When she is on the road, about the only time she has to herself is when she can slip out and go to a mall and wander around.

In her limited free time, she likes to crochet, read and play computer games. She enjoys movies, especially westerns, mysteries and romances. Generally, she doesn't care much for action or science fiction movies, because they are too "far out" or violent.

She has a wonderful group of friends, who love to spend time with her. On the road, she is with the members of the group for weeks at a time. She sees Susan, Tim and Megan as often as possible. Since a fire damaged their home, Steve and Standalee have been staying with Lily Fern. She sees her brother and sister and their families whenever she can.

In addition to all these personal contacts, she is part of a community that few outsiders would understand. Gospel performers are like a family in themselves. Because they are on the road, singing and performing all over the United States, often in combined programs, they see each other frequently throughout the year in some of the most unlikely places. The banter, support and general camaraderie among these people is a self-contained world. Standing jokes, sharing of news, expressions of concern for problems, impromptu jam sessions, all of the elements of a tight-knit group, perhaps better described as a "sub-culture," are present. Like any "family," there are little disagreements and cliques and special moments. The unifying force seems to be the intense love of music and serving God. They are human beings, with their little differences and peculiarities, but they are, as a group, genuine and loving people. They share a history and a goal.

After a Gaither taping, for which most of the people had stayed in the same motel, the coffee shop at breakfast time was occupied almost exclusively by gospel singers. The Statesmen, The Blackwoods, The Weatherfords and others shared humorous memories, reviewed the taping, commented on particularly interesting developments in the field, teased, joked, and consoled. Lily Fern's intention when going for breakfast was to work on this book. That couldn't happen with the number of people who came to the table to chat with her. She is at home in this setting, however, and is able to put her needs on the back burner for a while. She loves people in general, but she displays a special love and professional attitude with these old friends.

She is a good sport and participates actively in the teasing and joking, but she can also find time to encourage or compliment or just listen. For example, in a discussion with The Statesmen, after most of the others had left, she took time to commend Doug Young on his beautiful bass singing and to describe why she thought he was singing the way he should. In a quiet conversation with versatile Statesmen baritone, Michael Lo Prinzi, (who has since moved to the Blackwood Brothers) they discussed family situations and singing styles. She joked with tenor Wallace Nelms and lead Jack Toney, and they all listened with concern to a health report from the group's pianist-leader, Hovie Lister. There seems to be a wonderful "belonging" that these performers feel when they are together, and Lily Fern seems completely at home. The mutual respect among these seasoned road warriors for God is visible.

It is interesting to note that, in their youth, Bill and Danny Gaither were almost "Weatherfords:"

LFW: We thought we had them hired. We met and talked with them and they said they wanted to come. When Bill went home and told his dad, his dad said, 'Well, I don't think so. I think you're going to school.' I must add that God and Bill's father didn't make a mistake!

One thing that sustains the relationships among performers is their remarkable tolerance for practical jokes. In earlier chapters, Lily Fern's status as a "good sport" was established.

To understand the "coast to coast" pranks, one needs only to know Phil Enloe of The Couriers. As Lily Fern put it, "He is crazy anyway!" When The Weatherfords were in concert with The Cathedrals in California, a group known as Chosen Vision came to hear them sing. The members of Chosen Vision were dear friends of The Couriers. The Couriers are long-time friends of The Weatherfords, dating back to their days in Pennsylvania, which is Courier home turf. Chosen Vision is composed of Hugo Shirley, his wife, Esther and Carole Kossler. The ladies gave a love gift to The Weatherfords, and Lily Fern sent them a thank you note. Hugo was so impressed that he FAXed the note to Phil Enloe. Phil felt that he just couldn't pass up this opportunity. He FAXed a pseudo reply, supposedly from Lily Fern. The letterhead was "The Whetherferds--with Lily Fernando." The letter speaks for itself, if it is read carefully, with an understanding of Enloe's bizarre sense of humor:

With All My Heart

Feb. 15, 1997

Dear Chosen Mission,

Just a note to say how good it felt to have you all kiss up to me and my cling-on group as I was starring with The Catheters last week. Hugo, you were so sweet as you followed me around like a pitiful mongrel dog looking for a hand-out. I know it has become quite obvious that I have reached a lofty level in my career and everyone wants to be near me. Well, I must say not everyone is as persistent as you, darling. However, I must kindly say that you should realize that I must share myself with others when I am in the public. I know you suggested that we spend some time together alone, (talking music, right!) but, I need to kindly put you in your place. Yes, I am widowed, but I have no longer need for any romantic encounters; I have my public, and when they fall at my feet, it turns me on! You also mentioned that you would like to leave the, (how did you say it?) yokel group you are in and head for greener pastures. Well, Mr. Cherly, The Whetherferds will not be a wrung on your ladder to lift you to the heights that I soar in. You can keep your sweet smile, caressing hand shake, cheap chocolates and affair proposal. I have a career to think about for the moment. Next week, perhaps, but not today.

Tell your sweet wife and other lady friend that all of this goes for them, too. I don't know how to say this any kinder, but the next time you see me, unless you have a large cash offering or a second hand compliment to quickly convey, just keep on walking by. O.K.? O.K.!

Love and Kisses,

LILY FERNANDO

Like the good sport she is, Lily Fern laughed at the phony letter and showed it to friends. Then, at the next Grand Ole Gospel Reunion, Phil, Lily Fern and Hugo happened to meet. The subject of the letter came up as they chatted. Hugo explained that he got home late one night and didn't have much light on as he read the FAX, supposedly from Lily Fern. "I felt sick at my stomach. I really believed it was from Lily Fern, until I looked at it again and saw the phone number. Then I knew who came up with this!" They shared a laugh and a group hug.

When discussing her appreciation for a sense of humor, she revealed its value to her personally:

> LFW: I would probably have been in shackles if I hadn't had a sense of humor. You've got to have one. You have to be able to take it as well as dish it out. I think I've been able to do that. Usually, you can see humor in everything, if you really look for it. I know God has a sense of humor--he created me!

Another proof of her ability to laugh at herself is her participation in Charlie Waller's creation, a group called "The Strangemen:"

> LFW: One night we went out to eat with Charlie Waller. He described something he would like to do at the Grand Ole Gospel. He said, 'I would like to put together what I would call a good group. My idea of the cream of the crop. If I could pick my group, it would be you singing tenor, Jack Toney singing lead, Richard Coltrane singing baritone, Billy Todd singing bass and, probably, Buddy Burton playing the piano.' Now, Charlie doesn't brag on people a lot, and I know his preference is male quartets, so I was surprised. He said, 'In fact, I might do that. Would you do it?' I said, 'Sure.' He said, 'Would you disguise yourself as a man?' I said, 'Sure.' He said, 'I'm going to put together this group, and I'm going to have you disguised as a man and Buddy Burton disguised as a woman.' He really meant to have the other guys disguised, but they didn't want to do that. But Buddy and I didn't care. Buddy Burton's a crazy guy. Charlie decided to call the group 'The Strangemen.' So, that's how The Strangemen were born. I think most of us are trying to 'unborn' it, but Charlie doesn't want it 'unborn' and Charlie usually gets what he wants!

Audiences at the Grand Ole Gospel have trouble identifying the dignified Lily Fern Weatherford as the short, weird man with the pin stripe suit and slicked down toupee.

She is always up for the most subtle or the most slapstick humor. Also at the Grand Ole Gospel Reunion, she took part in Charlie Waller's "Let's Make a Deal," where audience members select performers to play the game for them. Lily ended up dangling a whipped cream covered doughnut from a pole, while David Reece tried to eat the doughnut without using his hands.

Her good nature and sense of humor have limits, as with any human being. Former Weatherford bass, Fulton Nash and his wife, Brenda, tell a story that Lily Fern did not find the least bit funny at the time it happened. Brenda reminded Fulton of the situation:

> BN: Remember when she had one of those migraines? It was on the bus. She was so sick she couldn't even talk clearly, so she was motioning to Earl to get a washcloth to wash her face, but she couldn't reach one and Earl didn't understand, so he called for you, because he couldn't make out what she was saying.
>
> FN: Yes. Well, we came in and we got a damp rag and tried to put it on her face, and she kept jerking her head around. She didn't want that on her face, and we didn't know why. We found out later. It was because she'd just cleaned the bus toilet with it, and we were trying to smear it all over her face. I think maybe her mouth needed cleaning out after that incident! She didn't laugh about it at that time, but she laughs about it now. Her headache was really bad.

As much as she is at ease with her family, friends, peers, and fans, she has had to come to grips with the need for privacy and the need to determine her own self-image and self esteem:

> LFW: When I'm in the public and on the platform, I try to sing and perform with dignity. But, when I get on the bus, then I fall apart. I don't mean I go to pieces, but then I can say, 'Oh, it's over and I can relax.' And I don't mean that I don't love that life--it's just that you've got to have a break. I really love my privacy. I'm not a loner, but I like to be alone.
>
> I like me now. There was a time when I was younger that I didn't like me. I felt inferior to people. I was very timid as a child, bashful, stuttering and couldn't talk to anybody. When I first started singing with Earl, he told me, 'You have a beautiful voice. You can sing.' And he began to build my confidence. And then probably people built my confidence. I think it was just developed over the years.
>
> But I don't want that to go so far that I think that I'm better than anybody else, because I certainly don't think I am. But at least I can hold my own.

Regarding influences on her singing, she points out that she didn't know anything about gospel singing when she first started. There was no such thing as "Southern Gospel." There was just church music and convention singing. A major influence was Bob Jones.

LFW: One of the finest singers I've ever heard is Bob Jones on the West Coast. He's eighty-two now and is still singing. I loved to hear him sing when he was a young man, and he's still got a phenomenal voice. He sings with his son's group now.

Lily Fern reels off names of some of her own personal favorites. About Glen Payne she says, "I've never heard him hit a bad note. He has great musical talent." Jake Hess is special to her because "he reaches the hearts of people. He sings in a way that isn't even orthodox. He's a stylist." Debra Talley "is probably my all-time favorite singer--secular or gospel. She has rich, full, beautiful tones." Another is Jeanne Johnson. "Jeanne is a *fine* singer."

As a girl, growing up in the forties, she was influenced by popular singers such as Jo Stafford, Patti Page, Rosemary Clooney, Doris Day, Dinah Shore and Lena Horne, all singing on the radio. She tried to copy their "smooth tones, those trills and slides."

She has many favorite song writers, including Mosie Lister, Audrey Meier and Henry Slaughter. She loves them because their songs reach people's hearts.

She is particularly critical of herself as a singer:

LFW: I could be getting better as far as projecting, if I had more control of my breathing. I need to do more vocalization. I need to raise my range a little bit. The better breath control you have, the longer you can hold a tone, and the prettier you can make those sustaining tones.

I think I have sung so long that I have confidence that I can do it. You have to have a certain amount of confidence to perform. When I first started, did I have confidence? No, I did not! Actually, I have never felt that I deserved the compliments that I get. I get calls from people I don't even know, telling me that I am their all time favorite singer, male or female. They say I have a beautiful voice. I can listen to myself sing, and I don't know where it comes from. I really don't. I just open my mouth and sing. I would have to think that it is pretty, or I wouldn't do it. I wouldn't want to sing, if I thought it wasn't good enough to be heard, but to me it's just a God-given talent. Maybe it's a good thing that I can't evaluate it.

Yesterday, I listened to some of my tapes and I thought, 'That was pretty.' But as far as what others say--I don't hear it. My brother said,

'You're the only one who doesn't think you're great.' And I said, 'Well, good. You wouldn't love me if you thought I acted like I thought I was great!' I never put a song on an album that I didn't think I could've done better if I'd had another chance.

I know when I'm singing effectively and getting across to people. There are times when I sing a song and the next time I sing it, I'll change the inflections. I can tell the way I'm singing is reaching more people than the night before. I think it involves your moods, too, and how God is using you at that particular time. If you have any heart at all, you're naturally going to try to get the message across a little better.

Earl and Lily Fern have always stressed smooth harmony and careful diction. Lily Fern explains, "We've always tried to say our words the same. Earl always said, 'Even if it's wrong, I want togetherness!'"

One of the primary elements of Weatherford success is the fact that they don't sing straight harmony. It is more difficult, but they believe that the closer you keep the tenor to the bass, the smoother the harmony will be. They change parts often and share the leads. They may invert the parts several times to keep the tenor from being too far from the bass. Lily Fern says that is the secret of the Weatherford sound.

She lists "In the Garden," "Something Beautiful" and "Because of Yesterday" as some of her favorite Weatherford albums, not only for the songs and the harmony, but because of the type of orchestration used. When asked what made "In the Garden" so special, she responded:

LFW: Probably a lot of things enter into it being called a 'benchmark' album. I've often heard it said that album was ten or fifteen years before its time. We were doing things that nobody else was doing. Just little things, like maybe a touch of modern harmony here and there. We were the first ones who ever did any of that. We would just throw something in now and then that would nearly knock your hat in the creek! A lot of singers would say, 'What did you do there?' And it was the combination of the personnel, I'm quite sure. Henry [Slaughter] was at the right time to expand his writing and ministry and he had written some good songs. He brought us 'What a Precious Friend,' and it looked like a chicken scratched on the paper! He and his wife, Hazel had been through a lot, and he sat down and wrote, 'I've a friend who's always near me,' and I don't sing that song without remembering his testimony. Maybe that's why it has such meaning when we sing it, but it's become a signature song for The Weatherfords.

Anyway, we got it on RCA and RCA promoted it. They said, 'We want an album that all kinds of people will enjoy--the First Baptist as well as the small churches.' And it did. So, I would say it was the time, the personnel, the innovations and the lives that were behind the songs. It was a phenomenal time for The Weatherfords.

As in every group, there were times of conflict and disagreement, but as Fulton Nash remarked, "Lily was right there to give Earl support, even though she didn't always agree." Brenda Nash believes that their focus and dedication kept them going. She said she thought "the covenant they made with the Lord when they dedicated their lives to His service through gospel music was binding upon their hearts, between each other and with the Lord."

Lily Fern recalls how Earl would sometimes test her at concerts by announcing that she would sing a song that he knew was difficult for her, or a series that was difficult, when she was not feeling "up to it." She laughs as she tells how she felt about it. "Earl is up in Heaven now, but I'm not sure I've quite forgiven him for that!"

She confesses that she hasn't always felt prepared to go on stage. Fortunately, someone taught her how to approach that situation:

LFW: There are times when a person just doesn't feel like going on stage. I never had many voice lessons--just a few--but I had a voice teacher who told me something that gets me through, and I try to pass it on to younger singers. Her name was Elizabeth Richert. She told me, 'Pray just before you go on and you'll do fine.' She said to pray, 'All of you, Lord, none of me.'

Much of her focus as a performer is her intention toward the audience:

LFW: You know that you're there to try to move them--to convey a message to them. So every song I sing, even if I sing it every night straight, I still want to get that message across to somebody in that audience. Maybe that is a form of love, or of just giving yourself to that audience.

There are times when I have to be on that I wish I didn't. I don't want to sound like I'm untouchable, because I'm not, but there are times before or after a performance when I'm just pulled from a lot of directions at once. That doesn't bother me at the time, but when I'm going back in to face that, I think, 'Oh, I wish I didn't have to do this today.' But I can turn that around, almost like living a dual personality. It's something that you do and you thrive on, but you sometimes don't feel up to it. You wish you could just go and sit down and enjoy something. And yet, if I didn't have that, I would be worried. 'Why aren't people talking to me?' So, it's a complex thing.

Most of the time, I'm really thrilled to talk to people, and it's not when I'm tired that it bothers me; it's when I have to be somewhere and there's no way to go unless you say, 'I don't have time,' and that's not good, so I just try to be as cordial as I can and still try to make my destination.

Lily Fern always tries to talk to all the people who come up to her after a performance, or at her booth, where the group sells their tapes and CD's. Unfortunately, she is often swamped with so many people that she can't get to all of them. Even then, an observer will see her smile and wave to those she can't talk to at that time. A warm hug and a personal greeting is always available, whether she is working her booth, preparing to go on stage, trying to get back to the bus or even trying to grab a sandwich.

Most people are congenial and pleasant with her, but occasionally, someone will be rude. Lily Fern tries to take it in stride:

LFW: A man came out of a concert once a long time ago, back when we wore big, teased-up hair-dos, and said something rude. I was standing at our booth getting ready to sell records. He didn't say, 'I enjoyed the concert,' or anything--just 'I've chased rabbits out of bushes that looked better than your hair.' And he walked out the door!

Sometimes someone will be so insistent to talk to her, that she can't deal with anyone or anything else. For example:

LFW: At the California Western States Quartet Convention, a man and wife came to the booth three or four times and kept inquiring about someone. I didn't really know the person that well, but he had been to one of our concerts in Florida about four years ago and had called me once about a year before this convention. So I had some information about him, but it was at home. I told them the information was at home and invited them to call me sometime. They kept returning to ask the same thing.

The next day, a group of us decided we were going to go shopping and we went to the mall. There was a big Mother's Day sale and we headed for a shoe department. Everybody scattered, looking for bargains. I walked over to a corner to look at some shoes and, when I looked up, this same man was sitting there. He said, 'Oh, hello! I'm so glad you came. Now, there's my wife over there. You go get her....' All this time he was waving, trying to get her attention. He went on, 'She'll want to hug your neck! She'll want to talk to you.' I didn't go get her, so he asked me to tell him again what I knew about this person. I said, 'No. No, this is *shopping*! This is a different business. When I'm shopping, forget anything else. You come to my booth tonight and I'll tell you whatever I can.' He didn't say any more and he never came back to my booth. I hope I didn't offend him, but I needed to have some time away and I was shopping!

While Lily Fern runs into a lot of funny situations, she also finds that people seek her out as a spiritual guide:

LFW: There must be something about my personality that makes people aware that I have compassion or empathy for their situations-- and I do. Sometimes they start to tell me something and, before they get the first sentence out, I can almost tell you what they're going to say. I don't know if that would be called the 'gift of discernment,' or what it is. There are some that make you think, 'Oh, boy. Another one of these!' But there are others who come and talk to you and you feel immediately that you just want to reach out and hug them--that maybe that will help get them through the day or something. And usually you want to pray with them. The only thing you can do in those situations is pray for them or with them. You want to show them that somebody does care and that the main one who cares is Jesus. And you want to point them that way. That's what I try to do, because I can't handle their problems; I can't fix their situations, but I can sure tell them about the One who can.

I feel like when anybody talks to me, most of the time they would rather that those things would not be told to anybody else. I don't tell those things unless it's something that's general. A lot of the time, there are things that are told to me that should not be told to anybody else. I know that it's not going to go any farther than me and the Lord. They have nothing to fear as far as I'm concerned.

Sometimes I feel that I can tell more about people than they know I can. And I don't think that's psychic, either. I think you must go back to discernment. God gives us common sense, I think. I pray for wisdom and for the right answers for these people. There again, you have to go back to the same old thing. When you ask God for something in all honesty, he's going to do it for you. I think that maybe people sense that in me, too. Because, if I can help somebody, nothing pleases me any better. I have prayed God to keep my life, mold my character and give me wisdom and strength.

Given the life she leads, she needs all the wisdom and strength she can acquire. Life on the road is not easy. Lily Fern she describes that life:

LFW: A typical day on a bus is probably a bus break-down! A typical day begins with leaving a motel. The night before we have agreed we must leave by a certain time, and hopefully we have included time to make a stop here and there. Whether or not we planned right, we end up running late. Anyway, we get something to eat. If it's early, just coffee and a doughnut on the bus; if it's around ten o'clock or so, I'll eat a good breakfast. We drive until maybe two or three in the afternoon, stop and get a half way decent meal--not fast food. I get sick of that. Then we go to the concert location, set up, do the concert, tear down and go to the next motel or truck stop.

Sometimes we just go to a truck stop and spend the night on the bus. A typical night at the truck stop is eating in smoke-filled restaurants, making your phone calls where all the guys are smoking. Once a week, if I don't get to go to a laundromat, I do my laundry at the truck stop. There's always someone in there and invariably these men who have been away from home are lonely and start talking. They'll talk your ear off if you let them. They all ask what I'm doing there. They know there's something a little different from the average woman who would come in there, and they want to know what it is. I tell them that I'm traveling on a bus and that I'm an entertainer in gospel music. The minute that you mention gospel or church, they get very sanctimonious. They snuff out their cigarettes, straighten their shoulders, and they tell about their grandmothers praying for them when they were little boys, and how they went to church and Sunday School and how their wives go to church every week and go to prayer meeting and pray for them. Then, I say to them, 'But do you do those things for yourself?' I've left more laundromats with drivers either crying or hating me, but I've never been insulted or mistreated at a truck stop. I think it is probably the safest place in the world for a woman to be alone, unless she doesn't want to be. We've been to millions of them. I can close my eyes and see 'Flying J's' and '76's' all over the place!

For someone who has spent so much time on the road, it is curious that about the only area of her life where Lily Fern will express a significant lack of confidence is as a driver. When asked if she ever drove the bus, she responded vehemently:

LFW: Noooo! *Never will!* Even if I could, I wouldn't let them know, because I'd have to take a shift! When I drive, I get to thinking. When I was driving and listening to tapes the other day, I found I was driving the way the mood of the music went. I thought, 'Hey, something's got to stop here!' If it was a slow song, I was going about twenty-five miles an hour. If it was a fast one, I was scooting down the highway. I feel I don't have good judgment when driving. Earl always felt better when I was in a bigger car, and I understand what he meant. I may not be quick enough. I've been driving for, oh, probably forty years, I suppose, but I still don't think I'm very capable. My kids don't like for me to drive for them. But I get there and back!

Driving got her in trouble with her granddaughter. When Megan was eight years old, she was coming home with Grandma. A man turned abruptly in front of them and Lily Fern had to slam on the brakes. She exclaimed, "You stupid idiot!" Megan gasped, "Grandma! I thought you were a Christian!" Grandma had to apologize. "I shouldn't have said that, but the man is still an idiot!"

Lily Fern recognizes that her life is somewhat fragmented, which results in some personality differences and some strange perceptions:

LFW: I think I have to be three different personalities. What's made me aware of this is that I have heard people express surprise that I have to work on a stopped up sink, or something. They see me singing on video tape and no other way. My home life is very domesticated. I love to cook, when I have time, and I think I'm a good cook. I'm not a gourmet cook. I'm good at finding different foods that are compatible with each other and making up recipes, where something will taste better with this flavor instead of that. I can taste food and go home and duplicate it to perfection. I've done that. And that's a different life than most people even think I can do. And I love to keep house. I don't like the work of it, but I like it when it's clean and it's been a challenge to me, but it's all clean.

And I think I'm a different personality with family--my children and grandchild. Because, for example, when I'm with Megan, I just want to be with her.

I don't think that's really being three different people. It's just adapting your way to the different things you have in your life. I hope I'm not really three different personalities. At least we don't fight with each other!

Friends and acquaintances find it difficult to believe that Lily Fern has been in the business for over fifty years. Lily Fern says she doesn't really feel her age, either:

LFW: I don't feel like I'm in my late 60's. When I think about it, I think that's unreal. I can't be that old! But there are times when my body seems to be saying, 'You're too old for this; cut it out!' I think it helps that I'm in pretty good health and most of the time I want to keep active. Sometimes I get in the mood that I just don't want to do anything, and I don't. The longer I stay in that frame of mind, the harder it is to get back in the swing of things, so I try not to get that way very often. I think once in a while I owe myself a day or two days or whatever, but I try not to really dwell on that. I have a tendency to really feel sorry for myself, if I would let myself. And that's bad. That's dangerous. So, I just don't. But now, if I really feel real, real bad, I'll just take a day and not do anything. This morning, I could have told myself, 'You're sixty-eight, and you need to stay in bed and listen to the thunder and the rain!'

But she remains active because of her driving goal, to serve God. She says that when she is tired or down, she just thinks of someone who was blessed by her singing, or a particular song, and that makes it absolutely worthwhile. She remembers several such incidents, such as the time when she had to get to the platform for a performance before over 20,000 people, and a man came and asked to talk to her. She knew she needed to go, but when she heard his story, she chastised herself for being in a hurry. He said he never went to church and was not interested in religion. His older brother was dying, so the man went to be with him. They watched the Gaither video, "Turn Your Radio On," and Lily Fern sang "Eastern Gate." The man said it just broke his heart. He went to church and was saved.

Lily Fern said that if in the fifty-four years of her ministry she never accomplished more than that, it would all be worth it. She told this story to her friend Pam, who works at the City Hall in Paoli. Pam said something Lily Fern will never forget: "When we leave this world and go to eternity, the only thing worthwhile we can take with us is another soul."

As she works toward that goal, she believes she is in the "perfect will" of God. "If I didn't, I would be actively seeking it, because I believe people can be in the perfect will if they are sincerely seeking it."

In terms of private time, she has found no need to establish ground rules with the group as she travels:

LFW: We don't really have any ground rules. I think it is just generally known amongst us that we are our own persons. We might go all day on the bus and hardly talk to each other. I don't think anything about that, and I'm sure they don't either. I personally thrive on my privacy at times. I can be sitting in the front of the bus, and they won't bother me. Sometimes they do, of course, and I'm sure I do them, too, but most of the time we are on our own.

It's the same with Steve and Standalee, when they had to move in with me for a while. I just go my way and they go theirs. You have to get a mind set when you live so close with people. What they do is none of my business, and what I do is none of their business. We understand that. About the only rules deal with financial matters.

Confrontations and temper flare-ups have been comparatively few.

For the most part, Lily Fern has accumulated friends all over the country. On only a few occasions has the old Goble temper flared.

She tells of a time when she confronted a preacher. They sang at a camp meeting and after the first day had been signed for a second, until Earl got a phone call that they didn't need them after all. When Earl asked why, the preacher said that Lily Fern sang on the stage with no hose and no toes or back in her shoes. Actually, she was wearing a fairly new product, seamless hose. She got so angry that she went and showed the preacher the hose and told him that he should have been looking somewhere other than at her legs anyway! Earl said she cost them a booking by confronting the preacher. Lily's response? "Oh, well!"

Incidents such as this are rare. Lily Fern values the friends and acquaintances she has throughout the country. She says:

> LFW: Next to salvation, friendship is one of the greatest gifts that God has ever given a man or woman. If I thought any of my actions would offend anybody or cause me to lose a friend, it would break my heart. I couldn't take that.

Lily Fern has simple criteria for the people she would choose as friends and for the kind of person who makes her uncomfortable:

> LFW: I would tend to choose as a friend somebody with a good sense of humor and basically the same beliefs I have. I wouldn't be comfortable with someone who drank a lot or was a wild-living person. I like anyone who has loving kindness and is broad-minded when they look at somebody with a fault in his or her life. I can't stand self-righteous people. They think they are 'holier than thou,' or God's chosen. Or a man who thinks he's God's gift to women. I'd be the first one to say, 'What woman would want you as a gift?'
>
> A person in the singing field who can really inhibit me is one who, any time you make a remark, has to correct that or change it. We have some of those in the singing field. I don't like that kind of attitude. A few times I have stopped them in their tracks, to the point that now I don't feel so inhibited. Most of the time, I only feel uncomfortable around people because of the way they act toward me.

Lily Fern is happy that most of those close to her have become Christians. That is a significant concern to her, although she is not one to "preach at" anyone. She tries to live by example and does not judge people.

She had been concerned about Florence, but as she reports:

> LFW: My sister got saved several years ago and, of course, my brother and his family are Christians, and my children are Christians. We're not going to give up praying for the others.

She didn't get to know her father's brothers and sisters very well until later in life, but she has come to know some members of "her generation" of his family--nephews, nieces, cousins--and is very impressed with them: "All of them that I have met have been fine Christian people."

For Lily Fern, about the only unfinished business relating to her family regards the adoption of her children.

> LFW: When we got Susan, we could ask anything we wanted about her past. The only thing I really wanted to know was that her parents were healthy. That was the only thing I was really interested in with all three children. Susan's mother came from a very wealthy family, but she had never been married, and when she got pregnant with Susan, her parents threatened to disown her if anybody found out. When Steve came along, his mother just could not sign the final papers for him. She tried three or four times, and just couldn't give him up. She was forced to, finally, because she had no way to take care of him. She was under very poor circumstances. She was quite a bit younger than Susan's mother had been. Both mothers knew that their children would be better off in a home with a father and a mother, so they signed the papers.
>
> I made so plain to Susan and Steve, over and over again, that their biological mothers loved them very, very much. I don't want them to think ill of them or think that they were not wanted, or that they were of bad blood, because that is not the case. As a matter of fact, I think those mothers are heroic for having enough love to give their children a chance at a better life.
>
> I've discussed this with both Susan and Steve many times. Susan says she never thinks about it. She has never shown any interest in her background or anything, but Steve's a little different. He's a bit more inquisitive and he's often said he wondered if he had brothers and sisters and if they had double-jointed thumbs like he has! He always has said that the most important concern is, 'I just wonder if my mother's a Christian, or if her children are Christians, or what kind of background they have.'
>
> I told both of them early on in life, and I still tell them that if there is ever a time that they want to find out, that I will do everything within my power to help them to find them. But, I've always warned them to be very, very careful, because we don't know those mothers--what they have told the families they have now, and we would not want to do anything to hurt those people and we would have to be very careful in any kind of an investigation that they would have to be protected as well as I was protected when I got Susan and Steve. Neither of the children has done anything about that, but I would go through that with them.
>
> I've always felt that my children love me very dearly, and Steve said to

someone, just the other day, 'She's the only mother I ever knew. There's not a thing that can keep me from loving her. I love her more every day.'

Lily Fern believes that if you are not secure in a child's love by the time they are grown, you never will be. She feels secure in that love:

LFW: Personally, I felt secure from the moment I got them. That just was never a worry to me and it wouldn't be now, even if they decided they wanted to look up their biological parents. If it would help Susan and Steven to feel better about their lives, I would help them, and I would not be afraid that they would love me any less. As a matter of fact, I think they would probably love me more, if I would help them in every way that I could.

She has the warmest feelings for those two mothers:

LFW: Every birthday, Christmas or special holiday that goes by, I think of those two brave women, who unselfishly gave their children up so those children could have a better life. I pray for them continually, that they will know the happiness that I have known. Because of *them*, I am a mother.

Lily Fern's life now consists of her children, her home, her friends and her work. She is a modern, vibrant woman, facing life on the road in the same way she always has. As many of her friends and co-workers have stated, she is a "trooper." A good part of her coping mechanism is a sense of humor. She is still the first one to laugh at herself.

For example, not long ago the group was scheduled for a Sunday evening concert, so Lily Fern did what she has done for years, when possible. They were to sing at six p.m., so she rested all afternoon and then got up to dress. She put on her shoes, the same ones she had worn in the morning performance, and they felt terrible. She thought, "My feet couldn't be so swollen. I've been lying down all afternoon!" She took the shoes off and examined them. They looked alright, so she put them on again and they still felt strange. She stood and looked in the full length mirror and thought, "What on earth?" They looked weird. Then she realized that she had them on the wrong feet. She just stood there alone and laughed at herself.

Her friend, Brenda Nash, tells of another situation:

BN: Lily's sense of humor and ability to laugh at herself act as a buffer to the stresses of a strenuous life style. One time when they were at our house, staying between some engagements, they had parked the bus in our driveway. Lily was getting ready to take her shower and she went out to the bus to get some clean underclothes. Our next door neighbor, Gene, was leaving on his way to work and, having been at the concert the night before, noticed Lily and waved at her. She had her clean underwear in her hand and, without thinking, she just waved it at him. She came in the house laughing at herself because she waved her underwear at our neighbor.

Lily Fern laughs at herself about another situation. She went grocery shopping in nearby Pauls Valley and parked right in front of the grocery store. She got her groceries and told the boy to put them in the gold Chrysler. He met her as she came out and said, "Ma'am, there's no gold Chrysler out there." Lily Fern said, "There is, too! I have a gold Chrysler." They went out into the lot and sure enough, there was no gold Chrysler. She went to where she had parked and leaned against a car to think about it. There were probably not ten cars in the acre lot, but no gold Chrysler. She said, "I have a gold Chrysler and I parked right here." Actually, she was right on both statements. She did have a gold Chrysler and she did park right there, but on this particular day, she had borrowed Steve's car, which she was leaning on. She told the grocery boy, "Never mind. Just put them in this car." She still sees the young man and he asks her if she has lost her car lately.

Traveling with her group, she takes a lot of teasing. One joke involves food. Lily Fern hates fast food. Most of the group members over the years like it. She always says she needs to have a halfway decent meal at least once a day. Steve and Kenny Payne, one of her more recent group members, had a standing joke. Whenever it was time to stop to eat, "the boys," as she sometimes called them, would break into a recitation: "She has to have a *halfway decent meal!*"

Perhaps the most interesting facet of Lily Fern's personality is her simple, solid philosophy of life and religion. The following statement probably sums up the essence of her goals and religious philosophy:

LFW: I want to help people--to let them see how to keep going, even with hardship. God has worked it all out. With God in control, there is no fear. It pays to serve the Lord. We have to have faith and trust. I believe that if an individual gives his or her life to Christ, God sheds the light on the path. God is committed to taking care of you, no matter what you are going through. The *Bible* says praise Him in all things, not just the good things.

She expands on this philosophy with an example:

LFW: God knows what's in your future. When you try everything you can do, then you should give up on it and turn it over to the Lord and move to something else. He always has something else for us to do. Sometimes there's something that you really want to get done, and you just cannot get it done. For example, I have sat down many, many times, trying to book a tour, and nothing would flow right on that tour, nothing! I could not get the dates I needed. I'd have a time on the schedule and a slot that I'd just have days open and I'd have to maybe change the whole schedule. If I'd just forget that and go on to something else and then go back, when those dates were impossible, there was always a reason for it. Either the bus was going to break down or something. I know that has happened two or three times. I couldn't figure out why in the world I couldn't book a date, why I could not get that schedule going. And, just before the time that we were supposed to have left, the bus would break down, and we would have been on the road, broken down. But, as it was, we were home where we could get the bus repaired. Either that, or somebody was very ill and we would have had to cancel dates anyway.

She was raised in a strict but loving home. She believes that "a child raised in a home like I was has no reason not to make Heaven her goal." She says, "They prayed it and preached it."

She takes the *Bible* literally. She speaks of the beauty of Heaven and the streets of gold. She ponders the concept of eternal sunshine and being in the shadow of God's smile:

LFW: He has to be smiling on us always. There will be nothing to frown about. I've often thought, 'What would it be like if God laughed out loud!' I've asked many preachers if we will know each other in Heaven, and the *Bible* says we will know as we are known, so I think we will know each other. There will be love, but everyone will be loved the same.

Paul said, 'I die daily.' I believe I have to give my life to Christ daily. There'd be so many wonderful things in Heaven--like no bus to ride, no bus break-downs, no suitcases to pack, no keys to lose--but the most wonderful thing would be God's smile.

Her concept of sin is perhaps more modern than her strict up-bringing would indicate. She believes that excess, harming the body and harming others are all sins, just like the "major" sins, and that all sins can be forgiven. She remembers, also, that God "hates the backbiter, the gossiper." She adds that a good definition of a gossiper is one "who spreads gossip like it was gospel." In other words, her concept of sin is not as strict as that with which she grew up.

She explains her idea of God's grace:

LFW: I'm not certain I know how to define God's grace, without giving an illustration. When Earl died, I could have almost lost my mind in a few moments there, and I thought, 'There's no way. What am I going to do?' Immediately, I felt God's peace come over me. And the words came to me, 'His grace is sufficient,' and it's almost like He died on the cross for our sins, but He also died that we might live through these problems that we have. I don't know if that's how to define God's grace or not, but He is there to help us carry those loads, whether we deserve it or not. We're not always going to be free of carrying burdens, but He is there to help us carry them.

Whether from her religious background or a simple sense of social justice, Lily Fern believes in strict accountability for actions. While she doesn't usually judge her fellow human beings, she believes in the strictest possible punishment for crimes such as child molestation or violence such as the Oklahoma City bombing. She is open-minded about cases where people harm only themselves, but wishes that they would change the harmful behavior.

Discussing current events and politics, she admits she no longer has any political leanings because of political corruption. In terms of candidates for office, she says, "I just grab for one and hope for the best." She adds that "Jesus Christ is all I can turn to in this world."

She is disappointed at evangelists and ministers whose worldly behavior exploits preaching the gospel. She says it makes it more difficult "for the rest of us, who are trying to walk the way. It hurts all of us."

The greatest blessing she has experienced lately is the atmosphere at the Gaither tapings:

LFW: It's easy to be fed spiritually at a Gaither taping. It may be the closed atmosphere, but when I go to those, I know I'm going to be spiritually blessed. We have joked that Bill Gaither is the only one we know of that could get that many gospel singers together in one room for three days without some killing each other!

Lily Fern is a very loving person. When asked how she deals with totally exasperating or mean-spirited people, she responded that she just asks God to love them until she can. "I have to love them, I know, but I don't have to love their ways." She distinguishes between the love of mankind in general and the deep love of her family, which she describes as providing a "wonderful, wonderful feeling of security."

Lily Fern has a security deeper than that of the knowledge of the love of her family and friends. It is obvious that she is secure in the love of her God and the sure promise of an eternity, reunited with Earl and those she has lost in this life. That is visible in her face when she sings "The Eastern Gate" on the Gaither video tapes. Her solid faith is reflected in her singing, her choice of songs, and her life in general. The sadness, faith and joy combined in the opening line, "I will meet you in the morning" brings a promise to all who listen.

She has no intention of retiring as long as she can raise her voice in the hope of bringing her message to the people who seek her out, whether to listen to her sing or to ask for her prayers. She is happy and content with her life. In a *Singing News* column written almost a year after Earl's death, Lily Fern concluded by saying, "When God puts a message in your heart, you have to tell it. When He puts a song on your lips, you have to sing it!"

Through the combined blessings of a sense of humor, a kind and loving nature, and a strong faith in God, Lily Fern has found peace after losing Earl. She pulled herself together and began a new stage in her career. Time will tell just how successful it is, but, if the comments of her family, friends and peers are any indication, Lily Fern Weatherford is already a success.

Chapter Twelve

A Living Legacy

Note: All of the materials about Lily Fern and The Weatherfords quoted in this chapter were directed to me, including letters, interviews and electronically recorded statements. While I was not able to reach all of the important people in Lily Fern's life during my research, I believe this collection includes a representative sample of the memories, reactions and feelings of family, friends, colleagues and peers. My sincere apologies to those I was unable to reach in the time available.

I have used alphabetical order for the simple reason that categorization is impossible, since, in the case of Lily Fern Weatherford, friends and colleagues become family, family members are friends and colleagues. Letters and comments have been edited due to space limitations.

Gail Shadwell

CLOID BAKER:

I talked to my father and mother, Ray and Alice <u>Fern</u> Baker to confirm what I remember as a 6 year old kid, in 1953, going to a Weatherford concert with my folks. About that time, my dad had been listening to WOWO, a Ft. Wayne, Indiana radio station, when Jay Gould announced that a special group, the Earl Weatherford Quartet, would be singing live on the station. If people liked their singing, they were asked to call the station and let Bob Sievers, the announcer, or Guy Harris, the station manager, know. Well, a lot of people did like the Weatherfords, so they called in and Dad tells me that they sang live every morning for about two years. While they were singing live on WOWO each morning, they also would schedule concerts at night in churches. It was one of these concerts, in Huntington, Indiana, that I remember at the age of 6. One of my memories is that of the big, black or blue Buick with a single wheeled trailer

With All My Heart

on the back to carry their sound equipment and 78 records in. I remember two "mikes," two large speakers and a very pretty young lady named Lily Fern. I did not know then how much a part of my life the Weatherfords would be.

My Dad bought three of those 78 records which my folks just gave me this year. Titles included "Two New Voices," "Swing Down Chariot," "In My Father's House," "How Many Times," "My God Is Real" and "How About Your Heart."

My mother had been very sick and in the hospital.... Dad bought the new Weatherford "In The Garden" album for Mom. My mother would play it over and over until she could go to sleep. The doctors told Mom she might live another 5 to 10 years. She just turned 74 this year in 1997. My mom started listening to Lily Fern sing in 1953 and still listens today, as Lily Fern sings in 1997. Wow, what a career! (By the way--my folks also recently gave me that same "In The Garden" album that was purchased in 1959.)

The Weatherford album that helped train my musical ear the most was that classic "In The Garden." As a young man, I traveled with many good gospel groups but I always compared their sound with the Weatherford sound. I still do today with my own group, Forgiven. The Weatherford influence goes even further. I met my wife, Debbie McQueen, while she was traveling with the Weatherfords and I was traveling with the Bill Gaither Trio, as bass player. We were married in 1972. Later in the 70's, Debbie and I were both able to travel full time with the Weatherfords. This was a dream come true for me.

I appreciate all of the support that Lily has provided to our trio in the years since we traveled with the Weatherfords. We are in the process now of planning a Florida singing tour in early 1998, with The Weatherfords and our trio. This will also be a shared vacation, which we have done several times over the past few years.

What do I think of Lily Fern Weatherford? I think Steve Weatherford says it best when he introduces Lily--"She sings with dignity, class and a style that compares with no other." There is only one Lily Fern Weatherford. Love and hugs to Lily Fern from a Weatherford member for life.

DEBBIE MCQUEEN BAKER:

When I think about Lily Fern Weatherford, there are several words and thoughts that come to my mind. She is a seasoned professional. She is always a lady and I would say that she has a lot of "class." There will never be another with the unique and beautiful voice that is hers alone. She is someone that you can call on when you are enduring problems in your life and you know that she will remember to bring your need before the Lord. She has endured hardships and gone through valleys, but always trusted in the Lord to meet all her needs. She is one of the funniest people to be around that I know and she really can make me laugh. I don't think she will ever really grow old because she is still as active today as the day I met her. She is probably the only "Mom" that I know that my own "Mom" trusted to take me under her wing as an 18 year old, traveling on the road full time. She is a special friend to me and I love her.

We were so excited when we heard about Lily's book being written. We were honored when we were asked to be a part of the book by writing about some memories we have made with Lily and her family. Actually, in the more than 25 years that she has been a part of our lives, we could probably write a book ourselves about all of the laughter, tears, mountains and valleys we have shared.

Although Cloid had heard the Weatherfords on radio when he was a boy..., I never had the pleasure of hearing them until after high school graduation. I was playing piano for a local group from Cincinnati, Ohio and was invited to attend a Weatherford service one evening. I loved the smooth, sweet sound and almost instantly Earl and Lily became special friends to me. It all happened so fast--their piano player had just resigned, they liked my style (or they were desperate), they offered me a job and within 2 weeks, at the ripe old age of 18, I literally met the Weatherfords by the side of the road, on their way through Dayton, Ohio and headed West.

After I was on the road for a little more than a year, we did a series of concerts with the Bill Gaither Trio and Henry and Hazel Slaughter. We worked one date in Wilmington, Delaware and besides meeting Bill and Gloria Gaither, I also met my future husband, Cloid Baker, who was bus driver and bass player for the Gaithers. Life on the road was never quite the same after that.... Earl used to tease me about "Clod Hopper," his nickname for the guy who was about to take me away from my second family. Lily and I were very close and I think we both knew that this was a special man in my life. So, When I told them that I would be leaving and getting married, it was like telling family and there was a happiness, but also a sadness that our times together in the future would be very limited.

We didn't have the chance to spend as much time as we would have liked to with Earl and Lily after my marriage, but we always kept in touch and any time the Weatherfords were singing around Indiana we would be part of the crowd. Any time we went, Earl and Lily would always call us up to sing with them and it would bring back old memories. In the late 70's we were singing week-ends with Cloid's dad, Ray, when it looked like we were going to have to quit because of his mom's health. We were kind of depressed about the situation and the terrible winter we were having in Indiana. Since the Weatherfords usually spend most of the winter in Florida, they suggested that we take a little vacation and join them. We took our 3 year old, Shawna, and left on a week's vacation. When we got to Florida, we found that their lead singer had just decided to leave and they wanted us to join the group again. So, Cloid and Debbie Baker became members of the Weatherfords, and Shawna traveled as a little Weatherford.

By then, Steve was beginning to be coached by Earl to sing bass on a few songs. We were on the road for several weeks at a time and Earl and Lily had a great time with Shawna. Every night, Shawna would sit toward the front of the church while we sang, and every night, Earl would introduce her so that she could stand up on the pew and meet people. He made her feel very special and she adored Earl and Lily. They bought her frilly dresses and she used to lie on Earl's big belly to fall asleep. Shawna told everyone about the "Weddafords," as she called them.

In 1977, we found out that we were going to have another baby. Although Shawna was a real "trooper" on the road and she had secured a third set of grandparents, we felt that it would be too much to take two children on the road full time. It was with bittersweet feelings that we talked to Earl and Lily and explained to them that we felt it would be better to get off the road to prepare for the baby. Although we left later that year, we have maintained an on-going close relationship with them over the years.

There are many times that we have taken trips to spend time with Lily and the boys since Earl's home-going. They have stayed in our home many times over the years. Lily gets sick of restaurants and when they stay here, she cooks us home-cooked meals while we are at work. Usually one of the standards is pot roast and mashed potatoes. She can whip up some really good gravy, too.

The last year before the National Quartet Convention left Nashville, I flew there to spend some time with Lily Fern. It has now become a yearly event for us. Louisville is only two hours from our home, so every year I drive down on Monday to spend the entire week with Lily. We share a motel room and we have a great time visiting with each other, with old friends and staying up most of the night!! Anyone who attends the National Quartet Convention knows what I'm talking about. It's a great reunion, but you literally wear yourself out trying to stay up all night and not miss anything. Cloid comes down later in the week because I'm not sure he could keep up with our pace for the entire week! It's a tradition now and we look forward to our week in September.

When I think about Lily Fern I can sum it up by saying that my life has been changed because I was fortunate enough to know her. She is a special person to me and my family.

DR. JAMES BLACKWOOD:

I count it a real privilege to have known Lily Fern Weatherford, and I have known her during most of the fifty years of her gospel singing career. I am proud to call her my friend.

I have the highest regard for her as a LADY and as a gospel singer. Many times I have expressed my opinion to others about her beautiful voice in an otherwise male quartet. For many who did not know differently, one would think her rich alto voice was that of a wonderful male first tenor. Her beautiful blend with the male members of the quartet gave the Weatherfords a unique sound that was easily recognizable by gospel quartet lovers.

The Weatherford's album on RCA Victor Records entitled, "IN THE GARDEN," is an all-time classic among gospel quartet recordings and was and is the BENCHMARK by which all gospel quartet albums are measured. Much of this credit goes to the rich voice of Lily Fern Weatherford.

Lily Fern's courage and dedication was clearly demonstrated during the illness and death of her husband, Earl. Her strength during that period was a wonderful example to all other singers.

Lily Fern, may you live to bless all of us for many more years with your lovely voice and sweet smile!

CAROLYN BRANHAM:

Meeting Lily Fern Weatherford was a desire that my deceased husband, Ralph Heath, had. Approximately five years prior to his death in 1995, we received a call from friends in Augusta, Georgia, informing us that the Weatherfords would be performing as a local church. We attended and our friends told Lily how much Ralph wanted to meet her and that it was Ralph's birthday. She acknowledged him from the platform, sang "Happy Birthday," and sang a special request for him of "What a Precious Friend."

After the concert, we had dinner with everyone in the group and later went to our friends' home, where the Weatherford's were staying. We talked and "cut the fool" until the wee hours, all the while learning to love the uniqueness and "down to earth" person we found in Lily. After the first meeting, Ralph would do his best to book dates for the Weatherfords in our area, trying to make sure they had a reason to come and stay in our home. They became "family" as a result.

We met Lily a few months after Earl's death and, though I understand the loss of her companion and the "hole" such a loss creates in one's soul, she always managed to be radiant. As Ralph would say, "A first class lady," no matter when or where you encountered her.

Lily has a special gift of how to be a friend. She never crowds your space, but she knows how to be available, if and when you need her prayers, cards of encouragement, or if you simply need to talk--a great friend and lady, to say the least.

As a performer, Lily is smooth and classy. Her voice is soothing and yet vibrant. Her stage presence is one of confidence and determination for the performance to go on, no matter how she may feel physically or any other burden of the heart that would pull the average person to a standstill. (A very professional woman.)

My favorite times with Lily are when we share "girl talk," when she stays in my home. There is no subject we won't breech. For us, it is interesting and usually produces many laughs and, on occasion (if we manage to get serious) a few tears. We have discovered the loss of our "two-peas-in-a-pod" husbands produces many conversations and comparisons in their personalities. Sad, funny and true.

Since the Weatherfords have stayed in my home many times, I see Lily in a mother mode occasionally. I have never met Susan, her daughter, but Steve has always been with her. She has the most respect for her son and is so grateful to serve the Lord standing performance after performance next to him. Steve is extremely proud of his mother and wants her to have the recognition she so richly deserves for the part she has played in the establishment of Southern Gospel music. He knows the hardships she has endured, all through the years, to persevere. Rearing two children, as she and Earl pursued their ministry, could not have been an easy chore. However, it has all paid off in having children that adore her and strive with her to keep the ministry going. She is blessed!

Though Lily is approaching the "golden years," she is as young at heart as a teenager. If her knees would take it, she could bounce off the walls with the youngest. She loves having a good time, laughter, and a <u>good</u>, clean joke--and sometimes a slightly tarnished one brings a smile! But first and foremost, she is very spiritual and will send a prayer to heaven in an instant. She has that "peace and joy" that "passeth all understanding," and it shows. The great thing about being around Lily is knowing how sincere her prayer life is and yet she is so balanced in the reality of everyday life.

When the Lord has given us abilities to do something over and beyond the average person, I believe He intends for us to develop them until we are one of the best. The Weatherfords have been doing just that since their conception. It shows up in their performances and I've seen with my own eyes (during their practice times while visiting me) how determined they are for perfection. They <u>never</u> just "belt out" a song. They sing it over and over, stop in the middle, pick back up at a weak point, and practice until the sound is the smooth "Weatherford" sound. Their harmony is so close that they can switch parts and you will never know it. It's truly amazing!

Beyond all that's been said, I can tell you, if you need a friend (and a good one at that), one who can sing, make you laugh and pray for you, seek out Lily Fern Weatherford. You won't be disappointed. I hope the Lord will let her sing until His return.

HASKELL COOLEY:

If anyone in Gospel Music deserves the honor of a biography, it is Lily Fern. I have known Lily Fern and The Weatherfords for many years. It was my great privilege to be the pianist for The Weatherfords in 1972 and 1973. I was most happy to be playing with a group that stressed smooth, blending, quality singing. They were and still are a credit to Gospel Music. Lily Fern and her deceased husband, Earl, were the main reasons for this. The perfect person to build this kind of singing around was Lily. Her voice is smooth, never harsh, always melodious, always blending, superb interpretation of lyrics, always on perfect pitch; in short, perfect technique. I have never heard anyone else sing, in any style of music, who is as easy on the ears.

I found Lily to be a dedicated Christian who is genuinely interested in the souls and lives of others. She is the epitome of kindness. <u>May she forever sing.</u> I am her biggest fan.

GLENN COUCH:

Thank you for giving me the opportunity to think back on the nearly three years I was privileged to work with Lily and The Weatherford Quartet. It was probably the happiest period of my life, in that the only thing I ever wanted to do was to sing in a great gospel quartet, and Earl and Lily gave me that chance.

Nearly always, when Lily Fern is being talked or written about--whether by gospel music fans or by fellow singers--it's her voice and vocal style that's talked about; but, when you get to know Lily better, you realize that as fine as it is, her voice is just one small part of a great woman. Lily is from the old school of "Team" singers. Today, nearly every gospel group is made up of three to five soloists who occasionally sing at the same time; but when Lily sings as part of a group, she is intuitively aware of every nuance of what others around her are doing and blends into the group sound, making the sum far greater than the parts and not even thinking about her own ego.

Lily's off-stage persona is the same as you see on stage. Anyone who's worked with Lily for any time at all recognizes that she is the consummate professional in the best meaning of the word. In forty-seven years of traveling with singing groups of all kinds, I've never worked with anyone easier to be around consistently than Lily Fern Weatherford. I don't mean to imply that Lily disappears into the background, but that she's a joy to be around.

The sensitivity, warmth, and love that reaches across the footlights never leaves her while traveling down the road in the old bus, or sitting across the table in her kitchen. I guess it's obvious that I love this lady and feel fortunate to call her a friend. Without her saying a thing, and probably not even being aware of it herself, she inspires those in her group to try to come up to her level. You know it isn't possible, but you try hard to come as close as you can.

I don't remember ever hearing Lily complain about anything. One time The Weatherford's bus gave up the ghost and we had to do a two month national tour crowded on to the Songfellows bus. Not only did we have two quartets (and friends) on the same bus, but we traveled from Pomona, California to Pennsylvania--four days and about six concerts--before getting the time to check into a motel for an honest-to-goodness bath or shower. Not too many women could handle that without complaint, but Lily kept her composure, took "spit baths" in church bathrooms and auditorium dressing rooms and walked on stage with a smile. I never once saw Lily lose her dignity.

There's only one Lily Fern Weatherford and her like will never be seen again, although the world could sure use a few million like her.

BOB CREWS:

To me, Lily Fern has one of the prettiest female voices in the gospel music industry. She is such a nice person and never received the credit due in all the years of her singing career.

Although the Harmoneers were never on stage with her that much, she has always blessed the fans with her singing. I am very proud to know such a person as Lily Fern Weatherford, and wish her many more years singing gospel music.

SUSAN CUNNINGHAM:

Mom said that you wanted me to write something about how I felt about her doing this book. I wish she had done it a long time ago. We have been trying to get her to do one for a long time. I think that every family would like to have a book of this sort that they can pass down to their children. I feel very fortunate that when Megan asks questions I will be able to either pull out a video or get out the book and let her read about her grandparents and their lives.

My parents were pioneers in their field, paving the way for many of the major groups of today, which I feel has never been mentioned enough. My mother has an interesting and worthwhile story to tell that will cross many boundaries. She has touched many people in her life already, and through this book, she will reach even more people with the message to which she has dedicated her life.

I think a lot of importance needs to be put on WHY she is a gospel singer, why she lives the life that she does and the DIFFICULTY of it, such as the two times the buses caught on fire, the breakdowns, the MANY times that they needed bus parts and it seemed they had no money and no resources, not even the means to get to the garage, but there was always a way provided to them.

They were treated badly by some pastors, although Mom and Dad went to great lengths to please them and keep them happy. A lot of times it didn't work. People should know the way they wouldn't tolerate members in the group who were not dedicated to God. People should realize that you do not hear stories about Mom and Dad the way you sometimes hear them about other gospel singers.

I admire the way that Mom treats everyone the same, no matter who they are. I have seen her, recently, in fact, get up from resting to talk to a fan and give an autograph, when the person knocked on her door and asked for it. She always has time to listen to their problems and pray with them. Not everyone is like that. She would die before she would hurt someone's feelings.

I hope these comments help to further tell the story of Lily Fern Weatherford.

TIM CUNNINGHAM:

When I count my blessings, having Lily for a mother-in-law is one of the ones I count first. She has the ability to make you feel loved in any situation. I would say honestly that in 15 years, we have never had one cross word with each other. She is so easy to talk to and be around. I don't think many son-in-laws can say that. I get a thrill out of watching people clamor around her at concerts. She talks to all and signs her autograph when asked, always with a smile, of course. If they only knew her like I know her. She is the most down to earth person you have ever met. I am so proud of her and all she stands for. She should be a model for young women all over. She is a lady in every way and a person of high moral stature, who has helped many people all over this country. She deserves every award that has ever been given for her unselfishness and giving to others. People like Lily don't come along very often. If you have a chance to meet her, don't pass it up. She is one of a kind.

ANN DOWNING:

Of course, the primary thing in my mind concerning Lily is we lost our husbands within four months of each other. I'll never forget that first Gaither video taping following Paul's and Earl's deaths----oh, I was dreading it, yet looking forward to it, too. It had only been a couple of months or so since Earl had died. Lily sang "Eastern Gate," a song I had sung with Paul many, many times. She made it through, as you have viewed on the video, and I have to say I'm glad Bill didn't ask me to sing it. We have through these past five years hugged and encouraged each other on a consistent basis. I have to say she is a sister in the Lord, but additionally a sister in pain. I feel a real bond with her--a wonderful singer, but a greater friend. You see, I think Lily is such a strong woman, because she not only kept on singing, she assumed leadership of a group. I didn't have that responsibility, but I realize God has been preparing her all these years. He is faithful through the years.

NEIL ENLOE:

In the 1960's it was our (The Couriers) delight to work many concert dates with the Weatherfords, then comprising Lily Fern, Glen Payne, Earl Weatherford, Armond Morales and on the piano was Henry Slaughter. Given their association with the great Cathedral of Tomorrow pastored by the beloved Rex Humbard, not to mention their vast weekly television audience, the Weatherfords were certainly a group to be identified with and to know as friends. We were grateful to gain inroads to new venues because of the outcry to hear the Weatherfords. We came along riding on their coattails. You never forget those who befriended and helped you in your days of struggle.

Earl Weatherford, always the soft-spoken leader, was a decent and fair man who had no enemies. I never heard a word of scandal concerning Earl. Both on stage and off he kept intact his dignity and his relationship with his Lord. He didn't feel comfortable singing solos, so he became a pro at making every other member of the group sound good by singing the blending background parts. I've come to realize that is a special gift.

But he always knew who could win the audience for the Weatherfords when it came time to sing. Standing by his side was his sweetheart, Lily Fern. She could indeed get the job done. The audience would like her. He knew that. Furthermore, he knew Lily Fern's relationship of endearment with her fans would last a lifetime. Smart man.

Proof of his cunning in recognizing talent was the birthing of the popular Cathedrals Quartet from members of the Weatherfords. Armond Morales went from the Weatherfords to the Imperials.

One style of interpretive singing which has always gained my appreciation is that of not forcing the lyric. If Orson Wells would make a comment on the singing style of Lily Fern, he might say, "She will sing no line before it's time!" While her audience eagerly hangs on to every lyric line, she has the unique ability to wait until the emotional anticipation of a word has fully blossomed before she releases it. Singing is story-telling, and she is the best.

Steve Weatherford has grown to become the "Earl" of his generation. Emcee, soloist, personality and communicator, Steve, like most sons, is out-doing his father. A more likable, jovial and sincere heart you'll never find. He has come to fill the huge gap left by the passing of his father. Totally at home on stage, he is the front man who is so valuable in the image-making of the group. Steve's versatile singing adds color to the Weatherford's sound.

But Lily Fern, she's the identifying sound in the Weatherfords. Some things never change. When you hear their music played, you immediately recognize the wonderful voice of Lily Fern and say, "That's the Weatherfords!" She was and remains the hook upon which the Weatherford sound hangs. All parts point to Lily Fern. She is the personification of the name, The Weatherfords.

Some of my most treasured recordings are those of the Weatherfords, both pre and post "IN THE GARDEN." This album is still a standard of excellence toward which the whole world of Christian music should aim.

Someday when I lay the microphone down for the last time, it will be people like the Weatherfords, who always have taken the high road in life, who will afford me my most meaningful memories of the noblest and best in gospel music. Lily Fern has been a sterling example of a lady, a mother, a Godly woman, a great gospel singer and a dear friend.

Thanks, Lily Fern, for making us all proud. We love you!

PHIL ENLOE:

I appreciate the opportunity to participate in the wonderful and thoughtful publication that you are working on with our mutual friend, Lily Fern Weatherford.

I tease Lily a lot and we have a great deal of fun together, so I took a little journalistic liberty and had some fun with her again in this far-out story. I figured everyone else will be showering her with a load of accolades, so I would take a different approach.

(The following story was included with Phil Enloe's letter. At last we know the truth about Lily Fern! Or at least Phil's version. G.S.)

A Living Legacy

An Unauthorized Synoptic Biography of
LILY FERN WEATHERFORD

by
Phil Enloe
of
The Couriers

Many, many years ago, my grandfather told me about a beautiful little girl who was born in a one room log cabin near the farming town of Slapout, Oklahoma located in the panhandle of the western plains. Throckmorton and Earleen Noodleberry named their only child, "Agnes Fernadette Noodleberry." Though millions know her today as "Lily Fern," I am probably the only remaining person who is aware of her humble beginning and her much guarded secret of how she became the most Famous Gospel Singer and Legendary Diva of Southern Gospel Music. Though her parents gave her the nickname, "Little Fernie," she grew to become a giant in her field of music. Contrary to popular belief, she was not born with a silver spoon in her mouth, but rather, with a pitchfork in her hand, gasoline in her veins and the voice of an angel.

The first time Little Fernie cried the Noodleberrys knew that she was destined for a great future on the performing and musical stage; she cried a triple high "C." Though Throckmorton was a hard working share cropper, he and Earleen were determined that Little Fernie would have a better life than shucking corn and shredding wheat. In Little Fernie's early years she honed her musical skills among the barn-yard animals. When she sang, the cows gave more milk, the chickens laid more eggs and the whole farm was in harmony. Please understand, this is no "Kiss and Tell" story; mainly because I have never kissed Lily; OK, maybe once! However, I believe by telling her "Rags to Riches" story, Lily Fern will finally be able to live at peace with herself as her fans realize that she is a "Share Cropper's Daughter."

One day, an old Greyhound type bus coughed and sputtered, then died right in front of Noodleberry Farm. Faintly legible and beneath a film of oil and diesel residue read "The Weatherford Quartet." Once the huge vehicle came to a rest, it was quickly engulfed in a bellow of smoke and steam. The Noodleberrys stood in awe, when from the encumbering haze walked the figure of a stately man. It was none other than the Earl of Gospel Music, Mr. Weatherford himself. No other Salesman of Song had ventured this close to the Noodleberry Farm and Throckmorton just knew that the bus breakdown was an omen for Little Fernie's future. Mr. Noodleberry offered to repair the road-weary coach and with precision custom engineering, he mended the aged rig with bailing wire and duck tape. Within a short period of time, the tired old vehicle was willing to travel a few more miles for the gospel. Just before leaving, Earl noticed Little Fernie watching from a distance. By now she was eighteen and a beautiful young lady. He fixed his piercing eyes on her loveliness and walked straightway toward her. He cupped his hand betwixt his lips and his right ear, then introduced himself in a mellow baritone intonation. "You are more beautiful than a flower," he acknowledged, and asked for her name. "My name is Agnes Fernadette, but my parents call me Little Fernie," she sang in a melodious soprano trill. The entire scene was as if it were from a Broadway Musical. It was love at first sight for the Salesman and the Farmer's Daughter. Earl and Mr. Noodleberry quickly agreed upon an exchange for the bus repairs and Little Fernie never looked back. Earl soon changed Little Fernie's last name to Weatherford at the nearest Justice Of The Peace and gave her the now famous stage name of "Lily Fern" that she still carries today.

Soon after the marriage Earl fired his temperamental tenor and Lily's amazing career began. Though The Weatherfords experienced many personnel changes through the years, the illustrious Lily Fern remains the stalwart of the group. She also transcended the fondest dreams of her parents and is unsurpassed in her unique style.

Earl and Lily's only son, "Percy Pitchford Weatherford," stage-named "Steve," assumed the reins of leadership after his father passed away.

So, there you have it; everything but the truth about Lily Fern Weatherford. The only real truth in my account of Lily Fern is that my world is always a little brighter when I am privileged to share a brief moment in the presence of one of the most gracious and gifted ladies in Gospel Music. She sings it and she lives it! There will never be another voice or life as grand as hers.

MEEKLY E. GOBLE:

In my love and appreciation for my sister, Lily Fern, superlatives aren't adequate to express what I feel for her and how I cherish her love and fellowship. Any time we are together, we just have so much fun and enjoy each other.

I deeply appreciate her close walk with the Lord. She is on Monday, Tuesday, Wednesday and all week, what you hear her sing on Sunday from the platform. She's as genuine a person as I know.

I've seen her go through some real trials, including traveling for fifty-plus years in the singing business, and many times I've heard her say, with a burdened heart, "I don't know how it's going to come out, but I know that God will provide--that God will see us through this." She was always right. The Lord did provide for her and she has helped me gain faith in my own life.

I love her so much and I love knowing that we can not only be loving brother and sister, but we can be good friends.

LARRY GATLIN:

I'm really happy for the opportunity to tell what I feel about Lily Fern Weatherford.

Let me start at the beginning. I was a big fan of The Blackwoods and The Statesmen. At that time, they were coming to Abilene and Odessa for concerts. I cried for three days when The Blackwoods' plane went down. At that time, I had never heard of The Weatherfords. The Singing Wills Family came to Odessa for a concert and we sang with them. Then they came home with us for dinner. I'll never forget! Mom made a big ham dinner for us, then one of the Wills said, "We've got something we want you to hear." They played The Weatherfords' "In The Garden" album. If you play that tape for me today, I can sing every part, do every introduction, every modulation in every song. They were fabulous. I still loved The Statesmen and The Blackwoods, but this just added to the texture of gospel music forever. It became part of the tapestry of my life. It had a tremendous impact.

I only saw the classic group once--Earl, Lily, Glen, Armond and Henry. They left Akron and broke up after that.

I actually got to know Lily Fern later. One day at a hotel in Tampa, Florida, I heard the sound no gospel singer can ever forget--the air brakes on a bus. I love that sound! I looked out and saw a bus pull up. It was the Weatherford bus. Later I called and got either Earl or Steve, I don't remember which, but he said Lily was down in the hotel laundry room. I went down to the laundry room and, sure enough, there was Lily Fern Weatherford doing the laundry. I went up and hugged her and we visited for a while. They were singing at a church there, and we were off on Sunday, so I got to go hear them.

You know that song, "What A Precious Friend," where she does that great "On His promise I'm relying....?" Well, when Bill Gaither called me to come to a taping, I told Bill I want to do that number with Lily Fern Weatherford, and he let us do it. I got to sing Earl's part. What a thrill!

I love Lily Fern! I'm glad someone's doing her story. I guess I could boil it down to this: I love, respect and cherish her.

NANCY HARMON:

First, let me say that for years I have held Lily Fern and the entire Weatherfords in the highest of esteem and regards.

I have not had the privilege of knowing them in a close relationship, as friends often do, but I would like to say that I have NEVER heard anything negative, or words spoken in any way other than PRAISE for the integrity of Lily Fern and the Weatherfords.

Gospel music is what it is because of people like Lily Fern, who have blazed a trail of COMMITMENT, DEDICATION, and PERSEVERANCE through every storm of life.... She POSSESSES what her song has always manifested...STRENGTH, HONOR and INTEGRITY, as well as praise and worship for the GOD who gives all songs.

I wish you the BEST in helping the world celebrate a lady who has touched thousands of lives.

LABREESKA HEMPHILL:

Lily Fern Weatherford is a very sweet and gracious lady. I have known her for many years, but thanks to the frequent Gaither tapings have had a chance to really know her. She is the same every time I see her; her easy smile and gentle spirit is an inspiration to me.

Lily is loved and respected by her peers as having her own smooth style of delivery when she sings. It takes determination and dedication for a woman to obey the call of God in her life when it takes her from the comforts of home. Having done this myself by raising and educating three children on the road, I know first hand. And now, playing the role of grandmother, which is most fulfilling but also takes effort and time, commodities that a traveling woman has in short supply.

Solomon asks the question in Proverbs 31, "Who can find a virtuous woman?" He then states, "For her price is far above rubies.... The heart of her husband doth safely trust in her, so that he shall have no need of spoil.... She girdith her loins with strength and strengtheneth her arms.... Strength and honor are her clothing.... Give her the fruit of her hands; and let her own works praise her."

Lily has helped to blaze the trail for others to proudly follow, heralding the message of a Risen Savior with dignity and honor. My life and the lives of countless others across this nation is richer because there was and is a Lily Fern Weatherford and I am happy to say she is my friend.

JAKE HESS:

Lily Fern is the "sound" of the Weatherfords. No matter who the members have been through the years, Lily Fern is the sound. The first time I heard The Weatherfords singing with Lily Fern, I was not where I could see the stage. I wondered, who is that guy singing tenor? Then I saw that it was a pretty little girl! Not only is Lily Fern one of the best female singers ever to be in the business, she is a lady. She has always conducted herself with class and dignity.

I am looking forward to reading the book.

LOU WILLS HILDRETH:

I first heard the incredible voice of Lily Fern Weatherford at an outdoor sing in DeLeon, Texas, in the early fifties. W.B. Nowlin had gathered talent from across the nation to sing at this annual festival. The Singing Wills Family, as we were billed then, always sang for this event, and we loved it, in spite of the heat and primitive venue. I will never forget this one--nor the smoothest quartet I had ever heard. Lily Fern, her husband Earl, Glen Payne, Armond Morales, with Henry Slaughter at the piano, sang with such authority and dignity the audience became quiet and respectful. Outdoor sings are notorious for unresponsive listeners, but singers and listeners alike knew THIS WAS A QUARTET. This was my introduction to a lady who would earn my love and respect in the next forty years, and whose singing is still awesome to me.

In Nashville during the seventies and eighties, I really considered it an honor to represent the WEATHERFORD QUARTET through Nashville Gospel Talent Agency. I came to know Earl and Lily Fern as precious friends during this period. These people wrote the book on integrity and consistency. The dignity shown by Lily Fern at the death of her beloved husband, Earl, is a pattern we can all look to when we face such a loss. She and her son, Steve, continue to give back to a needy world the values the Weatherfords are known for. I applaud the beauty of character and the magnificent singing of Lily Fern Weatherford.

BOB JONES, SR.:

Lily Fern just happened to have one of the nicest female voices on record anywhere. She made good use of the God-given talent she had and she and Earl set a standard for four part harmony singing that really has no equal in the entire gospel singing industry. Now that Earl has gone on to glory, she still carries on the traditional easy-to-listen-to, sweet and smooth sound that is my own personal choice. Her son, Steve, does a marvelous job as her right hand man and is an excellent singer himself. And today, in 1997, she still has it. No doubt there will be many in Heaven because of her commitment to Christ. We wish her many more years of service to the Lord.

WYNEMA (NEMA) SHAHAN KING:

When I think of Lily Fern, I think of "Precious Memories." She has always been and always will be the truest, dearest, best secret-sharing, and most fun-loving friend anyone could have.

We met at the Compton Nazarene Church in 1938. Her parents soon became my parents, and my parents became her parents, because every Sunday afternoon she was at my house or I was at hers. We were with each other during the week and share many school memories. We still go to the Enterprise Junior High School reunions together when we can.

Our big treat on Sunday afternoons was to go to Clifton's Cafeteria in Los Angeles or to the Chicken Pie Shop in Long Beach. How we loved those chicken pies! An what do we have when she comes to visit us now? Of course, chicken pies.

Lily Fern has loved to sing as long as I can remember. God has truly blessed her with a wonderful voice. I wasn't quite so lucky, but we still sat together on the front row at church and sang as loud as we could. During one service, we were singing "Such Love" at the top of our voices. My daddy, the song director, asked us to stand, turn around and sing a verse. We stood, faced the audience and started to sing. But what do 8 and 9 year old girls do? We started to giggle. We laughed so hard that we couldn't sing. We both got into trouble with our parents when we got home.

One Sunday, when she was 12 and I was 13, a really good-looking guy came in and sat on the row behind us. We kept sneaking peeks at him and giggling. As the years passed, we both thought he was so nice and even more handsome than ever. She said she had her eye on him first, but she did the "Christian thing" and let me have him. Now Glen and I have been married for over 50 years and we were very fortunate that she could come to help us celebrate our Golden Anniversary.

Lily Fern was truly a sister-in-heart to our whole family. She was a bridesmaid in my sister, Wanda Wall's wedding. By the time Glen and I married, she had already met Earl and was starting her singing career. Because of her traveling commitments, she wasn't able to be in our wedding. But I was so happy she was using the talents God had given her to minister to others.

And now, even though we are separated for long periods at a time, when we are together, it's as if we have never been apart. We pick up in the middle of a sentence, and never stop talking, reminiscing, sharing and giggling.

Yes, when I think of Lily Fern I really do think of "Precious Memories" and we are still making memories that will last forever. Glen and I, along with our children, Ron, Bob, Lynda May and their families, always look forward to visits from her.

I love you Lily Fern, my sister-in-heart, and always pray that God will continue to bless you and bring us together again very soon.

LILLIE KNAULS:

I must say I did not grow up hearing Southern Gospel music or ever seeing the wonderful folk I have met since I have been a part of the Gaither videos. So, what I will say will be short. Since meeting Lily Fern at a Gaither Video taping, I have LOVED her. Right away I felt LOVE from her. She has a quiet, gentle spirit and I always go to her and say, "Here we are--the two most beautiful "lilies" in this place!" She is so CUTE, too!

With All My Heart

HAROLD LANE:

My recollections of Lily Fern are somewhat limited due to limited interaction, yet I have always considered her one of the best vocalists in Southern Gospel Music. In fact, while listening to her sing, Glen Payne and I agreed we have never heard Lily Fern sing off pitch. I have high regard for Lily Fern's ability to sing with feeling.

As a credit to Lily Fern and her late husband, Earl, the Weatherfords have always had an outstanding group, no matter who the personnel of the group have been. Their sound has been consistently good throughout the years.

Most importantly, the songs she sings reflect the life Lily Fern lives. For example, when listening to her rendition of "What A Precious Friend Is He," it is clear to all that Lily Fern knows about Whom she is singing.

EVA MAE LEFEVRE:

Lily Fern Weatherford--what a joy! The first time I remember Lily and Earl must have been about 35 years ago--at the Cathedral of Tomorrow. Her moving, rich voice has been a constant blessing. Gospel music, like so many fields, has not been easy for women. I know! But Lily Fern was always a "trooper." She is always careful to credit the Lord with her successes. And, like I was blessed with Urias, she was blessed with a fine helpmate in Earl.

She is always such a delight at the "Old Timers" in Greenville, South Carolina. She has a precious sense of humor. I think she was in on a little joke on me there last year--I have not laughed so hard in years.

I am proud to say Lily Fern Weatherford and I have walked in some of the same footsteps--and always "Walking in the King's Highway." She is a shining example to the young women who will follow us--and I know she is taking many with her to Heaven!

MICHAEL LO PRINZI:

The first time I saw Lily Fern Weatherford was in the early 1960's; she was singing with The Weatherford Quartet. As I listened to them sing, I came away with the feeling that these folks really sang from the heart and their smooth, close harmony, song selection and presentation made for a wonderful evening of gospel music.

After that first encounter with the Weatherfords, I attended numerous other concerts by them. Lily Fern always exhibited the highest standard of professionalism, sincerity, and conveyed the love of God to her audiences.

Since getting to know her on a personal level, I find that my first impressions were correct. This gracious lady of Gospel Music is filled with goodness and always has a kind word for everyone. I feel it is an honor and privilege to be counted as her friend.

MARK LOWRY:

Unfortunately, I don't know Lily Fern as well as I'd like to. Our paths have crossed through the years, but not that often and I don't have any interesting stories about her (that she would want printed...<grin>). All I know about Lily is that she's a great singer, seems to be a good mom, and was a good wife! What better could be said about someone?

I remember when I lived in Atlanta--one night I was going to the movies. I noticed The Weatherford's bus was in the parking lot of the mall. I hopped on the bus and talked Lily Fern into going to the movie with me. She didn't really want to go, but I can be very persuasive. You see, a lot of the churches they work don't believe in movies, which I've never really understood. I mean, they're real whether you believe in them or not. Anyway, it was G rated. But, she was nervous. She put on a hat, wrapped a scarf around her face, and wore sunglasses. Not only can Lily Fern sing the house down, but she never wants to offend a weaker brother!

(Editor's note: Lily Fern's story is slightly different!)

ARMOND MORALES:

My memories of Lily Fern Weatherford start back in 1949 in Lynwood, California. I was a young man finishing high school and had no ambitions of being involved in music of any kind.

Well, Les Roberson and I attended the same church and he asked me to try out for the bass part for the Weatherford Stamps Quartet. I had done some singing at our church and high school choirs, and to my amazement, Earl took me on as the bass singer. That's when I first met Lily Fern. She was so instrumental to the sound of the Weatherfords. Like myself, I don't think she ever realized how far-reaching her gifted voice, that God had given her, would bless countless thousands of people across our nation.

She was a real trooper and a complete professional in every sense of the word. Traveling wasn't easy in those early years and she never complained. When it came time to sing she was always ready.

We worked together for 15 years (with me leaving and going to college and the army) from Los Angeles, California where we would sing on week-ends and do Live Radio in downtown L.A., to Fort Wayne, Indiana on W.O.W.O., where we had our radio show and booked our dates. From there to Akron, Ohio with the Rex Humbard Ministry for many years.

My time with Lily Fern and Earl taught me many valuable lessons for all parts of my life. Lily Fern was for me a wonderful person to be around. I'll always love her and appreciate the start she and Earl gave me almost 49 years ago. I'm glad to hear she is still singing and blessing people everywhere she goes.

You're a great lady and God bless you, Lily.

REV. BILL MATTHEWS:

I have been Lily Fern Weatherford's Pastor for many years. We love each other in the Lord Jesus. I thank God for her and the fact that she is one of the few Gospel Singers who really is true to Our Lord Jesus Christ. We do not see each other often. We are both on the road for Jesus one way or another. I just thank God for allowing me to be her Pastor. Many would desire to say this, but by the grace of God, I am.

REV. TED MILES:

I am pastor of the Houston Terrace Baptist Church of San Antonio, Texas, and it is an honor to be classed as a close friend of the Weatherfords. In fact, our families have been close for more than thirty years.

A friend told me one time, "If you ever have a chance, hear the Weatherfords," and in the mid-fifties, I went to Houston to attend a concert where the Weatherfords were singing.

They were featured along with the Statesmen and the Blackwood Brothers, and on this particular evening, they came on last. They came on stage, gathered around one mike, and started singing, "I Wanta Know." You never heard anything like it in your life! There was not a sound heard other than their singing, and when the last note faded away, about five thousand voices erupted. This was singing, the likes of which I had never heard before, but the way we instinctively knew it should be done. This was vintage Weatherfords, smooth as silk, but with a dignity that you felt. It was a night I shall never forget.

In 1964, they came to the Lakeview Baptist Church in San Antonio where I pastored. From that night on, we became fast friends, as family. I was, and am, a great admirer of Earl and Lily Fern. Earl was as close to me as my own brother. Years have passed, more than thirty of them since we first hosted the Weatherfords, but my admiration for them has grown to towering proportions, and a bond established that even death has not been able to break. I was honored when the family asked me to conduct the funeral of Earl's father, "Papaw," and again when asked to conduct Earl's funeral service. When my wife, Maggeline, passed away December 26, 1996, my children and I were comforted and uplifted when Lily sang so beautifully, "He Whispers Sweet Peace" and "Heaven Sounding Sweeter." We will forever be in her debt.

There has never been even a hint of scandal concerning the Weatherfords in all of these years, and I certainly do not expect any. It is so gratifying to see the group continuing on, abiding by the same standard of conduct and music that has characterized them from the beginning.

Their love and friendship is one of my most cherished possessions.

BRENDA NASH:

I read a card one time and in essence it said into each of our lives come unique individuals--special people who add so much to our life journeys. They bring a relationship--numerous priceless treasures. I feel this about Lily, because she has brought so many priceless treasures into my life to enrich and connect, bond, enhance and strengthen the relationship that we've had, which didn't come overnight. It came through years and occurrences and talks--and just living.

Little did I realize when I married a member of the Weatherford Quartet that Lily would become that unique individual to me. The Lord blessed so many of us through her phenomenal, anointed music and blessed some of us with her friendship. I am one of those who has been blessed with her friendship. She certainly is in my inner circle, the nearest and dearest friends. I feel so blessed of the Lord to have shared as a friend with Lily for almost thirty years. I've seen what a profound person she is, not only professionally, but personally.

Many can elaborate on her professionalism, but I'll share some personal notes-- characteristics that flow from the personage of Lily. What really stands out to me are her faith, humor, selflessness, dedication, endurance, strength, focus, organization and priorities. She is sensitive and humble, also. These are prominent characteristics. To me, her faith is her driving force. She loves the Lord and is so sensitive to his leading and to doing what is right. She and Earl answered the call to sing the gospel, and she has been faithful to that, even when it looked as if she couldn't crawl on that bus again. It was hard to leave the folks, the children at home--burying loved ones and having to leave before the funeral, but that covenant that she and Earl made came through at critical times. The Lord was her strength.

I am so blessed to have a friend in Lily Fern, and to be blessed by her music is wonderful in itself. Everyone can understand and receive that music, but she's my dear, dear friend. You think her music is rich? Yes, it is. But her friendship is richer.

FULTON NASH:

Probably some of the happiest days of my life were with the Weatherfords, and that's through thick and thin, through the bad and the good. They believed in me; they believed that I could be of some benefit to them and help them with the sound that they were seeking. Sometimes I think they just kept me around because there wasn't anybody else available and they were having a difficult time finding talent!

I enjoyed even the times when we broke down and Earl and I had to stay up all night working on the bus or, maybe, if I couldn't do anything, at least I stayed up with him. I held a flashlight while he tried to do something--and he was not a mechanic. He knew just a little more than I did. But at least we toughed out a lot of rough times together, and a lot of women wouldn't have been able to put up with all that. That's just a life that women don't want to have to contend with if they can possibly get out of it, but, boy, she just stayed with it!

Lily Fern is a pro in every sense of the word. She is topnotch. There is none finer, there's none better. I love her voice. Well, I guess I just love everything about her.

WALLACE NELMS:

I would be honored to make some comments about Lily Fern:

One of the first albums I ever bought was <u>In The Garden</u> by The Weatherford Quartet. In my opinion, this album will go down in history as the <u>greatest</u> Southern Gospel quartet album ever recorded. Why? It's perfect!!!. Lily Fern's singing on this album was flawless. Lily Fern is by far the "<u>greatest female Southern Gospel singer</u>" to ever set foot on a stage or record Southern Gospel Music in a studio. Anyone who doesn't agree with this--really has their right to be wrong. Not only is Lily Fern the "<u>greatest female Southern Gospel singer</u>" but a real "first class" lady. She has always been friendly with everyone, <u>all</u> the times I have been in her presence. I count it an honor to know her and consider her a true, Christian friend.

My desire for you is that the book you are writing about Lily Fern will be a huge success and be a blessing to the fans of Southern Gospel Music. I am sure it will allow fans to get to know Lily better.

DUANE NICHOLSON:

I am truly honored to share a few thoughts concerning Lily's long and illustrious ministry.

The Couriers association with The Weatherfords goes back to the early 60's. We traveled the back roads of Ohio and Pennsylvania together in cars and later in motor coaches. We also have had them share in our concerts in Harrisburg, Pa. They are always favorites not only among the audience, but with the groups that sing on the programs with them. The smooth harmonies and great selections of songs with meaning are unequaled.

Lily Fern is the same off stage as she is on. I have never heard her complain, or talk badly about any person in our long association. She is gracious and kind and a grand lady among ladies. She always has time to talk to you, and does not seem to understand that she will go down in Gospel Music history as perhaps the best female singer of all time. Now there are those who sing higher and those who sing louder and those who sing lower, but no one can match her ability to share a song with dignity, grace and smoothness and believability even after these many years.

What else can I say? She traveled with a husband who was consumed with singing, with few complaints about the hardships and problems that she had to face. When Earl died, she faced the supreme test with the same gracefulness and strength that had brought her through the years, and now continues with Steve, her son, to carry on the tradition of The Weatherfords.

I have the greatest admiration and respect for you, Lily Fern. You have shown many of us the way it should be done. May God give you many more years to minister in song and to bless us as singers listening to you and still learning from a Master.

CALVIN NEWTON:

Thanks so much for giving me the opportunity to be a part of Lily Fern's biography. Although until recently I was never privileged to sing with Lily Fern, I have always had the utmost respect for her and for Earl. Their reputation through their many years in serving God through Gospel Music has always been unblemished. Lily Fern's voice is clear, strong and true and, indeed, has been the standard for many young female singers. Her enthusiasm for our music never seems to wane, even after being a part of it for more than 50 years. I'm sure there were times after Earl left this earth, when she must have been tempted to "hang it up." But she persevered, and she's a real inspiration to all of us.

GLEN PAYNE:

It was my honor to hear Lily Fern sing nearly 50 years ago. She is truly a great singer. Then, in 1957, I had the honor of singing with her for about 5 years. She is the only female singer that gives a group that rich, full sound. Earl was like family to my family, and, of course, we miss him deeply. I count Lily Fern one of the great pioneers of Gospel Music.

Lily, Van and I love you very much.

NAOMI SEGO READER:

The singing ministry of The Weatherfords has always blessed me. I remember working with them in the sixties and was always over-overjoyed with their smooth sound.

Lily Fern is just the best when it comes to singing a song the way it should be. Age and experience has only made her better.

The Gaither and Charles Waller tapings have helped us to become better acquainted and even get to sing a song together on the "Praise Him" video by Charles Waller. "What a Day That Will Be" was the song and what a night that was. I counted it such an honor to sing with this great lady. I love and appreciate her very much.

DAVID REECE:

I first met Earl and Lily Fern back in the late 1940's while playing for the Rangers Quartet. I thought then, and still do, that they were some of the nicest people I had ever met and to be able to sing with and enjoy being with them on many programs was a great pleasure.

Lily Fern has the distinction of having a voice that you can hear anywhere, any time, and you know it's Lily Fern. I listen to some people sing and my feet go to sleep. Not so with Lily Fern. Her beautiful voice, her smile, her talent and overall beauty demand attention. She is truly one of the GREATS in Gospel Singing. I count it a blessing to have her as a friend.

HENRY SLAUGHTER:

Lily Fern Weatherford--the gospel singing lady who "sings the tenor part in a male group like a man should sing it." I heard this said of her by one of her peers while I was pianist/arranger for The Weatherfords. Then and now, I whole-wholeheartedly agree with that statement. The many recordings, television programs and videos and personal appearances verify and validate this fact. Those of us who worked with Lily Fern know it best and appreciate it most.

I salute her in her long and successful career in gospel music. Her outstanding abilities and accomplishments in gospel should have been recognized and honored more many years before they were. Too often, excellence and greatness are not recognized until many years after.

I am honored to have been a part of some of the great contributions Lily Fern Weatherford has made to the world of gospel music and the kingdom of God. I am glad to be one of those who shared gospel music ministry together, but also a long time, close friendship and Christian fellowship. I am one of her many, many fans.

GORDON STOKER:

I am sorry that I had never had the pleasure of meeting Lily Fern, or hearing her sing until I started doing some of the Gaither tapes.

Lily Fern is a lovely person, and I have enjoyed the couple of solos I have heard her sing when we filmed the shows for Gaither. I look forward to seeing and hearing her again.

RICK STRICKLAND:

I have sung gospel music since I was five years old. My professional career in gospel music started in 1983. I have always been a huge fan of gospel music and artists since I was a little boy. I remember watching gospel music on television when we only had black and white television sets. Every week I was glued to the set watching "The Gospel Singing Jubilee." I loved listening to and watching all the singers. I also listened to any gospel music on the radio that I could tune in. My Grandma Compton and I would go to any all-night sings in the area. Grandma would pack a sack of biscuits to have throughout the evening. I remember staying all night for the singing and hearing Hovie Lister preach the next morning.

I wanted to tell you a little bit about my early background and experiences with gospel music so you will understand that gospel music is my love. I have been a fan of many gospel artists that I have never met, but felt like I knew through their music. I have been very fortunate to know many of the legendary artists that still are contributing to the history of gospel music.

One of my favorites is Lily Weatherford. The first time I heard Lily sing, she gave me goose bumps. I love her voice. Lily has that certain class about her that makes her stand out from the rest. She sings with such ease, and her delivery is truly anointed. The Weatherfords' harmonies have always thrilled me. They have sung some of the most beautiful arrangements that I have ever heard.

Besides being an incredible vocalist, Lily has a wonderful personality. I love to talk to Lily every time I see her. And, by the way, Lily is my girlfriend. Our secret is out, Lily! I do love Lily a whole bunch.

DEBRA TALLEY:

Several years ago, I had the pleasure of meeting Lily Fern Weatherford, after only knowing her by reputation and recordings.

Glen Payne of The Cathedrals had sung with The Weatherfords for many years. He would tell me Lily Fern was his favorite female singer and I was second.

She was always known for her beautiful alto voice, quality, smoothness, and ability to blend with male voices. I felt honored to be included, in Glen's respected opinion, with this talented lady.

Some time later, the Talleys were in concert with the Weatherfords and the Cathedrals. I finally had the privilege of meeting the lady I had heard so much about.

It's been a joy to get to know Lily Fern and to see her Christian testimony lived. She has shown an incredible peace and joy even through the loss of her beloved husband, Earl. At a time when it might be easier to end the singing career they had together, she has chosen to keep their song alive by sharing her life experiences with audiences everywhere. The wisdom and grace that can only come from walking close to the Master is evident in Lily Fern. She is truly an inspiration. I respect and love her.

WALLY VARNER:

My acquaintance with The Weatherfords has been fairly recent. When I first became aware of them, I knew they were super good, but I was just leaving gospel performing. I was out quite a long time until the Gaither videos began. We finally got to re-new our acquaintance at the tapings. Roy and Amy Pauley got us together when The Weatherfords were touring in Florida. Polly and I looked forward to being with them after we got acquainted.

Unfortunately, Earl passed away not long after we got to know them, but we have enjoyed being with Lily Fern and Steve. We always make sure to see them whenever we can.

My comments about Lily Fern could be summarized by the fact that I consider her the "First Lady of Gospel." I love, appreciate and admire her. She is one of the sweetest, most talented and funny people I know.

MICKEY VAUGHN:

I am honored to be asked to comment for Lily Fern's biography. That is how much respect and admiration I have for her. We jokingly talked about me giving you the "dirt." Guess what--there isn't any!

When I think about Lily, four words come to my mind: professional, class, lady and consistency.

Lily is always professional in the way she conducts herself on stage, off stage, around her table, responding to fans--she is just as nice and sweet and patient with the fan who is obviously uneducated, poor or perhaps not too intelligent as she is with the "doctors, lawyers and Indian chiefs," etc. She is never condescending.

I guess class goes along with the above paragraph. Lily is a classy lady. The way she conducts herself, the way she dresses--class is kind of hard to explain. You either have it or you don't. My mother always told me that class has nothing to do with money. I have learned through the years that that is true. Lily Fern has it.

She is always a lady. I have never seen her act in any other way. I made the comment about her never being condescending. Believe it or not, strange as it may seem, I cannot say that about all gospel singers. Lily has earned respect because she is a lady.

Consistent--She is always cheerful, fun-loving, always has a smile. I attended Earl's funeral on a Saturday. As I was leaving Pauls Valley, I looked over at the Love's gas station and there was Steve gassing up the bus. The next morning the Weatherfords were singing at a church in a little town close to Dallas. I am sure it was very difficult for Lily to stand there and sing 24 hours after she had buried her husband, but she did.

And, she just happens to be the greatest woman singer I have ever heard. The first year the Weatherfords were in Greenville, I watched the other artists when the Weatherfords went on stage. The other singers stopped in their tracks and listened to the Weatherfords. They knew that was the way it was supposed to be done!

I have been a fan of the Weatherfords since the 60's, but Lily and I have only been acquainted personally for the last ten years or so. We just clicked, I guess. For one thing, we both have a warped sense of humor and love to laugh. Seems like every time we get together, something crazy happens to get us tickled. And when we get tickled at the same time, it is all over!

STEVE WEATHERFORD:

Recently, my mom has received word of two honors that will be bestowed on her: the Living Legacy Award of the Women's International Center and an honorary doctorate from Oakland City University. Of course, she is very honored, but I'm afraid that last one is going to radically alter the way things are done around the house. I'm going to have to call her "Dr. Lily Fern." I may have to call her "Dr. Mom!" Can you imagine? "Hey, Dr. Mom, I need a baloney sandwich, stat!"

Seriously, though, for fifty-four years, Lily Fern Weatherford has graced a stage somewhere in this world to sing gospel music almost every night. She has been through a lot of things, good and bad. She's seen a lot of gospel styles come and go. We were talking about that a few days ago, about how gospel music styles have changed. It seems that back in the '70's, every group that could had their picture taken in front of their bus. Then they stood on rocks and hung from trees for the group picture. Then came the "big hair."

Lots of styles have come and gone while Mom was singing, and, to this day, she has still been faithful to what the Lord has called her to do.

A lot of people out there in gospel music think she is one of the finest, if not the all-time greatest female vocalist in gospel. I've never seen a female gospel singer in any era who cold stand and sing on the stage with the class, quality and dignity of Lily Fern Weatherford.

What can I say? She's my mom and I love her.

GEORGE YOUNCE:

When I think of Lily Fern, I always remember how she loved baby pigs. She was just crazy about them. But as much as she loves baby pigs, she is horrified of spiders. I'll never forget the time when we were rehearsing one day and Jim Hamill secretly placed a rubber spider on page 32 of Lily Fern's song book. Jim then suggested we try the song on page 32. When Lily Fern opened her song book and saw that spider laying there, she hit the highest note I've ever heard her hit, and threw that book straight up in the air. As far as I know, that book is still up in space!

Lily Fern was always such a good sport, and a real trooper to travel with. She also, in my opinion, is blessed with one of the most smooth, rich and unique female voices that has ever come along in gospel music, or any other style of music. I will forever be grateful that in November of 1954, the Lord allowed me the privilege and opportunity to not only be able to sing with Lily Fern and Earl, but to learn from them, also. I truly believe that they are one of the reasons that I am still out here today.

DOUG YOUNG:

I've only known Lily Fern Weatherford personally for a short time, but I quickly learned to love her. I am very honored to know her and count her as a good friend. She is one of the sweetest ladies ever, with a beautiful voice, a great personality and a big heart. I love her dearly.

Afterword

For more than forty years, I've admired Lily Fern Weatherford. Up until the past ten years or so, that admiration came merely through listening to her velvet voice on the many Weatherford recordings I've heard and collected over the years.

Many have lodged complaints against me saying that I'm only a male quartet man, having little or no interest in female singers or mixed groups. This is an accusation that is far from the truth. There have been many great lady singers down through the years whom I have much respect for, and whose vocal talents I hold in high esteem--people like Mom Speer, Ginger Laxon, Ann Downing, Jeannie Johnson, Sue Dodge, Debra Talley and others. None, however, in my way of thinking had what Lily Fern had. She always had, and still has a beauty and smoothness that has never been matched, and probably never will be.

The experts, not necessarily all of today's singers and listeners, but those veteran performers and Gospel Music lovers who've been around long enough to have an overall view and perception of the industry, have long lauded Lily Fern Weatherford as the nation's truest female gospel singer. Not the loudest, not the flashiest or the most showy, she's simply Gospel Music's finest female singer of all time, and in my view, among the five greatest gospel singers we've ever had--period.

My wife, Amy, and I became close with Earl, Lily and their son, Steve, a little more than ten years ago. After taking in a Weatherford concert in St. Petersburg, Florida, we all introduced ourselves to each other for the first time. We, of course, knew them only from years of listening to their great recordings, and they knew me from my writings in the *Singing News* magazine. After the concert that evening, we shared a meal just across the street from the church, thus beginning a most cherished relationship.

During the past decade, Amy and I have become close to this wonderful family. We have watched them as they've rejoiced and as they've weathered storms. Of course, their biggest trial came in the summer of 1991, when death claimed the group's founder and leader, Earl Weatherford. I watched Earl during his last months as an oxygen tank was his constant companion. Still he somehow found enough strength, though barely, to walk on stage every night, right up until his death, to tell his audiences about Christ. I observed Lily Fern during those final months, and how she loved and cared for Earl, taking care of his needs with grace and tenderness. Yet, she took the stage every night during this unbelievably difficult time and lifted her voice with the conviction, professionalism and class that her audiences over the past century have come to expect.

Since Earl's death, Lily Fern has carried on with as much, or perhaps even more dignity that any other gospel performer.

I'm sure Lily Fern would tell you that she possibly could not have gone on without the help and great support of her son, Steve Weatherford, who after Earl's death, took the responsibility of the group's road and stage management, as well as continuing as the group's lead singer.

Lily Fern Weatherford is truly one of Gospel Music's treasures, lending to the industry a certain dignity and distinction, which in the minds of so many have set her apart from most others. Thank you, Lily Fern, for your class, your voice and for your life-long commitment, which now spans fifty-three years of full-time ministry. To those who would only watch and listen, you have taught many lessons, but the most valuable lesson you've taught us is that whatever our endeavors may be, to do them with steadfastness, and just as importantly, do them with dignity.

Roy Pauley, Columnist
The Singing News

Kenny Payne, Roy Pauley, Lily Fern Weatherford, Steve Weatherford

APPENDIX

Weatherford Members
1944 to Present

Anderson, Tommy	Hall, Billy Jo	Reynolds, Betty J.
Baker, Cloid	Hamill, Jim	Riggs, Claude
Baker, Debbie McQueen	Holbrook, Jim	Roberson, Les
Beeler, Glen	Hopkins, James	Roberson, Raye
Bressler, Ray	Houston, George	Robinson, O.D.
Brisendine, Bill	Huxman, Norman	Ross, Art
Bryson, Jack	Jarrett, Buel	Rowland, Dave
Caldwell, Jamie	Jones, Bob	Simmons, Ted
Campbell, Buddy	Jones, Lee	Slaughter, Henry
Carter, Ken	Jones Ray	Smith, Foster
Clark, Brenda	Keel, Ann	Smith, M.P. Rev.
Clark, Bobby	Kirk, Jerry	Sparks, Marlin
Clark, James	Koker, Danny	Tackett, Gayle
Clay, Vic	Lumpkin, Troy	Taylor, Jack
Cook, Don	Larson, Danny	Thacker, Bob
Cooley, Haskell	Lawson, Danny	Thompson, Tommy
Costley, Kevin	Loman, Ray	Tremble, Roy
Couch, Glen	Lyles, Al	Turman, Harold
Cox, Earl Jr.	Martin, Richard	Wagner, Bill
Dartt, Tracy	Morales, Armond	Wall, A.V.
Drake, Ralph	Nash, Fulton	Watson, J.B.
Engles, David	Oaks, Avery	Weatherford, Earl
Evans, Jerry	Payne, Dorothy Bright	Weatherford, Lily Fern
Evans, Mack	Payne, Glen	Weatherford, Steve
Feliciano, Ken	Payne, Kenny	Weston, Raymond
Fowler, Bob	Plowman, Bill	Weston, Rady
Garrett, Marvin	Pollizzi, Nathan	Williams, Ken
Gillis, Bob	Porch, Harold	Wood, Norman
Hall, Scranton	Pratt, Scott	Younce, George

Recent Awards

1990
Achievement Award
Great Plains Southern Gospel Association
Earl and Lily Fern Weatherford

1992
Living Legend
Grand Ole Gospel Reunion
Earl and Lily Fern Weatherford

1993
Female Entertainer of the Year
Great Plains Southern Gospel Association
Lily Fern Weatherford

1994
Female Entertainer of the Year
Great Plains Southern Gospel Association
Lily Fern Weatherford

1994
Hall of Fame
Great Plains Southern Gospel Association
Earl and Lily Fern Weatherford

1998
Living Legacy Award
Women's International Center
Lily Fern Weatherford

1998
Honorary Ph.D. in Humanities
Oakland City University
Lily Fern Weatherford

Cassette Tapes Still Available from
The Weatherfords, P.O. Box 116, Paoli, OK 73074

WO-1 Because of Yesterday

WO-2 From the Cross

WO-3 He Means All to Me

WO-4 Here We Are

WO-5 I'll Follow Jesus

WO-6 In the Garden

WO-7 Let's Just Praise the Lord

WO-8 Sing Out the Good News

WO-9 Something Beautiful

WO-10 The Last Sunday

WO-11 The Weatherford Tradition Continues

WO-12 Touch Through Me

WO-13 Tried, Tested and True

WO-14 Weatherford's 60th Album

WO-15 Time For the Hymns

WO-16 Both Sides of the River (CD also available)

WO-17 Listen to Those Smooth Weatherfords

WO-18 The Cross Made the Difference

WO-19 Faith and Prayer

WO-20 Come On Let's Sing

WO-21A The Weatherfords--Thru The Years

Most current album:
Standing on Tradition
(CD also available)

Index

A

Akron, OH 52, 69, 79-81, 84-85, 87-89, 96, 98-99, 101, 105, 118-119
Akron Baptist Temple 80-82
Allen, OK 147
Angels/Angels' Stadium 37
Apache, OK 7
"Place of Peace, A" 4
Ardmore, OK 124
Assembly of God Bible School 69
Assembly of God Church 117

B

Baker, Cloid 189
Baker, Debbie McQueen 190
"Because of Yesterday," 126, 174
Bemis Point, NY 86
Bethany, OK 2, 10, 148
Bethel Temple 117
Billington, Dr. Dallas 80-81
Blackwood, Dr. James 2, 168, 193
Blackwood Brothers 71, 169
Bob Jones and His Harmony Boys 43
Bradshaw Brothers and Don 143
Branham, Carolyn 193
Bryson, Jack 59-60, 68
Brush Arbor Jubilee 115-116
Buckeye, AZ 16-17
Burton, Buddy 171

C

Caldwell, Jamie 4
Calumet Church 10
Calvary Temple 79-82
Campbell, Kay and Lee 167
Catalina, CA 65
Cathedral of Tomorrow, The 6, 79-81, 83, 85, 87, 89-90, 94, 101, 103, 105-106
Cathedrals, The 87, 101, 169
Charleston, WV 74
Charlotte, NC 141
Chosen Vision 169
Clark, Bobby 101
Clark, James 142
Cleveland, OH 90
Clifton's Cafeteria 37
Clooney, Rosemary 173
Coltrane, Richard 171
Compton, CA 27-31, 33, 37, 54, 61, 65, 68
Compton Junior College 29-69
Cooley, Haskell 195
Cosby-Sexton Electrical 52
Couch, Glen 142, 196
Couriers, The 3, 92, 169
Crews, Bob 197
Cunningham, Megan 132-136, 162, 168, 179-180
Cunningham, Susan Weatherford 89-103, 106-110, 112-114, 116-117, 123, 125, 127-136,

142, 147, 157, 164, 168, 183-184, 197
Cunningham, Tim 132-134, 136, 168, 198
Curtis, J.W./Curtis Family 9, 17-19
Cuyahoga Falls, OH 80

D

Davenport, Gary 99
Davenport, Mary Lou 47, 98, 150-151
Davidson, Lewis and Ruth Humbard 83
Day, Doris 173
Derrick, Damian 163-164
Disney World 166
Downing, Ann 198

E

El Paso, TX 158
El Reno, OK 7, 58
Enloe, Neil 3, 10, 199
Enloe, Phil 170, 200-201
Escondido, CA 31

F

First Baptist 175
First Church of the Nazarene 9, 27
First Nazarene 10, 77
Folsum's Furniture Store 59
Fontana, CA 118, 121
Ford, Betty 5
Fort Wayne, IN 74, 77, 79-80, 82
Frank Stamps Quartet Co. 42
Fresno, CA 51
Frontier City 128

G

Gaither, Bill and Gloria 2, 42, 85, 151, 163, 165-166, 168-169, 180, 187-188
Gaither, Danny 85, 169
Gatlin, Larry 203
Gillis, Bob 72
Goble, Alonzo Elmer (Lon) 7, 9-10, 14-15, 22-25, 46, 48-51, 55-56, 61-63, 83, 95, 119, 149
Goble, George Thomas 7
Goble, Lillie Alice Summers 7, 9-10, 15, 22, 31, 37, 44, 49-50, 60-61, 83, 95, 119, 148-149
Goble, Martha Brown 3, 41-42, 52-55, 62, 150
Goble, Meekly Everette 10-14, 16-18, 20-21, 24, 26-27, 30, 33-35, 37, 40-42, 52-55, 62, 149-150, 202
Goble, Myrtle Mary 7
Gospel Music Trust Fund, The 163
Grand Ole Gospel Reunion 1, 3-4, 151, 155, 162, 165-166, 170-171
Grapes of Wrath, The 15, 17
Great Western Convention 4
Greeley, OK 106
Greenville, SC 155

H

Hall, Scranton 59
Hamblin, Stuart 85
Hamill, Jim 3, 74, 78-79, 85
Hanby, Marjorie 41
Harmon, Nancy 204
Harrisburg, PA 92
Hartford Music Co. 42

Hays, Don 145
Hemphill, LaBreeska 204
Henson, Rev. Clyde 117
Hess, Jake 144, 173, 205
Hildreth, Lou Wills 205
Holy Bible, The 9, 14, 20, 44, 110, 124-125, 185-186
Honey Creek, IN 7
Hopkins, James 101
Horne, Lena 173
Houston, George 86
Houston, TX 143
Humbard, Clem and Priscilla 83
Humbard, Juanita 83
Humbard, Mary 83
Humbard, Maude Aimee 83-84, 87, 90, 93-94, 96, 100, 103, 105
Humbard, Mom and Dad 83-84, 101
Humbard, Rev. Rex 6, 80-85, 87, 90, 94, 96, 101, 103, 105
Huntington, WV 74

I

Imperials, The 144
Independent Baptist Church 80, 82
"In the Garden" 2, 87, 174
IRS 118-119, 121-125, 127, 129

J

Jacumba, CA 19-22
Jeffries, Ann 5
Johnson, Jeanne 173
Johnstown, PA 105-106, 111, 113, 119, 121
Jones, Bob, Sr. 43-44, 47, 51, 172-173, 206
Jones, Roy 70, 72

Jones, Wayne and Leona Humbard 80, 83-84

K

KBIG 65
Keel, Ann 59, 66-68
Keppler, Mrs. 111-112
KFOX 65, 73
KGER 65
King, Wynema Shahan (Nema) 41, 152, 154, 156, 206
Kingfisher, OK 7, 9, 10
Knauls, Lillie 207
Knotts Berry Farm 55
Koker, Danny 78-79, 85
Kossler, Carol 169
Kuhlmann, Katherine 81

L

Lane, Gloria 5
Lane, Harold 208
Lanz, Bobbie Sue 47, 54, 84, 150
La Fevre, Eva Mae 208
Lister, Hovie 169
Lister, Mosie 79, 173
Living Legacy Award 1, 3
Logan, Bonnie Louise 47, 151
Long Beach, CA 33, 41, 51-52, 59, 65
Long Beach Pike 32
Lo Prinzi, Michael 169, 208
"Lord's Prayer, The" 68
Los Angeles, CA 19, 22, 24, 33, 36-37, 40, 98, 116, 121, 154
Louisville, KY 2
Lowery, Mark 209
Lynwood, CA 29, 51, 55, 57

M

Mackey Walker Trio 30
Marietta, GA 101
Martinsville, VA 141
Matthews, Rev. Bill 210
McAlister, Doyle 4
McAlister, OK 147
Meier, Audry 173
Mexican Border Patrol 21-22
Miles, Rev. Ted 210
Minneapolis, MN 142
Morales, Armond 3, 53, 68-69, 73-74, 86-87, 146, 209
Music Men, The 74

N

Nash, Brenda 121, 128, 142, 144, 167, 171, 175, 184-185, 211
Nash, Fulton 115, 121, 128, 140, 142, 169-170, 173, 210
National Quartet Convention 2-4, 141, 153, 160
Nazarene Young People Society 44
Nelms, Wallace 167, 211
Newton, Calvin 212
Nicholson, Duane 211
Norman, OK 43, 127

O

Oakland City University 5
Oak Ridge Boys 78
Ottumwa, IA 129, 139

P

Pacific Electric 33
Page, Patti 171
Paoli, OK 46, 58, 121-123, 148, 151, 167, 181

Pauley, Amy 166
Pauley, Roy 1, 166, 222
Pauls Valley, OK 46, 55, 98-99, 125, 147-148, 185
Payne, Dorothy Bright 41-42, 53, 73
Payne, Glen 3, 53, 86, 163, 173, 214
Payne, Kenny 4, 41, 73, 152-155 160-161, 185
Payne, Vernon 73
Penrod, Guy 154
Penrod, Rev. Joe 154
Phoenix, AZ 155
Powell, Rosa Nell Speer 2

R

Reader, Naomi Sego 215
RCA 175
Reece, David 171, 215
Richert, Elizabeth 175
Roberson, Camilla Raye Smith 53, 68-69, 73, 78
Roberson, Les 53, 68-69, 73, 78
Rockford, TN 72
Roosevelt, Franklin 56

S

Sacremento, CA 113, 116-117, 121
San Diego, CA 5, 19, 35, 40, 54
San Francisco, CA 51-52
San Gabriel Valley 16
San Pedro, CA 33
Shape Notes 42
Shenandoah, IA 78
Shirley, Esther 169
Shirley, Hugo 169-170
Shore, Dinah 173
Singing Conventions 41-43, 58

Singing News, The 1, 188
Slaughter, Hazel 84
Slaughter, Henry 3, 84, 86, 173-174, 215
Smiths, The 24
Smith, Rev. M.P. 9, 16
"Something Beautiful" 174
Song Fellows, The 115
Southern Gospel 2-5, 42, 74, 151, 162-163, 172
Southgate, CA 27
Speer, Brock 4
Speers, The 2, 85
Springfield, IL 73
Squier, Dennis 36, 53-54
Squier, Earl 31-32, 35-37, 51-54, 150
Squier, Florence Marie Goble 10-12, 17, 20, 22, 26-28, 30-32, 35-36, 40, 42, 49, 51-54, 148-150, 182
Stafford, Jo 173
Stamps-Baxter Music Co. 42, 70
Stamps-Baxter School of Music 70
Stamps, Frank 43
"Stand Together" 68
Statesmen, The 71, 168-169
Stoker, Gordon 216
Strangemen, The 171
Strickland, Rick 216
Summers, Dora 13
Summers, Elizabeth Vandora 7
Summers, Everette Arthur 7
Sumner, J.D. 159

T

Talley, Debra 173, 217
Terrell, Bob 74
Todd, Billy 171
Toney, Jack 169, 171
Trimble, Roy 142
Tucson, AZ 125, 147, 158
Turman, Harold 70, 72
"Turn Your Radio On" 180

V

Varner, Wally 217
Vaughan Music Co. 42
Vaughn, Mickey 218

W

Wacker Park 46
Wagner, Bill 71, 142
Waller, Charlie 151, 162-163, 171
Warsaw, IN 74
Washington, OK 46-47
Watson, J.B. 68
Weatherford, Earl Henderson 1-5, 14, 41-58, 60-63, 65, 68-74, 76-79, 81, 84-89, 91-101, 103, 106-110, 114-116, 118-119, 121-127, 131-134, 136-139, 141, 144-145, 143-149, 151-165, 172, 174-175, 179, 181, 188.
Weatherford, Elton Henderson 46
Weatherford, Mary Elvada 46
"Weatherford, Randall Wayne (Randy)" 95-101, 129, 137
Weatherford, Standalee Smith 4, 139-140, 166, 168, 181
Weatherford, Steven Earl 1, 3, 54, 100-102, 106-111, 113-114, 116-118, 123, 125-128, 136-141, 145, 147, 150, 152-155, 158, 160-161, 165-166, 168, 181, 183-185, 219
Weatherfords, The 1-5, 14, 41, 59, 68-69, 71-74, 78, 80, 84, 87, 101, 105, 116-117, 127-128,

147, 161-163, 166, 168-169, 175, 189
Weatherford, Vernon Carol 47
Western States Quartet Convention 176
"Where No One Stands Alone" 79
Wichita, KS 65, 78
Williams, Bette Jo 41, 47, 54, 85, 162
Williams, Earl 85
Williams, Jimmy Earl 54, 85
Wilmar, CA 16, 22, 24, 27-28
Winona Lake, IN 74
WKGR 65
Women's International Center 5
Wood, Norman 78
WOWO 74, 82
WPA 23-24

Y

YMCA 52
Younce, Clara 76
Younce, George 3, 74-78, 85, 163, 220
Young, Doug 169, 220
Youth For Christ 53
Yukon, OK 9, 121-122, 138, 150

Z

"Zion's Hill" 67